INDIA AS SEEN IN
THE KUṬṬANĪ-MATA OF DĀMODARAGUPTA

India as Seen in The Kuṭṭanī-Mata of Dāmodaragupta

Ajay Mitra Shastri

MOTILAL BANARSIDASS
Delhi Varanasi Patna Bangalore Madras

First Edition: Delhi, 1975
Reprint: Delhi, 1995,1996

ISBN: 81-208-1336-7

41 U.A. Bungalow Road, Jawahar Nagar, Delhi 110 007
120 Royapettah High Road, Mylapore, Madras 600 004
16 St. Mark's Road, Bangalore 560 001
Ashok Rajpath, Patna 800 004
Chowk, Varanasi 221 001

PRINTED IN INDIA

by Jainendra Prakash Jain at Shri Jainendra Press,
A-45 Naraina, Phase I, New Delhi 110 028
and Published by Narendra Prakash Jain for
Motilal Banarsidass,
Bungalow Road, Delhi 110 007

TO

MY *GURU*

MAHĀMAHOPĀDHYĀYA

PADMABHŪṢAṆA DR. V. V. MIRASHI

as a token of profound esteem and gratitude.

CONTENTS

FOREWORD

When I went to London in the early forties for my Ph.D. degree I was told by my teacher the late Dr. L. D. Barnett that if I wanted to study under him I had to avoid literary antiquarianism by which he meant gathering together tit-bits of literary information for my thesis and that I had to work on some solid subject pertaining to history, art or archaeology. At that time I had to agree with the views of Dr. Barnett; but after my return to this country I, in consultation with the late Dr. V.S. Agrawala, came to the conclusion that Sanskrit, Prakrit and Pali literature had strata of information which had to be sifted analytically to study the culture of a period which could be further checked by archaeological data. We in our humble way carried out research on this principle and were surprised at the richness and enormity of information contained in Indian literature for drawing a picture of the social and cultural life of the Indian people. Dr. Ajay Mitra Shastri in his *India as seen in the Kuṭṭanī-mata of Dāmodaragupta*, I am happy to say, follows the same principle and has studied the text so rigorously that hardly any information worth noting has escaped his attention. As a matter of fact his studies not only give a picture of the life and work of the people of Kashmir in the ninth century, but as Dāmodaragupta was a great traveller, the information which he has gathered in the *Kuṭṭanī-mata* gives a picture of the life and culture of northern India as well. After all, literary antiquarianism is not a pure bunkum but yields scientific data if used with caution.

Dr. Shastri is not only a good Sanskritist but is at the same time endowed with the historian's critical approach. This rare combination has enabled him more than anybody else to understand and analyse the text properly. Like his other writings the present work is marked by his great erudition and is a solid piece of historico-textual research. His researches on the date of Dāmodaragupta add a fresh chapter to the history of Sanskrit literature. In the various chapters of the book he throws interesting light on contemporary religious and socio-economic life, administration, education and literature and the state of fine arts. Of particular interest is his brief but enlightening discussion of the institution of courtesans in the eighth century A.D. Though the work is based on the *Kuṭṭanī-mata*, copious data have been drawn from archaeological sources and literary works like the *Rāja-taraṅgiṇī*, *Nīla-mata* and Kṣemendra's writings besides the *Kāma-sūtra* and the one-act plays incorporated in the *Caturbhāṇī* to supplement and corroborate the information supplied by Dāmodaragupta.

I once again offer my felicitations to Dr. Shastri for bringing out such an interesting study of a much neglected text. The information which he has critically studied is of great interest not only for a correct understanding of the institution of courtesans but also of other aspects of the life of the Indian people during the early mediaeval period.

MOTI CHANDRA

Prince of Wales Museum of Western India,
Bombay.
18.6.1974.

PREFACE

It was for the first time in the year 1965 that I went through the *Kuṭṭanī-mata* and realised the rich crop of cultural material which stood in the need of being properly harvested and made available to students of the cultural history of ancient India. Originally I thought of publishing a long paper, but with the progress of my study I realised that the subject required a sufficiently large monograph if I were to be judicious and honest to my undertaking. Accordingly, I engaged myself in an exhaustive, critical study of the text which, for obvious reasons, consumed much more time than expected earlier. The completion of the work was further delayed by other preoccupations and assignments demanding immediate attention. In the meantime, however, I published three papers on certain aspects of the subject in internationally reputed periodicals which attracted wide attention and evoked eloquent appreciation and encouraged me to complete the work in a comparatively shorter time than would have been the case otherwise.

As the celebrated poet-historian, Kalhaṇa, tells us, Dāmodaragupta, the author of the *Kuṭṭanī-mata*, occupied the high office of *dhī-saciva* or Prime Minister under Jayāpīḍa Vinayāditya, the Karkoṭa king of Kashmir, who flourished in the last quarter of the eighth and the first quarter of the following century A.D. The poem, therefore, may be justifiably supposed to reflect the contemporary Kashmiri life though, be it stated, it nowhere mentions the Happy Valley by name. As has been suggested in the opening chapter of the present work, the non-mention of Kashmir is probably deliberate, though we have unambiguous traces of the author's acquaintance with contemporary Kashmir. On the other hand, the scenes of the episodes narrated in the text are laid at Vārāṇasī, Pāṭaliputra and Mt. Abu which are all described in a realistic manner. The reliability of the account of Vārāṇasī and Arbuda, in particular, is amply borne out by literary and archaeological evidences. Although Kerala and Devarāṣṭra are also casually mentioned, the author does not evince much acquaintance with the South. It may, therefore, be reasonably assumed that the poem depicts contemporary North Indian life. Keeping this fact in view, I have spared no pains to corroborate and supplement the information supplied by our work from other sources, both literary and archaeological.

The present work is divided into seven chapters. The first chapter, which is introductory in nature, deals with such preliminary questions as the discovery and caption of the poem, its appreciation from a literary and historical standpoint and the sources of the stories related in it and Dāmodaragupta's life and times. An important feature of this chapter is a full discussion of the historical data enshrined in the poem which, it has been pointed out for the first time, bear out Kalhaṇa's evidence regarding Dāmodaragupta's date. It has further enabled us to fix more precisely the date of the Kalacuri royal poet Māyurāja Anaṅgaharṣa who can now be convincingly placed in the latter half of the eighth century A.D. The following chapter is devoted to a discussion of the political data furnished by Dāmodaragupta. Contemporary religious conditions form the subject-matter of the third chapter, while the next chapter is claimed by an analytical study of the data bearing on social life. These two chapters actually form the core of the present monograph. While dealing with the religious conditions it has been shown convincingly that the correct reading of the relevant name in verse 736 of the *Kuṭṭanī-mata* is *Kalaśeśvara*, and not *Kamaleśvara* which is found in a majority of manuscripts and adopted by all the modern editors of the text. As suggested by its title, our poem affords rich material on prostitution which, among other topics, is fully discussed in Chapter IV. In the next chapter attention is focussed on the information concerning educational practices and valuable literary references enshrined in the poem. It will be noticed that the work is particularly rich in information on erotics, poetics and dramaturgy. The second section of this chapter forms something like a running commentary on the poet's erudition to which attention has been invited in the opening chapter. The sixth chapter treats of data bearing on contemporary economic conditions including coinage in connection with which has been discussed, for the first time, the bearing of the mention of *Kedara* on the date of our poet. The wealth of information on the contemporary state of fine arts, particularly music, dance and drama, found in the text is analysed in the concluding chapter. The geographical references scattered in the *Kuṭṭanīmata* are studied in an appendix.

The work ends with a select bibliography wherein scrupulous care has been taken to enter only such of the titles as have actually been consulted and specifically cited in the text and footnotes.

Right from my student days Mahāmahopādhyāya Padmabhūṣaṇa Dr. V. V. Mirashi through his writings and with his singular devotion and rich contributions to the advancement of Indological studies has been a source of constant inspiration to me. And from the day I joined the Nagpur University some eighteen years ago his valuable advice and constructive criticism have always been available to me. All these years he evinced keen interest in my work which by itself served as a great incentive. I have, therefore, dedicated the present work to him as an humble token of my profound gratitude and respect for him.

At the end it is my pleasant duty to express my gratitude to persons from whom I have received valuable help in the completion of the present work. I gratefully remember on this occasion the late Dr. Moti Chandra who evinced keen interest in the progress of this work and blessed it with his foreword. I am grateful to Dr. G. T. Deshpande, formerly Professor and Head of the Department of Sanskrit, Nagpur University, for lively discussions I had with him during the preparation of the book. Sincere thanks are due to my colleagues Drs. G. B. Deglurkar and A.P. Jamkhedkar for supplying illustrations which formed the basis of Pls. XIII. 25 and XIX. 40, and to my student Shri Chandrashekhar Gupta, Registration Officer, Department of Archaeology, Govt. of Maharashtra, for valuable help in selecting some of the illustrations. My former student Shri P.R.K. Prasad, M.A., of the Archaeological Survey of India and the technical staff of my Department including Shri S. K. Pande, Shri S. K. Jagtap and Shri P. S. Joshi deserve my sincere thanks for the preparation of the plates appearing at the end of the book.

The index has been prepared by my wife Dr. Yogeshwari Shastri, M.A., Ph.D., and my son Ch. Avinash. To thank them will be observing too much of formality.

Last but not the least, I must record my sincere thanks to Messrs. Motilal Banarsidass, Delhi, for undertaking the publication of the work and showing full consideration all through the printing of the book.

In spite of utmost care bestowed on proof-reading, a few typographical errors have crept in the book, for which I crave the indulgence of the readers. In particular I should like to invite their attention to a serious inaccuracy regarding the page nos. mentioned on the title pages of Chs. VI and VII and the Appendix dealing with geographical references which has resulted from the spreading over of the material from p. 209 onward at the time of printing. Thus, in the last two lines of title page of Ch. VI (p. 191) we should read 210, 211 and 212 instead of 209, 210 and 211 respectively; on the title page of Ch. VII (p. 215) 217, 220, 224, 229, 230 and 231 instead of 215, 218, 222, 227, 227 and 229 respectively; and on the title page of the Appendix (p. 233) 235, 238 and 239 in place of 233, 236 and 237 respectively.

AJAY MITRA SHASTRI

Nagpur University
4th June, 1975.

ABBREVIATIONS

ABORI	:	*Annals of the Bhandarkar Oriental Research Institute.*
ASI, AR	:	*Archaeological Survey of India, Annual Reports.*
ASS	:	Anandashram Sanskrit Series.
BDCRI	:	*Bulletin of the Deccan College Research Institute.*
BI	:	Bibliotheca Indica.
BSS	:	Bombay Sanskrit Series.
BV	:	*Bhāratīya Vidyā.*
CII	:	*Corpus Inscriptionum Indicarum.*
EI	:	*Epigraphia Indica.*
GOS	:	Gaekwad's Oriental Series.
HDS	:	*History of Dharmaśāstra* by P. V. Kane.
HOS	:	Harward Oriental Series.
IA	:	*Indian Antiquary.*
JAHRS	:	*Journal of the Andhra Historical Research Society.*
JBBRAS	:	*Journal of the Bombay Branch of the Royal Asiatic Society.*
JBORS	:	*Journal of the Bihar and Orissa Research Society.*
JIH	:	*Journal of Indian History.*
JNSI	:	*Journal of the Numismatic Society of India.*
JOI	:	*Journal of Oriental Institute*, Baroda.
JRAS	:	*Journal of the Royal Asiatic Society of Great Britain and Ireland.*
K	:	*Kuṭṭanī-mata.*
KSS	:	Kashi Sanskrit Series.
MASI	:	*Memoirs of the Archaeological Survey of India.*
NSP	:	Nirnay Sagar Press.
RT	:	*Rāja-taraṅgiṇī.*
TSS	:	Trivandrum Sanskrit Series.

LIST OF ILLUSTRATIONS

Pl. XVI.31. Lady with a veil, Ajanta, Cave 10. G. Yazdani, *Ajanta*, Part III, Pl. XXIV.

32. Lady with hair arranged in two *veṇis*, Mathura. V. A. Smith, *Jaina Stūpa and Other Antiquities of Mathura*, Pl. XXXIV.

33. Lady with *dhammilla* hair-style, Ajanta, Cave 17. A. Ghosh, *et al*, *Ajanta Murals*, Pl. LVII.

34. Lady with *alakāvali* hair-style, Ajanta, Cave 1. *Ibid.*, Pl. XXXVIII.

35. Head of the figure of Gaṅgā with a combination of *alakāvali* and *dhammilla* hair-styles, Paunar.

,,XVII.36. Lady applying lac-dye to the sole of her foot, accompanied by an attendant holding a dye-container, Pārśvanātha Temple, Khajuraho. Kanvarlal, *op. cit.*, Fig. 180.

37. Lady applying collyrium, Pārśvanātha Temple, Khajuraho. *Ibid.*, Fig. 139.

,,XVIII.38. Lady playing with ball, Lakṣmaṇa Temple, Khajuraho. Kanvarlal, *op. cit.*, Fig. 32.

39. Lady at the game of ball, Sirsa, Allahabad District. Pramod Chandra, *op. cit.*, Pl. CLXII. 474.

,,XIX.40. Ram-fight, Ajanta, Cave 17, ceiling,

,,XX.41-42. Female figure playing with a parrot (41) and a *śārikā* (42), Markaṇḍa Ṛṣi Temple, Markandi. S. B. Deo, *op. cit.*, Pl. XXXIV. 2,1.

,,XXI.43. *Samudgikā*.

CHAPTER I

THE KUṬṬANĪ-MATA AND ITS AUTHOR

I. THE KUṬṬANĪ-MATA : ITS PAST POPULARITY, LOSS AND RE-DISCOVERY IN MODERN TIMES

Consisting of over a thousand stanzas in the Āryā metre,[1] the *Kuṭṭanī-mata* of Dāmodaragupta embodies, as suggested by its title,[2] a vivid exposition of the trickeries of whoredom by an experienced bawd to a young hetaira. Within a couple of centuries after its composition it attracted the attention of the connoisseurs and for a long time thereafter commanded great respect and popularity. This is borne out by the fact that many a stanza from this little poem is found cited in standard works on literary criticism and grammar and in several Sanskrit anthologies, more often than not without naming the source. Thus, three verses from the *Kuṭṭanī-mata* are quoted by a rhetorician of the eminence of Mammaṭa,[3] and another by the versatile Kṣemendra (11th century A.D.).[4] Śaraṇadeva, the author of the grammatical treatise *Durghaṭa-vṛtti* (1172 A.D.), adduces two verses from the poem,[5] and he is the only one amongst the ancient writers to mention the work from which he borrowed. Numerous other couplets from the work are found scattered in the *Alaṅkāra-sarvasva* of Maṅkha (*c.* 1150 A.D.),[6] the commentary

1. Madhusūdan Kaul's edition contains 1058 verses, while in Tripathi's edition, which is based on all the available manuscript material, we have 1059 stanzas. Verse 78 of Tripathi's edition is conspicuous by its absence in Kaul's where it has been relegated to a foot-note. Vide p. 9, fn. 7.

2. *Kuṭṭanī*=procuress; *mata*=advice, i.e., advice of a procuress. As will be shown in the sequel, the poem was also known as *Śambhalī-mata*. The words *kuṭṭanī* and *śambhalī* are synonymous.

3. *Kāvya-prakāśa* (edited by R. D. Karmarkar, Poona, 1950), vii.202= *Kuṭṭanī-mata* (hereinafter referred to as *K*) 697; viii.341 and ix. 356=*K* 103; x.452=*K* 97.

4. *Kavi-kaṇṭhābharaṇa*, v. 39 (*Kṣemendra-laghu-kāvya-saṅgraha* edited by Aryendra Sharma, Hyderabad, 1961, p. 78).

5. *Durghaṭa-vṛtti*, Vol. II (edited by Louis Renou with French notes, Paris 1945), pp. 80 (*Mātaḥ kiṁ vidadhāma iti Kuṭṭanī-mate* (=*K* 41) on Pāṇini, iii.4.99), 92 (*Kuṭṭanī-mate Vañcaka-vṛttyo veśyāḥ* (=*K* 485) on Pāṇini, iv.1.45).

6. *Alaṅkāra-sarvasva* (TSS, No. XLI, 2nd edition, 1926), p. 64 on *sūtra* 22: *K* 98. The *Alaṅkāra-sūtra* only appears to be the work of Ruyyaka, while the *Sarvasva* commentary was composed by Maṅkha. See Introduction to the *Alaṅkāra-sarvasva*; M. Krishnamachariar, *History of Classical Sanskrit Literature* (Madras, 1937), pp. 764-5.

on the *Maṅkha-kośa* by the author (Maṅkha) himself,[1] the *Gaṇaratna-mahodadhi* (1140 A.D.) of Vardhamāna,[2] the *Kavīndra-vacana-samuccaya* (*c.* close of the 10th century A.D.),[3] the *Sūkti-muktāvali* (1257 A.D.) of Jalhaṇa,[4] the *Subhāṣitāvali* of Vallabha-deva (not earlier than the latter half of the 15th century A.D.)[5] and a host of other works.[6] The poem is mentioned by name in the *Rāja-taraṅgiṇī* (iv.498) of Kalhaṇa, the *Durghaṭa-vṛtti* (on Pāṇini, iii.4.99; iv.1.45) of Śaraṇadeva, the *Kāvyānuśāsana* of the Jaina encyclopaedist Hemacandra[7] and the *Nāgara-sarvasva* of the Buddhist writer Padmaśrī, also known as Padma-śrījñāna.[8] Several verses of the last mentioned work are actually based on the *Kuṭṭanī-mata*.[9]

However, notwithstanding such a great popularity, by about the thirteenth century A.D. the poem dwindled into comparative obscurity as evidenced by the fact that the scholiasts

1. *Maṅkha-kośa* (edited by T. Zachariae, Bombay, 1897), on vv. 378 (*K* 64) and 630 (=*K* 312).

2. *Gaṇaratna-mahodadhi* (edited by J. Eggling, Delhi 1963), p. 39=*K* 411.

3. Edited by F. W. Thomas, Calcutta 1912, verse 138=*K* 1.

The correct title is actually *Subhāṣita-ratna-kośa* and the anthology was compiled by one Vidyākara (ed. by D. D. Kosambi and V. V. Gokhale, H. O. S., Vol. 32, 1957). Its verse 329 is the same as *K* 1.

4. *Sūkti-muktāvali*, verse 154=*K* 399.

5. *Subhāṣitāvali* (edited by P. Peterson, 2nd edition, Poona, 1961), Nos. 420=*K* 695; 1071=*K* 103; 1263=*K* 441; 1264=*K* 442; 1388=*K* 105; 1560=*K* 975; 2271=*K* 434; 2338=*K* 399; 2339=*K* 393; 2342=*K* 822; 2529=*K* 765; 2530=*K* 767; 2531-32= *K* 769-70; 2533=*K* 780; 2534 =K 786.

6. E.g., *Pañcatantra*, Kṣīrasvāmin's scholium on the *Amara-kośa*, *Śārṅgadhara-paddhati*, *Subhāṣita-ratna-bhāṇḍāgāra*, etc. Vide T. M. Tripatni (Ed.), *K*, pp. 472-73. As we shall see later, some verses attributed to our poet by Vallabhadeva and Veṇīdatta cannot be traced in the *K*.

7. *Kāvyānuśāsana* (edited by R.C. Parikh, Bombay, 1938), *Alaṅkāra-cūḍāmaṇi* on viii.8, p. 463; *Viveka*, verse 193, p. 464.

8. तत् कुट्टनी (v.l. कामिनी-) मतमुदीक्ष्य वराङ्गनानां
कान्ते विधेयमबलाचरितं प्रदिष्टम् ।
स्त्रीसौख्यलिङ्गमवधारयतां नराणां
चोक्तं स्वरागजननं सुतरामिहैव ॥

Nāgara-sarvasva (Bombay, 1921), xxxvii. 16.

9. *Nāgara-sarvasva*, xxxvii. 3-14, contain material directly borrowed from *K* 149-50, 152-56, 158-62.

of the *Kāvya-prakāśa*[1] and the *Nāgara-sarvasva*[2] exhibit complete ignorance about it. It is interesting to note in this connection that while quite a few early writers refer to the work by name, it is not named in any later writing.[3] The story of its resuscitation in our own times is not without interest. The credit of recovering it in modern times is undoubtedly due to the indefatigable labours of Dr. P. Peterson who, in 1883, lighted upon a thirteenth century palm-leaf manuscript of the poem in the Śāntinātha Temple Bhaṇḍāra at Cambay. Incomplete and inaccurate in many places, this manuscript refers to the poem by the name *Śambhalī-mata*.[4] Three years later, in 1886, Mahāmahopādhyāya Paṇḍita Durgāprasāda of Jaipur discovered two more manuscripts of the work. In these manuscripts the title of the poem is given as *Kuṭṭanī-mata*. Though these manuscripts were also incomplete and corrupt in many places, yet an edition of the work based on them was published in the Kāvyamālā series (no. 3, 1887). But the oldest and the first complete manuscript of the work was discovered by Mahāmahopādhyāya Dr. Haraprasāda Śāstrī in course of his tours for search of Sanskrit manuscripts in Nepal, in 1897-98. This manuscript, written in proto-Bengali characters,[5] was copied in the year 292 of the Newari

1. Māṇikyacandra (*c.* 1216 A.D.), the earliest commentator of the *Kāvya-prakāśa*, and Govinda (14th century A.D.), the author of the *Pradīpa* gloss, are reticent about the source of *Kāvya-prakāśa*, x. 452, which is really the same as *K* 97. Another commentator, Maheśvara, changes tne reading *Mālatyāḥ* to *Mālavyāḥ* and conjectures that the verse in question belonged to the *Mālavikāgnimitra* of Kālidāsa, while Kamalākarabhaṭṭa and Bhīmasena take it to belong to Bhavabhūti's *Mālatī-Mādhava*. All these suppositions are unfounded as the stanza under consideration is not found in either of these plays and reveal the commentators' ignorance of the real source, viz., the *K*.

2. As we have seen above, Padmaśrī, the author of the *Nāgara-sarvasva*, avers to have drawn upon the *K*. But his commentator, Jagajjyotirmalla (1617-33 A.D.), is completely ignorant about the poem and consequently misinterprets *Kuṭṭanī-matam* occurring in *Nāgara-sarvasva*, xxxvii.16, as *komala-matam*.

3. Later writers often give only the name of the author while quoting verses from the *K*. Some of them, who had neither access to the *K* nor knew the name of the author, prefixed the *K* stanzas by the phrase *kasy-āpi* (of some one). They evidently borrowed these verses from some secondary sources.

4. P. Peterson, *Report on the Search of Sanskrit Manuscripts in the Bombay Circle for* 1883-84, p. 23.

5. This is the oldest manuscript in Bengali characters so far discovered and as such has an important place in the history of the Bengali script.

era corresponding to 1172 A.D.[1] Along with it an incomplete manuscript in Newari characters was also discovered.[2] In their colophons the poem is entitled *Kuṭṭanī-mata*. These manuscripts formed the basis of Paṇḍita Madhusudan Kaul's critical edition of the work published by the Asiatic Society of Bengal in 1944.[3] Utilising all the manuscript material available to him, Paṇḍita Tanasukharam Manassukharam Tripathi prepared an excellent edition of this poem with brief notes of Paṇḍita Ratnagopāla Bhaṭṭa of Varanasi and his own exhaustive Sanskrit commentary, which was published posthumously in 1924.[4]

As we have seen above, manuscripts give the title of the work variously as *Kuṭṭanī-mata* or *Śambhalī-mata*. The author himself gives the caption of the poem in its second stanza; but unfortunately here also we have variant readings, viz., *kuṭṭanyā matam* and *śambhalyā matam*. *Kāminī-matam* is a variant for *Kuṭṭanī-matam* in the *Nāgara-sarvasva* (xxxvii.16), indicating that the work also passed under the caption *Kāminī-mata* which, however, does not appear to be an appropriate heading. The commentator, Jagajjyotirmalla, explains *Kuṭṭanī-matam* as *Komala-matam*, which really demonstrates his ignorance of the poem. The caption *Kuṭṭanī-mata* is found in a large number of manuscripts and is also vouched for by ancient writers like Kalhaṇa, Śaraṇadeva, Padmaśrī and Hemacandra who refer to the work by name. The title *Kuṭṭanī-mata* has, therefore, been generally adopted by modern scholars, and all the published editions of the work go under this caption. Be that as it may, the import of both the main titles, *Kuṭṭanī-mata* and *Śambhalī-mata*, is the same, both *kuṭṭanī* and *śambhalī* meaning procuress.

1. H. P. Śāstri, *A Descriptive Catalogue of Sanskrit Manuscripts in the Collections of the Asiatic Society of Bengal*, Vol. vii (Calcutta, 1934), no. 5086, pp. 75-86.

2. *Ibid*., no. 5085, p. 74. Also cf. no. 4740.

3. The printing of this edition commenced long ago, but it could not be brought out for several decades owing to peculiar circumstances. For an account of these hindrances, see Preface to Kaul's edition.

4. The *K* has been translated into German by J. C. Meyer, Leipzig 1903. It has been rendered into French also. Two editions of this work with Hindi translation came out in 1961, one by Atrideva Vidyalankara (Indological Book House, Varanasi) and the other by Jagannatha Pathak (Mitra Prakashan, Allahabad). But both these editions are most inadequate and replete with numerous errors.

II. DĀMODARAGUPTA AND HIS TIMES

Unfortunately, our knowledge about the life and times of the author of the poem, Dāmodaragupta, is meagre in the extreme. Like most of the luminaries on the horizon of Sanskrit literature, Dāmodaragupta also maintains complete taciturnity about himself except only once when he gives his own name and speaks of himself as the author of the *Kuṭṭanī-mata.*[1] We would have remained completely blank as regards his time, locale and patron but for a single stanza in that exhaustive *Chronicle of Kashmir* which informs us that Jayāpīḍa Vinayāditya, the Karkoṭa-Nāga king of Kashmir, appointed the poet Dāmodaragupta, the author of the *Kuṭṭanī-mata*, as his chief councillor (*dhī-saciva*) even as the demon king Bali had appointed Kavi (i.e. Śukra).[2] No other biographical detail is known about him from any other source.

There is a divergence of opinion about the date of Jayāpīḍa, the patron of our poet. According to the system of chronology followed by Kalhaṇa, Jayāpīḍa ruled for a period of thirty-one years, from 751 to 782 A.D.,[3] and S. P. Pandit holds this chronological scheme to be correct so far as the Karkoṭa kings are concerned.[4] But this chronology has not found favour with most of the modern historians who, basing on certain synchro-

1. कुट्टन्या मतमेतद् दामोदरगुप्तविरचितं शृणुत ॥ *K* 2.

2. स दामोदरगुप्ताख्यं कुट्टनीमतकारिणम् ।
कविं कविं बलिरिव धुर्यं धीसचिवं व्यधात् ॥ *RT*, iv. 496.

According to Mangeshrao Ramakrishna Telang, who contributed the Introduction to T. M. Tripathi's posthumous edition of the *Kuṭṭanī-mata* (p. 20), this fact is also recorded in the colophon found at the end of some manuscripts which runs as follows: *Iti śrī Kaśmīra-mahāmaṇḍala-mahī-maṇḍana-rāja-Jayāpīḍa-mantri-pravara—Dāmodaragupta-viracitaṁ Kuṭṭanī-mataṁ samāptam.* However, no such colophon is found at the end of the complete manuscript in proto-Bengali characters described by Haraprasada Sastri which merely avers that the *Kuṭṭanī-mata kāvya* was composed by *mahākavi Bhaṭṭa*-Dāmodaragupta : *Kuṭṭanī-mata-kāvyaṁ samāptam*; *kṛtir-iyaṁ Bhaṭṭa-Dāmodaraguptasya mahākaver=iti* (H. P. Śāstrī, *A Descriptive Catalogue of the Sanskrit Manuscripts in the Collections of the Asiatic Society of Bengal*, Vol. vii (Calcutta 1934), no. 5086, p. 85).

3. *RT*, iv. 657.

4. S. P. Pandit (Ed.), *Gauḍavaho* (2nd edition, Poona, 1927), Introduction, pp. lxxi ff. N. B. Utgikar, the re-editor of the *Gauḍavaho*, however, accepts the correction of Kalhaṇa's chronology suggested by Cunningham and others. See *ibid.*, pp. cclvi ff.

nisms furnished by the Chinese sources, hold that Kalhaṇa has antedated the reigns of the Karkoṭa kings by some years. The difference between the dates supplied by Kalhaṇa and the actual dates arrived at on the basis of the Chinese evidence has been variously estimated by scholars as twenty-five,[1] thirty-one[2] and thirty-eight years.[3] Without entering into this controversy, it may be concluded that Jayāpīḍa ruled in the last quarter of the eighth and early in the ninth century A.D. Our poet who, according to Kalhaṇa, was the chief minister of Jayāpīḍa, must also be taken to have flourished during the same period.

The above date, which is based on the contemporaneity of Jayāpīḍa and Dāmodaragupta, is also corroborated by a critical study of the valuable *historical data* afforded by the *Kuṭṭanī-mata* itself.

HISTORICAL DATA

1. *Enactment of Ratnāvalī*

Verses 880-928 of our poem[4] contain a graphic description of the enactment of the first act of the *Ratnāvalī*, and verse 926 is a verbatim reproduction of *Ratnāvalī*, i.24. The account is naturally brief and, to a certain extent, modified; but, as observed by Keith, there is no doubt that "it was played exactly in accordance with the stage directions which have come down to us embedded in the text of the drama as we have it".[5] Although Dāmodaragupta is reticent as regards its authorship,[6] there is

1. M. A. Stein, *Rāja-taraṅgiṇī* (Engl. tr.), Vol. I, Introduction, pp. 67, 94.

2. Cunningham, *The Ancient Geography of India* : The Buddhist Period (Indological Book House, Varanasi 1963), pp. 77-78 ; *Coins of Mediaeval India* (Indological Book House, Varanasi 1967), pp. 38-39.

3. Jan Yun-Hua, Some Fresh Reflections on Yaśovarmā of Kanauj and Muktāpīḍa of Kashmir, *JIH*, XLV (1967), pp. 161 ff.

4. See also vv. 801-809. Unless otherwise stated, all the references to the *K* pertain to Tripathi's editions.

5. A. B. Keith, *Sanskrit Drama*, p. 368.

6. The assertion of some scholars that Dāmodaragupta ascribes the play to a king (*ibid.*, p. 170; Nariman, Jackson and Ogden (Ed.), *Priyadarśikā* (Columbia University Indo-Iranian Series, Vol. 10, New York, 1923), Introduction, p. xli; R. S. Tripathi, *A History of Kanauj* (Varanasi, 1937), p. 180) or to Harṣa (S. N. Dasgupta and S. K. De, *A History of Sanskrit Literature*, Classical Period, Vol. I (2nd edition, Calcutta 1962, p. 256) is not borne out by the text.

abundant evidence, partly internal and partly external, to assure us that this play, as well as the two other plays, viz., the *Priya-darśikā* and the *Nāgānanda*, emanated from the pen of the royal author, Harṣavardhana Śīlāditya, who ruled over the kingdom of Sthāṇvīśvara (Thaneswar) and Kannauj in the first half of the seventh century A.D. (606-648 A.D.). The unity of authorship of all the three plays is evidenced by the occurrence of a common prologue attributing them to king Harṣadeva including a stanza speaking of śrī-Harṣa as an accomplished poet,[1] repetition of two common stanzas in the *Priya-darśikā* and the *Nāgānanda*[2] and of another in the *Priyadarśikā* and the *Ratnāvalī*,[3] and innumerable parallelisms as regards thoughts, situations, style, structure, diction and phrases. The common authorship of the three plays conceded, the following observation of the Chinese pilgrim, I-tsing, (671-695 A.D.), evidently made with reference to the *Nāgānanda*, conclusively proves Harṣa-Śīlāditya's authorship of all the three dramas. "King Śīlāditya," says he, "versified the story of the Bodhisattva Jīmūtavāhana (Chinese "Cloud-borne"), who surrendered himself in place of a Nāga. This version was set to music (lit. string and pipe). He had it performed by a band accompanied by dancing and acting, and thus popularised it in his time."[4] No early authority seems to have entertained doubt about his claim to their authorship. But the statement of Mammaṭa that Dhāvaka (v.l. = Bāṇa) received wealth from śrī-Harṣa (*śrī-Harṣ-āder = Dhāvak* (*v.*l. *Bāṇ*)*-ādīnām = iva dhanam*, *Kāvya-prakāśa*, on Kārikā 2) has led some late commentators, belonging to the seventeenth century and thereabouts, to impute sinister motives to Harṣa and to suspect the genuineness of his claim to the authorship of the *Ratnāvalī*.[5] It has accordingly been averred by these later exegetes that Dhāvaka composed

1. *Ratnāvalī*, i.5; *Priyadarśikā*, i.3; *Nāgānanda*, i. 3.
2. *Priyadarśikā*, iii.3 = *Nāgānanda*, iv.1; *Priyadarśikā*, iii. 10 = *Nāgānanda*, i.14.
3. *Ratnāvalī*, iv.21 = *Priyadarśikā*, iv.12.
4. J. Takakusu, *A Record of the Buddhist Religion as Practised in India and the Malay Archipelago* (Oxford, 1896), pp. 163-64.
5. Why the scholiasts chose the *Ratnāvalī* alone for calling Harṣa's authorship in question cannot be ascertained. But it was regarded as the best of Harṣa's plays and is, therefore, frequently referred to by the rhetoricians. Consequently by challenging his authorship of this play they refused, though implicitly, to concede his title as an author.

the *Ratnāvalī* but allowed it to pass in the name of Harṣa for pecuniary considerations.[1] But in view of the conclusive evidence, internal as well as external, bearing on the question, noticed above, the accusation of these scholiasts, who were removed from Harṣa by nearly a millennium, cannot be taken very seriously, and there are no cogent reasons to doubt Harṣa's authorship of the *Ratnāvalī*, as well as of the remaining two plays.[2]

The elaborate account of the performance of an act of the *Ratnāvalī* which, it may be incidentally pointed out, is the earliest known reference to the play, indicates the great popularity enjoyed by it in the days of Dāmodaragupta. An interval of about a century must be allowed between the composition of the play and its attaining such a popularity as is reflected in our poem.[3]

2. *Reference to Bhāskaravarman*

Verse 561, containing a reference to a certain Bhāskaravarman, may also point in the same direction. We are told that when Bhāskaravarman passed away, he was accompanied on the funeral pyre by his beloved who was unable to bear the pangs of separation from her lover even though she was dissuaded

1. The accusing commentators are Jayarāma, Vaidyanātha, Nāgoji and Paramānanda. Vide Nariman, Jackson and Ogden. *Priyadarśikā*, Introduction, p. xlvii.

2. Bāṇa, it may be noted, eulogises Harṣa's poetic talent which could hardly find expression in words and stresses his originality in composition, pouring forth, in art-poesy and in stories, a nectar unquaffed (from other sources). See *Harṣa-carita* (edited by Führer with the *Saṅketa* commentary, BSS, No. LXVI, Bombay, 1909), pp. 112, 121.

It has been recently suggested that Bāṇa makes a veiled allusion to the *Ratnāvalī* and has actually modelled his *Harṣa-carita* on it. Vide V. S. Pathak, *Ancient Historians of India* (Bombay, 1966), pp. 39-43.

For a full discussion on Harṣa's authorship of the *Ratnāvalī* see Nariman, Jackson and Ogden, *Priyadarśikā*, Introduction, pp. xxxix-xlix, lxxvii-lxxxvi; R. S. Tripathi, *l. c.*, pp. 180-87; A. B. Keith, *Sanskrit Drama*, pp. 170-71.

3. The *Nāgānanda* is, however, referred to by I-tsing as early as the last quarter of the seventh century A.D. The play had a strong Buddhistic appeal and could not escape the notice of the discerning Chinese pilgrim who was in search of everything appertaining his religion. The *Ratnāvalī* is undoubtedly the master-piece of Harṣa from the point of view of dramatic art and its great popularity, especially among dancing girls, may have been due, at least partly, to its sexual appeal.

from doing so by the king.[1] That our author intended to represent Bhāskaravarman as a monarch is evidenced by the intervention of the ruling chief, who was evidently his successor. The identification of this Bhāskaravarman, however, poses a difficult problem which does not admit of a definite solution in the present state of insufficient information. It is worth mentioning in this connection that the poet has mentioned by name a number of personages to illustrate the treacherous character of a procuress (vv. 35-38), the selfless love of a hetaira (vv. 559-566) and the like;[2] but they are undoubtedly fictitious figures invented to exemplify the various aspects of a prostitute's craft. Likewise, Bhāskaravarman, too, may be an imaginary figure. Even if we were to regard him as an historical personage, it is not easy to identify him. The only Bhāskaravarman known to sober history is the homonymous king of Kāmarūpa who was a contemporary of Harṣavardhana and the Chinese pilgrim Yuan Chwang. There is nothing improbable in Dāmodaragupta having heard of king Bhāskaravarman, particularly as he appears to have been thoroughly familiar with Harṣavardhana and his times.[3] That our poet was not averse to history is amply borne out by his valuable reference to the Kalacuri king Anaṅgaharṣa, to be noticed shortly. And if the two Bhāskaravarmans are regarded as identical, this allusion supplies an interesting piece of information about the Kāmarūpa king so far not available from any other source. But in the absence of an independent evidence on the point, the question must be left open.[4]

1. भास्करवर्मणि याते सुरवसतिं वारिताऽपि भूपतिना ।
तद्दुःखमसहमाना प्रविवेश विलासिनी दहनम् ॥ *K* 561.

2. Several men and women are mentioned by name, evidently to give a semblance of reality, for illustrating the conversation of procuresses, courtesans and their lovers. Vide vv. 331-67, 743-55, etc. These and Purandara, Sundarasena, Guṇapālita, Hāralatā, Mañjarī, etc., are fictitious names.

3. See vv. 801-809, 880-929 describing the *Ratnāvalī* of Harṣa.

4. P. C. Choudhury (*The History of Civilization of the People of Assam to the Twelfth Century A.D.* (Gauhati, 1959), p. 348) regards the identification as extremely doubtful, for Bhāskaravarman probably remained a celibate throughout his life. This view is evidently based on Bhāskaravarman's other name Kumāra, which literally taken would denote a bachelor, a celibate, an unmarried person. B. N. Shastri (Is Bhāskaravarmā, the King of Kāmarūpa, referred to in Kuṭṭanī-mata of Dāmodaragupta ?, *Summaries of Papers*, All-India Oriental Conference, XXIII Session, p. 117) concludes that Bhāskaravarman of the *K* is not a historical figure.

3. *Mention of Turuṣka Army*

Another piece of valuable evidence on the question under review is furnished by verse 10 which describes the Turuṣka army as strong in cavalry (*Turuṣka-sen-eva bahula-gandharvā*). By Turuṣkas here are undoubtedly meant the Arabs who were busy invading the different parts of northern and western India in the eighth century A.D.[1] Although the Arabs had been harbouring covetous designs against India and had carried out several raids earlier,[2] their first real success was the conquest of Sindh by Muhammad-ibn-Qasim in 708 A.D. Thereafter they raided a number of localities in North-Western India, Uttar Pradesh, Rajasthan, Malwa, Gujarat and Kashmir with widely varying results. Lalitāditya Muktāpīḍa (*c.* 724-60 A.D.), the celebrated king of Kashmir, probably inflicted a crushing defeat on the Muslim marauders.[3] In view of these facts, an intimate knowledge of the constitution of the Arab forces, as implied in the mention of the dominant position of the cavalry, could have been possible only about the middle of the eighth century A.D. Dāmodaragupta, therefore, could not have flourished before this date.

4. *Anaṅgaharṣa*

We may now proceed to take note of two precious references which clinch the issue by supplying us with both the upper and lower limits for the flourishing period of Dāmodaragupta. One of these is the mention of the demise of Anaṅgaharṣa, a patron of arts and letters, as a recent event.[4] The prominence attached to him by our poet more than justifies the general notion of the scholars that he was a royal personage. But so far he has not been identified satisfactorily. The general con-

1. Verse 11 of the Gwalior *praśasti* of Bhoja I also refers to the Arabs as Turuṣkas. Vide *EI*, XVIII, p. 108. verse H.

2. R. C. Majumdar and A.D. Pusalkar (Ed.), *Classical Age* (*The History and Culture of the Indian People*, Vol. III), pp. 167, 169.

3. *Ibid.*, pp. 130, 134, 173-74. Earlier, in 713 A.D., king Candrāpīḍa of Kashmir asked for the help of the Chinese emperor against the Arabs who, under Muhammad-bin-Qasim, had reached the frontier of Kashmir about this time. Though the Chinese emperor did not oblige him, Candrāpīḍa successfully defended his kingdom unaided. Vide *ibid.*, p. 132.

4. वयमपि देवनिकेतनमनङ्गहर्षे गते त्रिदिवलोकम् ।
आश्रितवन्तो गत्वा (v.l.-न्तोऽगत्या) तीर्थस्थानानुरोधेन ॥ *K* 800.

sensus among scholars, however, is in favour of regarding him as identical with the emperor Harṣavardhana of Thanesar and Kannauj. The first to propose this identification was probably Prof. K. H. Dhruva[1] who suggested that Harṣavardhana was also known as Anaṅga-Harṣa after *Ratnāvalī*, i. 22, wherein Udayana, king of Kauśāmbī, describing the matchless beauty of the queen Vāsavadattā, states rhetorically that the god Anaṅga (= bodiless, i.e., Cupid), failing to enjoy the touch of her hands, would definitely resent the loss of his body.[2] Mr. Tripathi acquiesces in this suggestion[3] and cites numerous instances of poets being nicknamed after some of their famous verses or expressions.[4] N. C. Mehta also commends this identification.[5] This view, which is apparently prompted by the fact that the stanza referring to Anaṅgaharṣa is immediately followed by one mentioning the *Ratnāvalī* plausibly attributed to Harṣavardhana on independent grounds, though tempting and largely followed, does not carry conviction. The strongest argument against this view is that Harṣavardhana is not referred to by this name even once by either Bāṇa or Yuan Chwang whose writings form the major source of our information about him. Had he been actually known by this name, we must justifiably expect it to occur in the prologues of his three plays or in his official records. But it is conspicuous by its absence there. We must, therefore, look for our Anaṅgaharṣa somewhere else.

The discovery and publication of the *Tāpasa-Vatsarāja*,[6] a play based on the Udayana cycle of legends, have thrown

1. K. H. Dhruva (Ed.), *Priyadarśikā* (1915), Introduction.

2. अनङ्गोऽयमनङ्गत्वमद्य निन्दिष्यति ध्रुवम् ।
यदनेन न संप्राप्तः पाणिस्पर्शोत्सवस्तव ॥

Ratnāvalī, i.22.

3. Vide his commentary on *K* 800, p. 285. However, he confounds the author of the *Ratnāvalī* with that of the *Tāpasa-Vatsarāja*.

4. E.g., Dīpaśikhā-Kālidāsa or Dhūma-Kālidāsa = Kālidāsa; Ātapatra-Bhāravi or Chatra-Bhāravi = Bhāravi; Niśā-Nārāyaṇa = Nārāyaṇa; Tāla-Ratnākara = Ratnākara; Yamunā-Trivikrama = Trivikramabhaṭṭa; Indu-Murāri = Murāri; Karṇikāra-Maṅkha = Maṅkha, etc.

5. N. C. Mehta, A Dramatic Production of the Eighth Century : the Development of the Modern, *JBORS*, xiv (1928), pp. 358 ff.

6. It has been edited on the basis of the only available manuscript by Yadugiri Yatirāja. Bangalore 1929. The manuscript is very defective and both the beginning and the end are lost.

very interesting light on this problem. According to its *prastāvanā* (prologue), it was composed by king Mātrarāja, also known as Anaṅgaharṣa, the son of Narendravardhana. The author is described as verily the moon among all the kings (*Nanu tasy-aiva sakala-narendra-candramasaḥ śrī-Narendravardhana-sūnor = Anaṅgaharṣ-āpara-nāmnaḥ śrī-Mātrarājasya ku(kṛ)tau kṛt-ānurāgo janaḥ samprati*).[1] Ever since the discovery of this play there has been no doubt about the identity of its author with Māyurāja,[2] the author of the *Udātta-Rāghava*, a play dramatising the *Rāmāyaṇa* story with alterations and omissions of such of the events in Rāma's life as cast a slur on his character, for the purpose of the author, as indicated by the title of the drama, was to represent the hero as entirely free from all defects. This identification was first suggested by M. Ramakrishna Kavi on the basis of the fact that Sarvānanda in his commentary on the *Nāmaliṅgānuśāsana* quoted a verse from the *Tāpasa-Vatsarāja* as Māyurāja's,[3] showing thereby that the scholiast regarded Māyurāja as just another name of Mātrarāja Anaṅgaharṣa. This identification has been further confirmed by the recent discovery by Dr. V. Raghavan of a manuscript of the *Udātta-Rāghava*, which was till then known only from citations in later works on rhetorics that gave the author's name as Māyurāja.[4] The prologue of this play as found in the only known manuscript is literally the same as that of the *Tāpasa-Vatsarāja* which conclusively proves that both the dramas proceeded from the same pen. The concluding portion of the *bharata-vākya* (benedictory stanza at the end) of the *Tāpasa-Vatsarāja* is lost irretrievably, but that of the *Udātta-Rāghava*, which has fortunately come down to us, refers to king Anaṅgaharṣa.[5] It would thus

1. *Tāpasa-Vatsarāja*, p. 1.
2. But *contra* S. K. De in *JRAS*, 1924, p. 664.
3. *JAHRS*, i, p. 157.
4. *Vakroktijīvita* (edited by S. K. De, Calcutta 1928), pp. 225, 244; *Daśarūpaka*, ii, 59; iii.24 (Māyurāja referred to as the author of the *Udātta-Rāghava*) : iv.13, 28; *Nāṭyadarpaṇa*, pp. 66, 116, 194; *Abhinava-bhāratī*, Ch. xix, etc. Hemacandra (*Kāvyānuśāsana*, Vol. I. p. 457) mentions Māyurāja as the author of a *kāvya*. Also vide Bhaṭṭanātha Svāmin, Māyurāja, *IA*, xli (1912), pp. 139-43; M. R. Kavi, Tāpasa-Vatsarāja, *JAHRS*, i, pp. 195 ff.
5. आस्तां नाद्य विवेकिता प्रतिदिनं नन्दन्तु विप्राः परं
सन्तरस्तावदमी भवन्तु सुखिनो यावद् धरित्रीधराः ।

follow that the real nomenclature of the author of both these plays was Mātrarāja Anaṅgaharṣa, and Māyurāja, mentioned in later Sanskrit works as the name of the author of the *Udātta-Rāghava*, was only a simplified (or Prākritised) form of Mātrarāja.[1] According to a stanza attributed to Rājaśekhara, Māyurāja was the foremost among the Kalacuri poets.[2] Soḍḍhala in his *Udayasundarī-kathā* describes Māurāja as a feudatory chief (*sāmanta*).[3] Mātrarāja (or Māyurāja) Anaṅgaharṣa was thus a Kalacuri ruling chief. But unfortunately he is not referred to in any Kalacuri inscription, and consequently we know absolutely nothing about his career except only his poetic achievements.

Widely divergent opinions are held as regards the date of the royal poet Mātrarāja Anaṅgaharṣa. There prevails a similar uncertainty about the territory over which he ruled. M. Ramakrishna Kavi regarded the *Tāpasa-Vatsarāja* as older than the *Ratnāvalī* of Harṣa and Māyurāja as a Kalacuri ruler of Māhiṣmatī. He proposed to place Mātrarāja about 600 A.D. and took him to be a contemporary of or earlier by about half a century than Bhavabhūti chiefly on stylistic grounds.[4] Bhaṭṭanātha Svāmin, on the other hand, points out that the plot of the *Udātta-Rāghava* deviates much more from the story of the *Rāmāyaṇa* than that of Bhavabhūti's *Mahāvīra-carita* and consequently thinks that Māyurāja must be placed later than Bhavabhūti and prior to Rājaśekhara, somewhere between 750 and 880 A.D.[5] M. Krishnamachariar thinks that Māyurāja Anaṅgaharṣa was a Kalacuri king of Māhiṣmatī who flourished

चन्द्रः प्रौढतरः ᴗ–सहृदयाः गाथा तथायं जनो (?)

गच्छन्त्वाप्तसुहृत्समागमसुखे नानङ्गहर्षोदयम् ॥

The information about the manuscript of the *Udātta-Rāghava* was communicated by Dr. V. Raghavan in a letter to Mahāmahopādhyāya Dr. V. V. Mirashi. I am grateful to the latter for allowing me to utilise this information.

1. Alternatively Māyurāja may have been obtained from Mātṛrāja through the intermediate stage, Māūrāja.

2. मायुराजसमो नान्यो जज्ञे कलचुरिः कविः ।
उदन्वतः समुत्तस्थुः कति वा तुहिनांशवः ॥
Quoted in Jalhaṇa's *Sūkti-muktāvali*, p. 46.

3. *Udayasundarī-kathā* (G.O.S.), p. 150.

4. *JAHRS*, i, pp. 150 ff.

5. *IA*, xli (1912), p. 143.

before the middle of the eighth century A.D.[1] Mahāmahopādhyāya Dr. V.V. Mirashi opines that he was one of the Kalacuri chiefs of Kālañjara who lived after Vāmadeva and before Śaṅkaragaṇa I of Tripurī, somewhere in the first half of the eighth century A.D.[2] Dr. S. K. De holds that the *Tāpasa-Vatsarāja* belongs to a period earlier than the middle of the ninth century A.D. as it was known to Ānandavardhana and Abhinavagupta as well as to Kuntaka.[3]

In the absence of any evidence to the contrary, the identification of Anaṅgaharṣa mentioned by Dāmodaragupta with the homonymous author of the two aforesaid dramas must be regarded as fairly certain, and as he is generally placed about the middle of the eighth century A.D., we may reasonably conclude that our poet could not have lived before the latter half of that century.

The reference to king Anaṅgaharṣa is important from another point of view also. As the date of Dāmodaragupta is indisputably settled by the evidence of Kalhaṇa's *Rāja-taraṅgiṇī*, it enables us to ascertain, more precisely than hitherto possibel, the lower limit of the flourishing period of Anaṅgaharṣa Mātrarāja. The earliest rhetorician to cite a stanza from one of the plays of Anaṅgaharṣa, albeit without naming the author or the work, is Ānandavardhana (855-883 A.D.),[4] while the first to mention Māyurāja Anaṅgaharṣa by name is, as we have seen above, Rājaśekhara (late 9th-early 10th century A.D.). Thus the evidence available so far could only warrant the general conclusion that Anaṅgaharṣa flourished not later than the middle of the ninth century A.D.[5] Professor Mirashi had no doubt suggested for Anaṅgaharṣa Māyurāja some date in the first

1. M. Krishnamachariar, *History of Classical Sanskrit Literature*, pp. 632, 638. According to him, Murāri, in his *Anargha-Rāghava*, makes a veiled allusion to Anaṅgaharṣa.

2. *Inscriptions of the Kalochuri-Chedi Era, CII*, iv, Introduction, p. lxxi.

3. S. N. Dasgupta and S. K. De, *A History of Sanskrit Literature, Classical Period*, Vol. I, p. 301.

4. *Utkampinī*, etc. (*Dhvanyāloka*, on iii. 3-4, p. 304 of K.S.S. Vol. 135, Varanasi, 1940)=*Tāpasa-Vatsarāja*, ii. 16. The *Tāpasa-Vatsarāja* has been quoted, among others, by Abhinavagupta, Rājaśekhara, Kuntaka, Mammaṭa, Maṅkha, Bhoja, Jalhaṇa and Hemacandra also. Vide pp. 17 ff. of the Sanskrit Introduction to the play.

5. As has been pointed out by S. K. De in *A History of Sanskrit Literature, Classical Period*, Vol. I, p. 301.

half of the eighth century A.D.,[1] but till now it was in the nature of a mere conjecture as no definite evidence could be adduced in support of this position.[2] The *Kuṭṭanī-mata* reference under study settles this problem once for all, as it proves beyond doubt that Anaṅgaharṣa could not have flourished later than the third quarter of the eighth century A.D.[3] And that he did not live much earlier and that his demise was quite a recent happening still fresh in public memory in the time of Dāmodaragupta is evident from the manner in which he refers to him. We are told that on the demise of Anaṅgaharṣa, a dance-master (*nartakācārya*) who had till then apparently enjoyed his patronage, went to Vārāṇasī as it was a holy place (*tīrtha*) and there trained some dancing girls in the performance of the *Ratnāvalī*, a drama emanating from the pen of Harṣavardhana. Now, as Harṣa lived up to about the middle of the seventh century A.D. and assuming that his writings must have taken at least about half a century to have attained such a great popularity, king Anaṅgaharṣa Mātrarāja, at whose court the *nartakācārya* must have frequently been required to direct the enactment of the *Ratnāvalī*, could not have lived much earlier than the middle of the eighth century A.D. Anaṅgaharṣa must, therefore, be placed somewhere in the eighth century A.D. preferably in its second or third quarter. It shows also that Anaṅgaharṣa Mātrarāja enjoyed a high reputation as a patron of fine arts, and probably of men of letters too, in his own life-time, something quite rare in those days; so much so that his fame reached the distant Kashmir in such a short time.

5. *Reference to Kedāra*

The reference to *kedāra* as a coin denomination (verse 606) shows that Dāmodaragupta did not live much later than the reign of Jayāpīḍa Vinayāditya. The *Kāśikā-vṛtti* (on v. 2. 120) also mentions the *kedāra* as a coin[4]. There is no doubt

1. *Inscriptions of the Kalachuri-Chedi Era, CII*, iv, Introduction, p. lxxi.

2. This explains the prevalence of widely divergent opinions on the question. As has been shown above, Anaṅgaharṣa is assigned by scholars different dates ranging from about 600 A.D. to the end of the ninth century.

3. In case we accept Kalhaṇa's chronology for Jayāpīḍa's reign, Anaṅgaharṣa will have to be placed before the middle of the eighth century.

4. For a possible allusion to this denomination in the *Bṛhatkalpabhāṣya*, see Ch. VII below.

whatsoever that it referred to the coins of ancient Kashmir copied closely from the gold and base gold coins of the Kidāra Kuṣāṇas. Like the gold issues of the Kidāra Kuṣāṇas, the Toramāṇa copper coins, gold and silver coins of Pravarasena II, gold coins of Narendrāditya and the copper and electrum coins of all the Karkoṭa kings from Durlabhavardhana to Jayāpīḍa Vinayāditya bear, as a rule, the name Kidāra or its abbreviations (Kida, Ki or Ke) under the left arm of the standing king on the obverse.[1] The name Kidāra reminds us of the originator of this type of coins, the first Little Kuṣāṇa chief Kidāra. It is evidently these Kashmir coins that were known as *kedara*. It is instructive to note in this connection that Jayāpīḍa was the last ruler of Kashmir on whose monetary issues we come across the name Kidāra or its abbreviations.[2] We may, therefore, justifiably conclude that our author could not have flourished long after Jayāpīḍa's rule.

The foregoing discussion of the historical evidence afforded by the *Kuṭṭanī-mata* points to the late eighth and early ninth century A.D. as the flourishing period of Dāmodaragupta. In view of this the statement of Kalhaṇa associating our poet with the reign of Jayāpīḍa must be accepted as correct. However, as we shall see in the sequel, the *Kuṭṭanī-mata*, in all likelihood, reflects the moral degeneration obtaining in Kashmir immediately following the demise of Jayāpīḍa. It would follow, therefore, that the period of Dāmodaragupta's literary activities lies probably early in the ninth century A.D.

The duration of Jayāpīḍa's reign holds a pride of place in the literary history of India in general and Kashmir in particular. He spared no efforts for the revival of learning, "which had hidden itself far away", in Kashmir "which was its original home".[3] He showered wealth and honours on scholars and poets. He restored the study of the *Mahābhāṣya* of Patañjali, which had been interrupted, by bringing from abroad competent expositors.[4] He attached to himself and elevated to higher rank such of the officers as were learned.[5] He was ever on the

1. For these coins see Cunningham, *Coins of Mediaeval India*, pl. iii; V. A. Smith, *Catalogue of Coins in the Indian Museum*, Vol. I, pp. 268-69.
2. For a full discussion of the numismatic data vide *infra*, Ch. VII.
3. *RT*, iv. 486.
4. *Ibid.*, iv. 488.
5. *Ibid.*, iv. 494.

in consequence of which "in the lands of other kings there was a dearth of learned men".[1] The noble example set by the king look-out for and collected all competent scholars at his court was followed by his feudatories and subordinates also.[2] Jayāpīḍa was not only a liberal patron of learning, but was himself a great scholar and poet. Kalhaṇa describes Jayāpīḍa's achievements in this field with his characteristic insight. Jayāpīḍa studied grammar from Kṣīra, a master of grammatical science, and thereby gained distinction.[3] He distinguished himself as a poet,[4] and a stanza is attributed to him in a later Sanskrit anthology.[5] He felt proud in competing with the learned men, and, if Kalhaṇa is to be relied upon, he was more famous as a scholar than as a king, and his reputation for scholarship survived him for a long time.[6] Among the literateurs who adorned his court were included, besides Dāmodaragupta and Kṣīra, the following:—(1) Udbhaṭa, the author of the *Alaṅkāra-sāra-saṅgraha* or the *Udbhaṭ-ālaṅkāra*, a scholium on the *Kāvyālaṅkāra* of Bhāmaha, known as *Bhāmaha-vivaraṇa*, *Bhāmaha-vṛtti* or *Kāvyālaṅkāra-vṛtti*, and another commentary on the *Nāṭya-śāstra* of Bharata; he is also known to have written a poem entitled *Kumāra-sambhava*.[7] According to Kalhaṇa, Jayāpīḍa had appointed him as his *sabhāpati* (chief *paṇḍita*) on a daily allowance of one lakh *dinnara* coins.[8] (2) Vāmana, the author of the *Kāvyālaṅkāra-sūtra* and its commentary (*vṛtti*).[9] He should be distinguished from the homonymous joint author of the *Kāśikā-vṛtti*; for the *Kāśikā* being known to the Chinese pilgrim I-tsing[10] must

1. RT, iv. 492.
2. *Ibid.*, iv. 492.
3. *Ibid.*, iv. 489. He has to be distinguished from Kṣīrasvāmin, the author of the *Kṣīra-taraṅgiṇī* (a gloss on the *Dhātu-pāṭha* of Pāṇini), a commentary on the *Amara-kośa* (called *Amara-koś-odghāṭana*) and some other grmmatical treatises, who flourished in the eleventh century A.D. Vide Yudhishthira Mimamsaka and R. S. Bhattacharya (Ed.), *Kṣīra-taraṅgiṇī* (Amritsar, Vikrama Samvat 2014), Introduction, pp. 30 ff. Unfortunately nothing is known about Kṣīra, Jayāpīḍa's teacher in grammar.
4. Kalhaṇa (iv. 550) informs us that scholars were even in his days moved to sadness when remembering the verses which Jayāpīda had composed in the dungeon in Nepal, and in which he had described his condition.
5. *Subhāṣitāvali*, No. 661.
6. *RT*, iv. 490-91.
7. P. V. Kane, *History of Sanskrit Poetics* (Delhi 1961). pp. 48-49. 133-39; S. N. Dasgupta and S. K. De. *l. c.*, pp. 533f.
8. *RT* iv. 495.
9. P. V. Kane, *l.c.*, pp. 139f.
10. Takakusu, *l.c.*, pp. 175f

be considerably older than Jayāpīḍa's time. (3) Manoratha. He was a senior contemporary of Ānandavardhana and an opponent of the *dhvani* theory. He obviously wrote some work (or works) on poetics which, however, has not come down to us.[1] A few stanzas are attributed to him in the *Subhāṣitāvali* of Vallabhadeva.[2] (4-6) Śaṅkhadatta, Caṭaka and Sandhimat are not known from any other source.[3]

The reign of Jayāpīḍa thus witnessed an unprecedented efflorescence of literary activity in which so many giants, each a gem in his chosen field, participated.

Although the Dharmaśāstras enjoin the *gupta*-ending names for the Vaiśyas, this injunction does not appear to have been strictly adhered to as we have instances of the members of other social cadres also bearing such names.[4] Such names are known to have been adopted even by the Brāhmaṇas.[5] Thus on the basis of the name-ending alone we cannot aver that our poet was a Vaiśya. On the contrary, there is definite evidence to show that Dāmodaragupta belonged to the first cadre of the Brāhmaṇical social order. Kṣemendra, while quoting a stanza from the *Kuṭṭanī-mata* in his *Kavi-kaṇṭhābharaṇa* (5.39) prefixes to the name of our author the title *bhaṭṭa* which was distinctive of the Brāhmaṇas. In epigraphic records this title is attached as a mark of reverence to the names of the learned Brāhmaṇas.[6] It is still borne as a surname by certain sections of the Brāhmaṇas.

1. *RT*, iv. 497. Ānandavardhana cites a verse which derides the *dhvani* theory and makes out a case for the *alaṅkāras*, *vakrokti* and *vyutpatti* as the very essence of poetry. According to Abhinavagupta, this stanza belonged to Manoratha. Vide *Dhvanyāloka* (K. S. S., Vol. 135, Varanasi 1940), pp. 26-27. Ānandavardhana was a contemporary of Avantivarman (855/56-883 A.D.), while Manoratha was a court poet of Jayāpīḍa. Manoratha must, therefore, be taken to be a senior contemporary of Ānandavardhana.

2. Nos. 51, 58, 440.

3. *RT*, iv. 497.

4. The Gupta emperors, for instance, appear to have been Kṣatriyas. Vide G.H. Ojha, *Rājapūtāne kā Itihāsa*, pp. 113-14.

5. E.g., Viṣṇugupta, more popularly known as Kauṭilya and Cāṇakya, Abhinavagupta and his ancestor Atrigupta.

6. *EI*, xxiii, p. 77, l. 18, p. 129, l. 32, p. 152, l. 36; xxvi, p. 123, etc. A Brāhmaṇa village is referred to as *bhaṭṭa-grāma*. Vide *ibid.*, xxv, p. 160, text line 20.

That Dāmodaragupta was an adherent of Brāhmaṇical Hinduism admits of no doubt. He no doubt makes a few allusions to the Buddha and some tenets of Buddhism, but they do not seem to emanate from a Buddhist's pen. We find many a reference to Vaiṣṇavism some of which shed lurid light on the condition of this sect in Dāmodaragupta's time. But at one place we come across a derisive description of a Vaiṣṇava ascetic forming a laughing stock of the people,[1] which would hardly behove a follower of Vaiṣṇavism. References to other divinities and cults are few and far between. As against this, Śaivism claims the largest number of references of which many are indicative of the highest veneration and even smack of sectarianism.[2] This should leave no room for doubt that Dāmodaragupta owed allegiance to Śaivism. This does not mean, however, that he was a bigot; like an average Hindu, he was rather eclectic in religious matters as evidenced by numerous allusions of a religious import.

The *Kūṭṭanī-mata* is so far the only known work of Dāmodaragupta. But there are four stanzas quoted as his in the *Subhāṣitāvali* of Vallabhadeva,[3] which cannot be traced in the *Kuṭṭanī-mata*.[4] It is likely, therefore, that our poet was the author of some other poem or poems also, but nothing is known

1. *K* 748-52.

2. See the description of Vārāṇasī, vv. 3 ff. The author makes the prince of the distant Devarāṣṭra pay a visit to Vārāṇasī in order to worship Śiva.

3. आरोग्यं विद्वत्ता सज्जनमैत्री महाकुले जन्म ।
स्वाधीनता च पुंसां महदैश्वर्यं विनाप्यर्थैः ॥ २३५ ॥
यद् धीमतातिवेगेन व्यासेन सहसा बहु ।
भाषितं शतशस्तेन तत्रैव च रुचिं कुरु ॥ २३३० ॥
चक्रिता च मृताचार्यं चेलं चर्चा च लीनता ।
चकारचञ्चुता चेति सप्त जीवनहेतवः ॥ २३३१ ॥
उपयुक्तखदिरवीटकजनिताधरभङ्गभयात् ।
कुलटा वाटकनिकटे तृष्यन्त्यपि वारि नो पिबति ॥ २३३६ ॥

4. Dāmodaragupta must be distinguished from Dāmodara and Dāmodarabhaṭṭa whose stanzas are cited in the *Padya-veṇī* (edited by J. B. Chaudhuri, Calcutta 1944) compiled by Veṇīdatta about the middle of the seventeenth century A.D. None of the stanzas quoted under their names is found in the *K.*

about them at present. It is possible that some of his other writings may come to light in future. However, there is no doubt that the *Kuṭṭanī-mata* was his *magnum opus* and his renown as a poet principally rested on it.

III. THE STORY

In short, the story of the *Kuṭṭanī-mata* runs as follows:

In the city of Vārāṇasī there lived a courtesan, Mālatī by name. Even though possessed of all the conceivable physical charms, she could attract only low-born, unmerited, diseased and ugly clients as she was not quite familiar with the tricks behoving her profession (3-21, 40). Once, while on the terrace of her house, she heard somebody reciting an Āryā which exhorted that an hetaira should give up the pride of her youth and beauty and strive to learn the ways and means of captivating the hearts of men (22-23). Taking it for a timely advice, she went to an old experienced procuress, Vikarālā, to seek her counsel in this matter. Having saluted her with her head bowed down on the earth, she eulogised Vikarālā's extraordinary success as a courtesan and bawd and then solicited her instructions (24-42). Vikarālā paid glowing tributes to Mālatī's peerless beauty which by itself, said she, was capable of winning the hearts of wealthy young men (43-57). Then she gave the following advice :

She (Mālatī) should entice Cintāmaṇi, son of an influential government officer. His father being away in the capital, he is the master of his own affairs and as such he can be easily won over. To accomplish this object she should despatch a shrewd female messenger (*dūtī*) to him. The messenger should first offer him betel and flowers and then narrate the pathetic condition that her mistress has reached pining in love for him, her matchless beauty and other accomplishments and try to attract him towards Mālatī by all means at her command (58-136).

When thus entangled, Cintāmaṇi comes to her residence, he should be suitably received and conducted to the bedchamber. Mālatī's mother should welcome him there and express gratitude for his visit. After she has left the bedroom, Mālatī should offer her person and satiate his sexual appetite by a variety of love sports (137-64). She should then pretend jealousy with Cintāmaṇi's wife by praising the latter's good fortune to have secured such a good husband and entreat him not to deprive her (Mālatī) of his love. And in order to convince him of the sincerity of her love she should narrate the following episode of Hāralatā and Sundarasena[1] (165-75):

In the city of Pāṭaliputra there lived a learned, pious Brāhmaṇa named Purandara. He had a very handsome and learned son, Sundarasena by name. One day when he was seated in a lonely place enjoying the company of his trusted friend, Guṇapālita, he heard an Āryā stressing the importance of peregrination for education. Thereupon Sundarasena resolved to embark upon a long sojourn and conveyed his decision to Guṇapālita. The latter described the difficulties experienced in a long journey. When they were thus conversing, they heard some one reciting another Āryā which emboldened them to brave these hardships (175-232).

In course of their peregrinations they arrived at the Arbuda mountain which they climbed. There Sundarasena happened to see a beautiful damsel named Hāralatā. Hāralatā also saw him and got enamoured of him. In her frantic longing for Sundarasena she landed herself in a pathetic condition. Having failed to dissuade her from this unstinted love unbecoming of a courtesan, her friend Candraprabhā betook herself to Sundarasena and apprised him of Hāralatā's love-lorn condition. Notwithstanding Guṇapālita's loud warnings against the genuineness of a wench's professions of love, Sundarasena decided to honour Hāralatā's love and went to her residence hearing on his way the conversation of the prostitutes, rakes and procuresses. He spent about one year and a half enjoying various kinds of pleasures in the company of his beloved. Just then he received a missive from his father rebuking him for having fallen in the trap of an hetaira in complete disregard of his high family tradition and asking him to return home immediately. He was at a loss to decide the future course of action, but on Guṇapālita's advice resolved to obey his father. Hāralatā accompanied them up to a banyan tree where Sundara-

1. S. K. De (*A History of Sanskrit Literature*, Vol. I, p. 197) wrongly gives the name of Hāralatā's lover as Sudarśana.

sena bade her good bye and proceeded further. He had hardly covered a little distance when he learnt from a fellow-traveller the tidings of the sad demise of Hāralatā. Broken-hearted, he at once returned to the banyan tree under which his sweetheart had breathed her last and mourned her death, while Guṇapālita consigned her mortal remains to the flames of fire. Sundarasena, unable to stand the grief, was about to follow his beloved on the funeral pyre when he heard a timely Āryā dissuading him from such a cowardly act. Sundarasena, however, could not bear the shock of her death and, accompanied by Guṇapālita, embraced ascetic life (233-497).

By all the means at her command, Mālatī should convince Cintāmaṇī that her love is not inspired by any pecuniary consideration (498-527). Once such a conviction is brought home, she should try to squeeze all his wealth by various cunning devices. She should, for instance, pretend to quarrel with her mother, the latter rebuking her for having rejected rich and generous clients for the sake of Cintāmaṇi and asking her to return forthwith all her belongings and the former professing her selfless love for Cintāmaṇi and handing over all the ornaments in the fit of the moment. On hearing these angry exchanges, Cintāmaṇi may bring to his mind some examples of the sincere love of the hetairae and being convinced of the genuineness of her love may eventually decide to please her by giving away everything belonging to him (528-84). If this fails, she should try the following stratagem: through her friend she should have it conveyed to Cintāmaṇi that on his failing to turn up last night his sweetheart, with all the jewellery on her person, went to meet him and was on the way robbed of her ornaments by the thieves (585-604). This device also failing, she should resort to other tricks such as a usurer demanding back his money which she had borrowed for Cintāmaṇi by pledging her pearl necklace (605-10), pretending to make an offering to the deity which she had earlier promised for securing his health when he was ill (611-13), and burning the house after removing everything therefrom and announcing wholesale destruction (614).

Having extracted all his belongings, she should strive to drive him out by such devices as showing disregard for him, giving him a separate seat, jealous speech, heart-breaking laughter, praising his rivals, accusing him of talking too much, obstructing his talk by opening some new topic, condemning his conduct, avoiding his company and making the maid utter harsh words. These tricks also failing, Mālatī should tell him that though she still loved him she could not afford to disobey her mother all the same and therefore he must get out at least for some time (615-63).

Having thus ousted Cintāmaṇi, she may proceed to woo again a man whom she had earlier discarded after his wealth was exhausted, provided, of course, he has regained his wealth. She may convince him of her sincerity by attributing their previous separation to a misunderstanding caused by a villain. In order to inflame his sexual appetite, she may recall to his mind earlier enjoyments. She should desert him again after his regained affluence has disappeared. In short, the behaviour of a strumpet is exemplified by the maxim of a mango which is first chewn fully and then thrown away or by that of a fish whose skin and bones are cast away after eating the flesh (674-735).

Then, in order to bring her advice home to Mālatī, Vikarālā narrated the following anecdote of the dancing girl Mañjarī and prince Samarabhaṭa :

Once prince Samarabhaṭa, son of Siṁhabhaṭa, king of Devarāṣṭra,[1] accompanied by some attendants, visited Vārāṇasī with the object of offering worship to the god Vṛṣabhadhvaja (i.e. Śiva). Hearing the conversation of the rakes and wenches on the way, he reached the temple and offered worship. Thereafter he was suitably received in an assemblage of dancers, actors and actresses, musicians, strumpets, traders and business magnets. On his inquiry about the state of music and dance in Vārāṇasī, the dance-master (*nartakācārya*) present there described the deplorable condition of these arts after king Anaṅgaharṣa's demise pointing out that the courtesans were interested more in their clients than in the pursuit of fine arts. He, however, introduced the prince to a pretty dancing girl, Mañjarī by name, who, he said, was an accomplished actress and requested him to witness the first act of the *Ratnāvalī* performed by his pupils. The prince appreciated the performance, particularly Mañjarī's role as Sāgarikā, adequately rewarded the dance-

1. S. K. De (*ibid.*, p. 198) wrongly describes Samarabhaṭa as the king of Benares.

master and returned to his residence. But he was deeply enamoured of Mañjarī, and when he was just describing her physical charms to his minister, there appeared Mañjarī's messenger who narrated graphically her mistress's affected love-lorn condition, thereby blazing his sexual appetite still further. On hearing Samarabhaṭa's favourable reply, Mañjarī, accompanied by her maid, came to the prince's residence, gratified him with a variety of love plays and deserted him after squeezing all his wealth (736-1056).

In conclusion, Vikarālā urged Mālatī to follow her instructions if she wished to amass great wealth (1057).

Convinced of the advice of Vikarālā, Mālatī came back home (1058).

IV. SOURCES OF THE STORY

It would appear from the above outline that the theme of the *Kuṭṭanī-mata* depends for its development on two stories, viz., (i) of Sundarasena and Hāralatā, and (ii) of prince Samarabhaṭa and Mañjarī. While the former symbolises ungrudging, selfless love, the latter serves to illustrate the deceptive character of the prostitute's craft. The two stories, it would be clear, are not in any way connected with one another. Even if they are taken individually, there is nothing charming about them. They look like two independent offices functioning in the same building. That Dāmodaragupta could create such a beautiful poem out of these disconnected anecdotes is by itself an eloquent tribute to his poetic talents.

We have absolutely no knowledge as regards the source of these stories. Attention may, however, be invited to some similar stories found in other works. Particular interest in this connection attaches to the *Kathā-sarit-sāgara* of Somadeva[1] and the *Bṛhat-kathā-mañjarī* of Kṣemendra[2] which represent the Kashmirian version of the celebrated Paiśācī compendium of stories, the *Bṛhat-kathā* of Guṇāḍhya. The Śaktiyaśolambaka of these works contains an interesting anecdote which runs as follows:—

1. Edited by Durgaprasad and K. P. Parab, 4th edition, Bombay, 1930. Translated into English by C. H. Tawney and edited by N. M. Penzer, Vols. I-X, London.

2. Edited by Sivadatta and K. P. Parab, 2nd edition, Bombay, 1931.

Ratnavarman, a wealthy merchant of the city of Citrakūṭa, had a son named Īśvaravarman. When the latter was on the verge of manhood, his father entrusted him to a bawd named Yamajihvā in order that he might learn the tricks of courtesans and not be deceived by them. Thereafter Īśvaravarman left for Suvarṇadvīpa for the purpose of trade. On his way, he arrived at a town named Kāñcanapura and set up his camp on its outskirts. Leaving his companions in the camp, he entered the town and went to a temple to witness a spectacle. And there he saw an hetaira named Sundarī and fell in love with her. He had lived with her for two months and exhausted much of his wealth when his friend advised him to resume the journey. With much reluctance he secured Sundarī's permission to part company. In the meantime, Sundarī and her mother Makarakaṭī hatched a stratagem and had a net spread out in a well lying on the road the traders must take. On the next day when Īśvaravarman set out on the journey, Sundarī and Makarakaṭī went up to the well to bid him farewell. There he made his sweetheart return, and he had hardly resumed his journey when Sundarī flung herself into the well over the net. Hearing the loud cries of her mother and the maids, Īśvaravarman and his friend came back there. Sundarī was brought out of the well, and she feigned regaining consciousness. Taking this incident as symbolising Sundarī's deep-seated love for him, the merchant's son gave up the idea of continuing the journey, and notwithstanding Arthadatta's advice against reposing confidence in a courtesan, he continued to live with Sundarī; and when he was stripped of all his wealth, Makarakaṭī had him turned out of his beloved's abode. When this episode was conveyed to his father, he somehow had his son brought back home. The remainder of the story does not concern us in the present inquiry.[1]

Making due allowance for the inevitable differences in accordance with the different objectives the two authors had before them, the close resemblance between the two stories of the *Kuṭṭanī-mata* on the one hand and the above story of the *Kathā-sarit-sāgara* and the *Bṛhat-kathā-mañjarī* on the other cannot be

1. *Kathā-sarit-sāgara*, x. 1. 54-175; Tawney and Penzer, vol. v, pp. 5-13; *Bṛhat-kathā-mañjarī*, xvi. 2. 36ff. There are some very insignificant differences between the two versions of the story.

denied. Taking first the story of Sundarasena and Hāralatā for comparison, Sundarasena of our story may stand for Īśvaravarman of the other story; the roles of their friends, Guṇapālita and Arthadatta, are almost identical; fathers of both Sundarasena and Īśvaravarman are perturbed at the news of their sons falling victims to the stratagems of the strumpets. The banyan tree of the *Kuṭṭanī-mata* and the well of the *Kathā-sarit-sāgara* and the *Bṛhat-kathā-mañjarī* also compare well. But whereas Vikarālā aimed at illustrating the rare unstinted love of a courtesan, the object of Somadeva and Kṣemendra was to demonstrate the untrustworthy character of the love of a wench. Hence Hāralatā, being unable to bear the pangs of separation from her lover, actually dies, while Sundarī feigns death with the object of beguiling her victim, Īśvaravarman.

This story bears a close resemblance with the other story of the *Kuṭṭanī-mata* also. Both Samarabhaṭa and Īśvaravarman fall into the clutches of the strumpets after seeing their performance, one at a Śiva temple at Vārāṇasī and the other at a temple at Kāñcanapura. And the heroes of both the stories are discarded after they are divested of all their riches. The only differences between the two stories are that (1) while Samarabhaṭa was a prince, Iśvaravarman was a trader; (2) in the *Kuṭṭanī-mata* story, even though Samarabhaṭa was enamoured of Mañjarī, it was the latter who took initiative, whereas in the other story the initiative was taken by Īśvaravarman, not by Sundarī, and (3) whereas Īśvaravarman's friend Arthadatta tried to save Īśvaravarman from the clutches of the wenches, Samarabhaṭa's minister tried to detract his master from the strumpet by attracting him to another equally great vice, viz., involvement with others' wives. But these differences are very minor and in no way affect the general tone of the two anecdotes. It is possible, though by no means certain, that Dāmodaragupta may have borrowed both of his stories from an original anecdote like the one outlined above.

It must also be pointed out here that there is a close similarity between the description of the physical features of the bawds Yamajihvā and Vikarālā[1] and their instructions to their

1. तत्र स्थूलहनुं दीर्घदशनां भुग्ननासिकाम् ।
शिक्षयन्तीं दुहितरं कुट्टनीं तां ददर्श सः ॥ *Kathā-sarit-sāgara*, x.1.60.

student strumpets.[1]

In this connection two other stories of the *Kathā-sarit-sāgara* and the *Bṛhat-kathā-mañjarī* also deserve attention. In one of these stories we read how Kumudikā, a courtesan of Ujjayinī, was prepared to sacrifice everything including her own life and helped Vikramasiṁha, king of Pratiṣṭhāna, regain his lost kingdom only to secure the release of a poor Brahmin's son, Śrīdhara by name, for whom she had genuine love.[2] The other story features Rūpiṇikā, a prostitute of Mathurā, who cherished selfless love for a poor Brāhmaṇa and persisted in it even against the explicit desire of her mother.[3] It is not impossible that our poet may have got the idea of depicting the sincere love of Hāralatā for the Brāhmaṇa Sundarasena from some such story.

The *Kathā-sarit-sāgara* and the *Bṛhat-kathā-mañjarī* are no doubt later than the *Kuṭṭanī-mata* by about three centuries and as such Dāmodaragupta could not have derived his story from Somadeva and Kṣemendra. But as averred by the two Kashmi-

अथ विरलोन्नतदशनां निम्नहनु स्थूलचिपिटनासाग्राम् । *K* 27.

1. धनेन पूज्यते पुत्रि सर्वो वेश्या विशेषतः ।
तच्च नास्त्यनुरागिण्या रागं वेश्या त्यजेदतः ॥
दोषाग्रदूतो रागो हि वेश्यापश्चिमसन्ध्ययोः ।
मिथ्यैव दर्शयेद् वेश्या तं नटीव सुशिक्षिता ॥
रञ्जयेत् तेन सा पूर्वं दुह्याद् रक्तं ततो धनम् ।
दुग्धार्थं च त्यजेदन्ते प्राप्तार्थं पुनराहरेत् ॥
समो यूनि शिशौ वृद्धे विरूपे रूपवत्यपि ।
वेश्याजनो यो मुनिवत्स चार्थं परमश्नुते ॥
चाटुक्रममनुरागं प्रणयरुषौ विरहजनितशोकार्तिम् ।
प्रकटयति वाररमणी नटीव शिक्षाभियोगेन ॥
प्रवयसि यौवनशालिनि हीनकुले सत्कुलप्रसूते च ।
रोगवति दृढशरीरे समचित्ता योगिनश्च गणिकाश्च ॥

Also cf. *K* 33 and *Kathā-sarit-sāgara*, xiv.4.82; *The Ocean of Story*, vol. viii, p. 60.

2. *Ibid.*, vol. v, pp. 15-18; *Kathā-sarit-sāgara*, x.2.1-53; *Bṛhat-kathā-mañjarī*, xvi.3.84-113.

3. *Ibid.*, ii.76-131; *Kathā-sarit-sāgara*, ii. 12.78-194; *The Ocean of Story*, vol. i, pp. 133 ff.

rian authors themselves, their works are only abridged Sanskrit versions of that vast compendium of story-literature, the *Bṛhat-kathā* of Guṇāḍhya in the Paiśācī dialect. This work, originally composed in the Sātavāhana period, was a treasure-house of narrative literature, and many Sanskrit and Prākrit literateurs have borrowed their themes from it. It is, therefore, very likely that the stories of Sundarī, Kumudikā and Rūpiṇikā may have been found in the original *Bṛhat-kathā* wherefrom Dāmodaragupta seems to have derived his stories introducing only such changes as were necessary for his purpose.

Before we leave this topic, attention must be drawn to an incident described at length in the *Rāja-taraṅgiṇī* of Kalhaṇa. The poet-historian narrates in detail how the Karkoṭa king Jayāpīḍa went to a temple of Kārttikeya at Puṇḍravardhana to view the dancing and singing performed in accordance with the precepts and fell in love with the dancing girl Kamalā which ultimately resulted into their life-long union.[1] The resemblance between this anecdote and the story of Mañjarī and Samarabhaṭa is quite obvious. Both Jayāpīḍa and Samarabhaṭa went to temples, one to the temple of Vṛṣabhadhvaja (i.e. Śiva) at Vārāṇasī and the other to a temple of the god Kārttikeya at Puṇḍravardhana in Bengal and both fell in love after watching a performance there. But whereas Kamalā's love for Jayāpīḍa was genuine, Mañjarī was actuated by pecuniary considerations. The incident narrated by Kalhaṇa does not belong to the domain of legends; it is real history. According to Kalhaṇa, this episode took place in the time of Jayāpīḍa, the patron of Dāmodaragupta, himself. It must have been widely known to the people and also to our poet; it is quite possible that Dāmodaragupta utilised some such incident and made a story out of it. However, whatever has been stated here about the sources of the stories of the *Kuṭṭanī-mata* is only a possibility; no certainty attaches to it.

In this connection reference must also be made to the general immorality prevailing in Kashmir in the time of Dāmodaragupta. The vice of prostitution was ubiquitous and even kings were not immune from it. A perusal of the *Rāja-taraṅgiṇī* shows the gravity of the havoc that prostitution wrought in the history of Kashmir.

1. *RT*,. iv. 421 ff.

Durlabhaka-Pratāpāditya II, the second king of the Karkoṭa dynasty, was overwhelmed by passion for Narendraprabhā, a lady of bewitching beauty and wife of a merchant named Noṇa, and married her after overcoming initial reluctance.[1] Vajrāditya, also known as Bappiyaka and Lalitāditya and father of Jayāpīḍa, was of a cruel character, wicked and a slave to avarice. He had a large number of women in his seraglio, with whom he diverted himself in turn, like a stallion with the mares, and ended his days through consumption, which was caused by excesses in sensual enjoyment.[2] Jayāpīḍa was one of the greatest rulers of ancient Kashmir. But he turned wicked in the later part of his reign, and under the malignant influence of his officials (the *kāyasthas*) he oppressed his subjects. Being a prey to avarice, he imposed heavy levies on farmers, confiscated the property of the people including the *agrahāras* of the Brāhmaṇas and had a large number of people butchered unnecessarily and consequently met with a violent end.[3] He was succeeded by his son Lalitāpīḍa who, avers Kalhaṇa, was a slave to his passions; he did not attend to regal duties, and the kingdom became the prey of courtesans and was defiled by immorality; he squandered the riches he had inherited on buffoons and the like; parasites got a foothold in the royal palace through their relationship with courtesans and initiated him in the arts of whoredom; he gave up diadem and bracelets, the signs of royalty, and enjoyed the company of women; he was happy in the enjoyment of prostitutes, befriended persons well-versed in narrating the stories about courtesans and clever in jesting and showered affection on parasites who insulted modest old men and thus kept them away; he made respectable old councillors feel ashamed by making them dress themselves in the garments marked with the foot-prints of courtesans.[4] Lalitāpīḍa's son and grand-successor, Cippaṭa-Jayāpīḍa, also called Bṛhaspati, was born of a concubine, Jayadevī, the daughter of a spirit-distiller (*kalya-pāla*) named Uppa. Cippaṭa-Jayāpīḍa's maternal uncles took advantage of their relationship with the king and almost completely plundered the royal

1. *RT.*, iv. 13-37
2. *Ibid.*, iv.393-98
3. *Ibid.*, iv. 620-55.
4. *Ibid.*, iv: 660-73.

treasury.[1] Conditions were not much different during the reigns of his successors, Ajitāpīḍa, Anaṅgāpīḍa and Utpalāpīḍa, when terror and chaos reigned supreme.[2] The situation improved only in 855/56 A.D. when Avantivarman ascended the throne of Kashmir. In short, in the period of some forty years following Jayāpīḍa's reign the destinies of the people of Kashmir, to a great extent, lay with courtesans and concubines. The example set by the kings must have been followed by the subjects. Our poet, who was very closely associated with the royal court, must have observed this state of affairs with his own eyes and felt disgusted. As he had himself been the prime minister, of the state during the reign of the great Jayāpīḍa, he could not have remained merely a passive observer of this deplorable state of affairs. In all likelihood it is this pitiable condition that the poet has really depicted in his poem. The names of characters had to be altered as a matter of course. When the poet, dilating on Mañjarī's physical charms, makes Samarabhaṭa say that one who has tasted the pleasure of her embrace is sure to remove from his mind his duties towards the subjects,[3] he seems to have in his mind such of the contemporary rulers of Kashmir as, engrossed in the enjoyment of courtesans, showed scant regard for their royal duties. Nay, the veil of the poem is transparent enough, and we may even succeed in identifying the king whom Dāmodaragupta had in his mind. The story of prince Samarabhaṭa contains probably a veiled reference to the debauchery of king Lalitāpīḍa, son and successor of Jayāpīḍa Vinayāditya, in whose reign our poet must have continued to live.

To sum up, the above-mentioned stories of the *Kathā-sarit-sāgara* and the *Bṛhat-kathā-mañjarī* which appear to have been included in the original *Bṛhat-kathā* of Guṇāḍhya, the episode culminating in the marriage of king Jayāpīḍa and the dancing girl Kamalā and the general immorality obtaining in Kashmir during the period under review, all appear to have contributed their own share towards the formation of the story of the *Kuṭṭanī-mata*.

1. *RT.*, iv.676 ff.
2. *Ibid.*, iv. 689-715.
3. सकृदपि यैरनुभूतस्तत्तनुपरिरम्भसुखरसास्वादः ।
विद्धि नराधिप तेषां दूरीभूतं प्रजाकार्यम् ॥ *K* 1039.

V. WHEN WAS THE KUṬṬANĪ-MATA COMPOSED ?

Basing on Kalhaṇa's statement that Jayāpīḍa appointed poet Dāmodaragupta, the writer of the *Kuṭṭanī-mata*, his *dhī-saciva*, Shri T. M. Tripathi has suggested that Jayāpīḍa must have made this appointment after testing Dāmodaragupta's ability through the *Kuṭṭani-mata*, i.e., Dāmodaragupta composed the *Kuṭṭani-mata* prior to his appointment as *dhī-saciva*.[1] This, however, does not appear to be very probable. If, as shown above, the *Kuṭṭanī-mata* reflects the moral depravity characterising the history of Kashmir for some four decades after Jayāpīḍa's reign, it would follow that the poem was composed during this period, most likely during Lalitāpīḍa's reign.

VI. DĀMODARAGUPTA AS A POET

Dāmodaragupta was a poet of considerable merit. That in spite of the coarseness of its contents the work attained great popularity within a comparatively short time after its composition and was extensively quoted by rhetoricians, grammarians and compilers of anthologies is symbolic of the esteem which the posterity cherished for Dāmodaragupta and his work. Limitations of space forbid a detailed examination of the literary merits of the *Kuṭṭanī-mata*, which is not also the purpose of the present monograph. Reference may, however, be made to some interesting features of the poem.

Dāmodaragupta selected for his work the Āryā metre (including its varieties like Gīti) which is regarded by some as particularly appropriate for a poem based on the sentiment of love.[2] The use of Āryā for this purpose appears to have been hallowed by tradition dating from very ancient times. It is interesting to note in this connection that the *Gāthā-sattasai*, an anthology of stanzas primarily dealing with love, compiled by Hāla-Sātavāhana and the *Āryā-saptaśatī* of Govardhana are composed in the same metre.[3] It is likely that Dāmodaragupta was inspired by the *Gāthā-sattasai* to adopt this metre for his work which, it must be pointed out, is the earliest datable

1. *RT*, iv. 495; Rasa-dīpikā commentary on *K*, p. 449.
2. *Ibid.*, p. 457.
3. Āryā is in Sanskrit what Gāthā is in Prākrit.

independent poem in Sanskrit treating of erotics. Kṣemendra also employed Āryā while dealing with prostitution in his *Kalā-vilāsa.*[1]

Figures of speech (*alaṅkāras*) are employed extensively by the poet. Those of word (*śabd-ālaṅkaras*) are used rather sparingly, while those of meaning (*arth-ālaṅkāras*) are very common. Among the former are included *vṛttyanuprāsa,*[1a] *śleṣa,*[2] *yamaka,*[3] *yamakāvali*[4] and *vyapetayamaka,*[5] the most prominent among the latter being *anumāna,*[6] *aprastutapraśaṁsā,*[7] *arthāntaranyāsa,*[8] *atiśayokti*[9] and its varieties *arthātiśayokti,*[10] *bhedakātiśayokti,*[11] *rūpakātiśayokti*[12] and *saṁbandhātiśayokti,*[13] *kāvyaliṅga,*[14] *kāvyārthāpatti,*[15] *rūpaka*[16] with its variety *mālārūpaka,*[17] *virodha,*[18] *virodhābhāsa,*[19]-*vyatireka,*[20] *upamā*[21] including its kinds *luptopamā,*[22] *nyūnopamā,*[23] *prativastūpamā,*[24] *pratyayārthopamā,*[25] *śleṣopamā*[26] and *vācakalupto-*

1. But he did not use this metre in the *Samaya-mātṛkā.* The metre did not find favour with most other Sanskrit poets of love.

1a. 103, 641.
2. 296, 766, 769, 966, 979.
3. 768, 966.
4. 305.
5. 643.
6. 182, 483, 709, 720, 750, 971, 973, 1005-6.
7. 118, 119, 132, 486, 516, 517, 552, 722, 825.
8. 106, 130, 245, 269, 286, 293, 297, 428, 1003.
9. 97, 777, 876-77, 977.
10. 978.
11. 784.
12. 769.
13. 814, 962.
14. 125, 183, 291, 295, 488, 547, 625, 721, 772, 784, 985, 987, 996-1000.
15. 975, 977, 1020-21, 1038, 1040.
16. 257-60, 268, 289, 299, 426, 429, 650, 699, 734-35, 1037.
17. 179-80, 208.
18. 179-80, 323, 764, 768, 769, 967, 968, 988.
19. 248-49, 264-66, 311-15, 484, 643, 766, 777, 1011.
20. 111, 354, 575, 577-78, 651, 655, 765, 768, 769, 774, 988.
21. 110, 271, 716, 775.
22. 764.
23. 258.
24. 366, 367.
25. 120.
26. 9-19, 101, 241, 247, 776, 965.

pamā,[27] and *utprekṣā*[28] together with its varieties *svarūpotprekṣā*[29] and *hetūtprekṣā*.[1] Of other *arthālaṅkāras* reference may be made to *anujñā*, *atadguṇa*, *anyokti*, *ākṣepa*, *asaṅgati*, *asama*, *apahnuti*, *kaitavāpahnuti*, *asatsamuccaya*, *udātta*, *kalpitabhrāntimān*, *dīpaka*, *dṛṣṭānta*, *nidarśanā*, *parikara*, *parisaṅkhyā*, *paryāyokti*, *punaruktavadābhāsa*, *punarukti*, *pratīpa*, *bhāvika*, *mudrā*, *lalita*, *vakrokti*, *vibhāvanā*, *vikalpa*, *vinokti*, *viśeṣa*, *viśeṣokti*, *viṣama*, *vyājastuti*, *lokokti*, *sama*, *samādhi*, *sandeha*, *samāsokti*, *samuccaya*, *saṁbhāvanā*, *sahokti*, *svabhāvokti* and *hetu*.[2] We have several examples where more than one figure of speech, sometimes as many as four or five, are employed in a single stanza.[3] Many verses furnish instances of the use of the *alaṅkāras* in combinations (*saṅkara* or *saṁsṛṣṭi*). Thus we have combinations of *unmīlita* and *arthāntaranyāsa* (112), of *ākṣepa* and *arthāntaranyāsa* (114, 243), of *ākṣepa*, *śleṣa* and *arthāntaranyāsa* (296), of *asatsamuccaya* and *kaitavāpahnuti* (393), of *rūpakātiśayokti*, *śleṣa* and *vibhāvanā* (413), of *viṣama* and *arthāntaranyāsa* (976), of *atiśayokti* and *kāvyārthāpatti* (977), of *samuccaya* and *viṣama* (986), and of *anumāna* and *paryāyokti* (1005-6). It stands to the credit of Dāmodaragupta that in most cases the *alaṅkāras* employed by him appear natural and add to the charm of the poem, and do not hamper our understanding as in the later decadant Sanskrit poetry.

Dāmodaragupta was a shrewd story-teller. He adopted a unique device for achieving the progress of the story. The usual method employed by poets to keep the story going is a direct narration or introduction of some new characters. But our poet did not tread this hackneyed path. Characters in

27. 330.
28. 108, 242, 244, 246, 369, 725.
29. 202.
1. 487, 899-900.
2. *Anujñā* : 146, 546 ; *atadguṇa* : 771; *anyokti* : 715, 1037; *ākṣepa* : 114, 1023; *asaṅgati* : 502; *asama* : 1013-14; *apahnuti* : 971; *kaitavāpahnuti* : 393; *asatsamuccaya*: 393; *udātta* : 179-80; *Kalpitabhrāntimān* : 981; *dīpaka* : 319, 320, 321, 645; *dṛṣṭānta*: 705; *nidarśanā* : 991; *parikara*: 681, 777, 987; *parisaṅkhyā*: 186-91, 11-17; 308-10, 547, 955-57, 1007; *paryāyokti* : 488, 969, 1005-6; *punaruktavadābhāsa*: 655, 763; *pratīpa* : 122, 133, 773; *bhāvika*: 727; *mudrā*: 714; 1037; *lalita*: 991; *vakrokti* : 488; *vibhāvanā*: 51, 770, 980, 1025; *vikalpa*: 205; *vinokti* : 488; *viśeṣa* : 962; *viśeṣokti*: 104; *viṣama*: 414, 976, 986, 987, 998, 1033; *vyājastuti* : 786, 983; *lokokti* : 366, 367; *sama* : 625, 650, 987. *samādhi* : 184; 274; *sandeha*: 681; 979; *samāsokti*: 636; 766, 899-900, 974; 985;. *samuccaya* : 131, 272; 968; 986, 1001; *sambhāvanā*: 125; *sahokti*: 725; *svabhāvokti*: 952-54; *hetu*: 767, 768, 785; *leśa* : 721.
3. E.g. 179-80, 134, 488 (4 *alaṅkāras*), 643, 768, 769, 777, 987 (4 *alaṅkāras*), 996-1000, 1037 (5 *alaṅkāras*).

the *Kuṭṭanī-mata* are very few indeed; Mālatī and Vikarālā, whose dialogue forms the main theme of the poem, are but secondary characters; the four principal characters of the pcem are Sundarasena and Hāralatā, and prince Samarabhaṭa and Mañjarī. To these may be added a messenger (*dūti*) each of Mālatī, Hāralatā and Mañjarī, and Sundarasena's friend Guṇapālita and Samarabhaṭa's minister. However, these characters taken unaided, the story would not have progressed. Dāmodaragupta, therefore, devised a novel method which consists in the introduction of some Āryā or Gīti stanzas said to have been sung not by any of the characters but by someone else in his own context but overheard by the characters concerned. It is these stanzas that give movement to the story. Whenever the story seems stagnating and the characters are at a loss to decide the future course of action, such Āryās or Gītis are introduced to indicate the timely action. Thus it is on hearing an Āryā recited by somebody in his own context that Mālatī makes her way to Vikarālā to get her advice (23). Another Āryā, also sung by somebody casually, inspires Sundarasena to undertake an educational excursion (212), and another Gīti (232) makes him firm in his resolve when his friend, Guṇapālita, tried to dissuade him by narrating the sufferings experienced by travellers in those days. Likewise, Sundarasena was encouraged to ascend the Arbuda mountain and respond favourably to Hāralatā's love by hearing such Gīti stanzas (255, 326-328). Similarly, Sundarasena decides to carry out his father's behest and return home (426-427, 466) and desists from accompanying his beloved on the funeral pyre (492) on hearing such stanzas. If Mālatī goes on an *abhisāra* in a rainy night it is because of an incitement reportedly provided by a Gīti (588). Again, the description of the benefits and thrills of hunting and cessation thereof are occasioned by similar verses (949, 959). Lastly, Samarabhaṭa finds, in a similar Gīti stanza (1043), support to his favourable response to Mañjarī's message of love. This device is unique in the whole range of Sanskrit literature.

The general framework of the *Kuṭṭanī-mata* is patterned on the Purāṇas. It begins and ends in the Purāṇic fashion. Mālatī calling on Vikarālā and eulogising her remind the reader of the Purāṇic descriptions of the pupils attending upon a sage, while Vikarālā's residence thronged by a multitude of lovers may be compared to a *gurukula*. As in the Purāṇas, Vikarālā's instructions to Mālatī are illustrated by sub-stories (*upākhyānas*). The story of Mañjarī and Samarabhaṭa resembles the *itihāsa* or *prarocanā* introduced in order to convince the pupils of the effectiveness of the teaching. And lastly, the closing description of Mālatī, satisfied with Vikarālā's teaching resulting in the removal of her ignorance, bowing at Vikarālā's feet and going home is also in conformity with the Purāṇic style.[1]

As pointed out by S. K. De,[2] the *Kuṭṭanī-mata* is the earliest datable work of an erotico-comic, if not fully satiric, tendency, and to Dāmodaragupta belongs the credit of introducing this particular genre in Sanskrit literature. He deserves all praise for the fact that in spite of the dangerously coarse content of the poem he never loses balance. Although the droll-life is dilated with frankness and fullness of details, the treatment is elegant throughout. The style is simple but effective. Brilliant flashes of wit and humour are scattered all over the poem. Dāmodaragupta was a great humourist who never missed an opportunity of humour afforded by the context. It is noteworthy in this connection that ancient Indian writers on literary criticism postulated a close connection between the sentiment of love (*śṛṅgāra*) and that of humour (*hāsya*). Bharata, for instance, thought that *hāsya* originated from *śṛṅgāra* and that *hāsya* is but an imitation of *śṛṅgāra*.[3] There is plenty of satire pervading the whole poem, but generally it is indirect. A few examples of such witty, humorous dialogues, taken at random, are cited below.

Duhitara eva ślāghyā dhig=lokaṁ putra-janma-santuṣṭam/
Jāmātara āpyante bhavādṛśā yad=abhisambandhāt // 146.

Fie upon those that are delighted at the birth of a son. Praiseworthy are, indeed, the daughters through whom are obtained sons-in-law like you.

Avidagdhaḥ śrama-kaṭhino durlabha-yoṣid=yuvā jaḍo vipraḥ/
Apamṛtyur=upakrāntaḥ kāmi-vyājena me rātrau// 393.

A foolish and uncultivated Brahmin youth, hardened by

1. G. T. Deshpande in *Chanda* (Marathi), vol. ii, no. 2, pp. 63-4.
2. *A History of Sanskrit Literature*, p. 197.
3. Cf. *Śṛṅgārād=dhi bhaved=dhāso...; Śṛṅgār-ānukṛtir=yā tu sa hāsyas=tu prakīrtitaḥ*, *Nāṭyaśāstra*, vi. 39, 40.

rough work, but unable to get women, came to me last night; he was, indeed, an untimely death in the guise of a lover.

Madya-vaśād=abhiyoktari mṛta-kalpe- talpa-bhāga-magnāyāḥ/
Avirodhita-nidrāyāḥ sukhena me yāminī yātā// 395.

The inebriate lover being as good as dead, I lay in a corner of the bed and spent the night peacefully, my sleep being undisturbed.

Śṛṇu sakhi kautukam=ekaṁ grāmīṇaka-kāminā yad=adya kṛtam/
Surata-rasa-mīlitākṣī mṛt-eti bhītena mukt-āsmi// 399.

Hear, O Friend, the unique thing that a rustic lover did me today (i.e., last night). In the ecstasy of the moment I had closed my eyes when he took me for dead and, being afraid, took to flight leaving me alone.[1]

Dāmodaragupta's characters are life-like and vividly portrayed. He was a master of word-pictures in which the interest of the poem mainly lies. His descriptions are full-blooded and they present before our eyes a complete picture of the thing described. As examples mention may be made of the descriptions of Cintāmaṇi and prince Samarabhaṭa and the mating of Mālatī and Cintāmaṇi and of Hāralatā and Sundarasena. One of the most touching examples of word-pictures is the description of Hāralatā just before her death supporting her strengthless body by clutching the branch of a banyan tree with one hand and with the other pressing her bosom so that her heart might not break, fixedly looking at her gradually disappearing lover through the tears that spontaneously welled up and coursed down the cheeks. It is, indeed, a picture of pathos in concrete shape:

Vaṭa-śākh-ālambi-bhujāṁ śvasit-oṣṇa-samīra-śuṣyad=adhara-dalām/
Paryastāṁ bibhrāṇāṁ tan=mārga-vilokan-ānimeṣa-dṛśam// 468
Lolāyamāna-veṇī-tiryak-kṛta-kaṇṭha-bhūṣaṇa-viśeṣām/
Galad=aśru-vāri-pūrṇāṁ patit-āṁśuka[2]*-niḥsah-āṅga-latām//*469
Rundhānām=iva hṛdayaṁ sphuṭad=itara-kareṇa kuca-yug-āśrayiṇā/

1. As suggested by Tripathi (p. 101), this stanza is based on *Gāthāsattasai*, iv. 60 :

अज्जं मोहणसुहिअं मुअत्ति मोत्तू पलाइए हलिए।
दरफुडिअ वेण्टभारोणआइ हसिअं फलहीए ॥

2. Tripathi prefers the reading *patitāṁ saṁśuṣka* in place of *patit-āṁśuka*. But the latter reading is preferable.

Pariśeṣitāṁ vilāsair=utsṛṣṭāṁ jīva-loka-kartavyaiḥ// 470
Aṅgīkṛtāṁ vipattyā vaśīkṛtāṁ marma-ghaṭṭanair-viṣamaiḥ /
Hāralatām=aparisphuṭam=antaḥparikṛṣyamāṇa-bhāratyā / 471
Mā mā tāvad=yāta kṣaṇam=ekaṁ yāvad=eṣa niṣkaruṇaḥ /
Vana-gulmair=na tirohitam=ity=abhidadhatīṁ jahuḥ prāṇāḥ//
472

With one of her hands clasping fast a branch of the banyan tree, her petal-like lower lip drying up with the hot breathing wind, her upturned and unwinking eyes looking at his path, the braid of her hair swinging, her beautiful neck-ornament lying aslant, drenched with dripping tears, her garment carelessly falling on the ground and her creeper-like body becoming helpless, the palm of her other hand resting on her bosom, as if preventing her heart from breaking, abandoned by amorous sports, free from worldly duties, adopted by calamity as its own, overwhelmed by heart-rending shocks, uttering in a choked voice, "Do not fly out, oh my breath, until this merciless fellow (Sundarasena) is hidden by wild bowers," she breathed her last.

The lamentation of Sundarasena over the sad demise of Hāralatā (475-479, 482-489) constitutes another example of pathetic outburst.

A student of the *Kuṭṭanī-mata* is called upon to answer a few questions, to wit, Why did the poet delineate the thrills of a courtesan's love? Did he derive sadistic pleasure in seeing innocent young men ruined by courtesans' treachery? If not, what purpose did he expect to be served by a vivid and illustrated narrative of the stratagems of strumpets? It is not difficult to answer these questions. Although Dāmodaragupta was primarily a poet and his work has turned out to be a beautiful piece of art, it is not necessary to suppose that he had no objective whatsoever before him. He was undoubtedly perturbed at the pitiable state of morals, described above, of Kashmir in the administration of which he had to play an important role, and he certainly wanted to do his bit to ameliorate this condition. His objective evidently was to warn the people against the vices of prostitution by citing instances of persons, under fictitious names, who were impoverished because of addiction to whores. He makes his purpose known only in the concluding stanza of the poem wherein we are told that one who listens to the poem adhering to its purport is never duped by parasites, courtesans, rogues and procuresses.[1] And the poet has succeeded remarkably well in achieving his objective while at the same time maintaining the poetic character of the work, never allowing us to feel the presence of the reformer. The reader is so much engrossed in the poem that he is always face to face with the various facets of the poet, he feels himself identified with him. It is only at the end when we have perused the whole poem, when we have dived deep into it and when we have completely identified ourselves with the poet and when our mind is still engrossed into the ecstasies of the poem that we are suddenly shaken by the poet who states that it is with some obj ect that he has composed the poem and that while enjoying the poem we should not lose sight of this fact. And once that we come to know of the purpose of the poet in describing the seducements of strumpets, we begin reflecting over the whole poem piece by piece and we find eloquent reverberations of the same warning everywhere. When after viewing the charms and j oys of courtesans' love we find their lovers ruined, when we find the cortesan's mother instructing her into the trickeries of her profession with special emphasis on the art of cheating men, we are at once shocked, as if we were awakened from a slumber, we come back to the realities of life, we begin to perceive the hidden meaning of all the apparently loving acts of the strumpet and thus we find the poignant notes of warning present everywhere in the poem. This sort of indirect warning administered through such poignant notes is undoubtedly much more effective than a compelling clause of law. The author appears to be one who did not believe in the efficacy of 'does' and 'don'ts'.

Because of the moralising lesson the *Kuṭṭanī-mata* is intended to transmit it has been sometimes classed, both by ancient and modern writers, as a didactic poem. Thus, according to Hemacandra's *Kāvyānuśāsana*, a story aiming at drawing some moral by means of the lives of animals, birds or low persons is known as a didactic story (*nidarśana-kathā*), and as instances are

1. काव्यमिदं यः शृणुते सम्यक् काव्यार्थपालनेनासौ ।
नो वञ्च्यते कदाचिद् विटवेश्याधूर्तकुट्टनीभिरिति ॥ *K* 1059.

mentioned the *Pañcatantra*, *Dhūrta-viṭa-saṁvāda*, *Kuṭṭanī-mata*, etc.[1]

The *Kuṭṭanī-mata* may justifiably be regarded as a social criticism, a comic satire on the moral depravity of certain classes of contemporary society, and in this respect forms a companion volume to the *bhāṇas* and *prahasanas*. It bears greater resemblance to the former in that there is an indirect exposure of human frailty as in the *bhāṇas* and not direct ridicule as in the *prahasanas*.

VII. DĀMODARAGUPTA'S ERUDITION

The domain of creative literature is wide enough to comprehend within its fold everything on the surface of the earth, and, as stated by Bharata with special reference to drama, there is no knowledge, no craft, no learning, no art and no combination that is not seen in it.[2] In ancient India, therefore, a poet was expected to be well-read and conversant with all varieties of subjects and his preparatory training so comprehensive as to include all the then known disciplines and, of course, commonplace things. Rudraṭa envisaged a sort of omniscience in a poet,[3] while Bhāmaha appreciated the heaviness of a poet's mental burden.[4] Special interest in this connection attaches to Ch. 8 of Rājaśekhara's *Kāvya-mīmāṁsā* which enumerates the Śruti, Smṛti, Itihāsa, Purāṇa, Mīmāṁsā, logic (including Sāṅkhya, Nyāya, Vaiśeṣika, Buddhist and Jaina philosophies and Lokāyata), Samayavidyā (including Śaiva-siddhānta,

1. तिरश्चामतिरश्चां वा चेष्टाभिर्यत्र कार्यमकार्यं वा निश्चीयते तत् पञ्चतन्त्रादिवत्, धूर्तविट-कुट्टनीमत-मयूरमार्जारिकादिवच्च निदर्शनम् ।

Kāvyānuśāsana, Alaṅkāra-cūḍāmaṇi, viii. 8, p. 463.

धूर्तविटकुट्टनीमतमयूरमार्जारिकादि यल्लोके ।
कार्याकार्यनिरूपणरूपमिह निदर्शनं तदपि ॥

Ibid., Viveka, 193, p. 464.

1. *Nāṭya-śāstra*, xix.143. Cf. Bhāmaha, *Kāvy-ālaṅkāra*, i.9; Vāmana, *Kāvya-ālaṅkāra*, i.3 ff.; Rudraṭa, *Kāvy-ālaṅkāra*, i.18; *Kāvya-prakāśa*, i.3.

2. *Kāvy-ālaṅkāra*, i.19.

3. *Kāvy-ālaṅkāra*, V. 4.

4. *Kāvya-mīmāṁsā* (G.O.S., no. 1, 3rd edition, Baroda 1934), pp. 35ff. To these Rājaśekhara adds four new principles, viz., *ucita-saṁyoga*, *yoktṛ-saṁyoga*, *utpādya-saṁyoga*, *saṁyoga-vikāra*, which, however, can hardly be regarded as sources of poetic theme.

Pañcarātra, Bauddha Siddhānta, etc.), the three Rāja-siddhāntas, viz., Arthaśāstra, Nāṭyaśāstra and Kāmasūtra, Loka which comprehends cultured and uncultured modes of life pertaining both to all the people and limited circles, and miscellany (including the sciences dealing with elephants, jewels, archery and Yoga, etc.) as sources of poetic themes.[1]

In consequence of this stress on versatility poets in ancient India were not unoften anxious to exhibit their mastery over various sciences. A perusal of the *Kuṭṭanī-mata* shows that our poet was familiar with a variety of subjects some of which he had assiduously studied. Proofs of a close and protracted study of Vātsyāyana's *Kāma-sūtra*, which is mentioned by name (77, 123), are found at every step. Dāmodaragupta's treatment of prostitution may be justifiably described as a running illustrated commentary on the Vaiśika section (VI) of the *Kāma-sūtra*. Vv. 812-861 dealing with involvement in others' wives are also based on its Pāradārika section (V). Dāmodaragupta was also acquainted with the writings of some other authorities on erotics, to wit, Dattakācārya, Rājaputra, Madanodaya and Viṭavṛtta or Vitaputra (77, 123). Bharata's *Nāṭya-śāstra* is another source Dāmodaragupta has heavily drawn upon. The descriptions of Cintāmaṇi and Samarabhaṭa, Sundarasena's wailing over the demise of his beloved, and, above all, the account of the performance of the *Ratnāvalī* afford enormous evidence of Dāmodaragupta's study of the *Nāṭya-śāstra*. Among other subjects with which he evinces his acquaintance mention may be made of the Upaniṣads (570), grammar (12, 13, 782, 980), prosody (10, 14, 313, 339, 465-66, 968 780,), Śruti (199, 422), Smṛtis (296, 419), the *Rāmāyaṇa* (786, 859, 861, 1000, 1004, 1014), the *Mahābhārata* (78, 194, 252, 984), the Purāṇas (86, 486, 487, 860, 1013, 1014, 1027), Daṇḍanīti (210, 318), poetics (627, 783, 791-92), Āyurveda (427, 1025, 1027, 1033), music (576, 940-44), Dhanurveda (951-57), Aśvaśāstra (500), Sāṅkhya (318), Yoga (996, 999, 1011), Mīmāṁsā (824), Buddhism (266, 778, 781) and Jainism (367). This many-sided learning is in full consonance with the noble tradition of high scholarship which characterised Jayāpīḍa's reign. The high position our poet occupied in the body politic of Kashmir enabled him to gain a first-hand experience of men and things traces whereof are noticeable all over the poem. He appears to have travelled extensively in northern India; his accounts of Vārāṇasī, Pāṭaliputra and Mt. Abu appear to be realistic.

VIII. KUṬṬANĪ-MATA AS A SOURCE OF CULTURAL HISTORY

Dāmodaragupta has brought practically all the important aspects of contemporary life within the purview of this little poem. As one might naturally expect, the work affords precious information about the life and practices of prostitutes who formed an important element of contemporary Indian society. In the account of Purandara and Sundarasena and the former's letter to the latter we get interesting glimpses of contemporary system of Brāhmaṇical education. The account of the peregrinations of Sundarasena and Guṇapālita gives us good idea of the difficulties experienced by travellers in those days when there were no swift means of communication as at present. The description of Cintāmaṇi and Samarabhaṭa furnishes valuable information about dress and ornaments as well as about the social types they represent. We also get casual but pleasing glimpses of the then religious beliefs and practices, social organisation, food and drinks, family life, position of women, sports and pastimes, administrative set-up, economic conditions and the state of fine arts. The work also supplies some valuable pieces of historical information which has already been discussed above.

The principal venue of the story of the *Kuṭṭanī-mata* is located at Vārāṇasī. Mālatī and Vikarālā, round whom the entire poem centres, lived at Vārāṇasī. The episode concerning Mañjarī and Samarabhaṭa is also reported to have occurred at Vārāṇasī. We, therefore, naturally get valuable details about Vārāṇasī which was then one of the major centres of Indian culture. It is worth mentioning in this connection that the description of Vārāṇasī, in some important details, is confirmed by other evidences. In the anecdote of Sundarasena and Hāralatā we find some information about Pāṭaliputra and Mt. Abu also.

Although there is no direct reference to Kashmir, there can be no doubt that the poem gives a fairly accurate picture of contemporary Kashmiri life. In fact, as shown above, the purpose of the author in composing the poem was to ridicule, though indirectly, the moral depravity of the higher sections of society in Kashmir. We also get casual allusions to the corruption prevailing in contemporary administration of Kashmir and the neglect of their duties by the kings.

The *Kuṭṭanī-mata* is of importance to a student of literary history also inasmuch as it contains the earliest reference to the enactment of Harṣavardhana's *Ratnāvalī* as also to Anaṅgaharṣa Mātrarāja, himself a poet and a patron of letters. Allusions to other works enable us to know the curriculum of literary studies in those days. The *Kuṭṭanī-mata* has thus turned out to be an invaluable source-book of the cultural history of India, more particularly her northern half, during the early mediaeval period.

CHAPTER II

POLITICAL THEORY AND ADMINISTRATION

I. POLITICAL THEORY

Prakṛtis

We get only a few casual allusions to some basic concepts of ancient Indian political thought. It was held by almost all the political thinkers of ancient India that a state is constituted by seven elements (*aṅgas* or *prakṛtis*), viz., *svāmin* (the head of the state), *amātya* (ministers), *janapada* or *rāṣṭra* (the country including its people), *durga* (the fortified city), *kośa* (the treasury), *daṇḍa* (the army) and *mitra* (the ally).[1] Dāmodaragupta makes a very interesting reference to these constituent elements. We are told that by coming into contact with everyone of the subjects, being steadfast in their respective duties, being strengthened by various means and by exacting heavy taxes from the subjects the elements of state become invincible.[2]

Upāyas and Guṇas

Another verse with a *double entendre* alludes to the several means (*upāyas*) and measures of policy (*guṇas*) which a king was advised to adopt in order to extend his dominions and to keep his enemies in check.[3] Earlier authorities like Vālmīki (v. 41. 2-3), Manu (vii. 109) and Yājñavalkya (i. 346) give the number of the *upāyas* as four, namely, *sāma* (conciliation), *dāna* (offering gifts), *bheda* (causing dissensions) and *daṇḍa* (punishment). Some later works, however, increase the number to seven by adding three more, to wit, *māyā*, *upekṣā* or *akṣa* (dice) and *indrajāla* or *vadha* (murder).[4] It is interesting to note in this connec-

1. *Arthaśāstra*, vi.1.1; *Manu-smṛti*, ix.294; *Yājñavalkya-smṛti*, i.353, etc. Some authorities give the number of the *aṅgas* as eight. Vide P. V. Kane, *History of Dharmaśāstra*, iii, p. 17.

2. प्रतिपुरुषं सन्निहिताः कृत्यपरा विविधविकरणोपचिताः ।
बहुलार्थग्राहिण्यः प्रकृतय इव दुर्ग्रहा गणिकाः ॥

K. 318.

3. बहुलोपायाभिज्ञा गुणविषये सततमाहितप्रीतिः ।
बलिनः स्थापयति वशे करभोरुर्विग्रहेण मृदुनैव ॥

K. 988.

4. Vide *HDS*, iii, pp. 171ff.

tion that following in the footsteps of political thinkers writers on erotics also developed the seven means to be adopted for pleasing one's beloved.[1] The *guṇas* or measures of foreign policy are six, viz., *sandhi* (peace or entering into a treaty), *vigraha* (war), *āsana* (indifference), *yāna* (marching or augmenting one's own power), *saṁśraya* (submission to the enemy) and *dvaidhībhāva* (dual policy, i.e., resorting to peace with one and war with another).[2] At another place the first two policies, peace and war, are contrasted (265).

Upadhās

Verse 210 describes Guṇapālita as one whose integrity had been ascertained by means of all the *upadhās* (*sakal-opadhā-viśuddhaḥ*, 210). *Upadhā*, as used here, is a technical term peculiar to ancient Indian polity and was employed to denote the secret tests devised to determine the purity of high government officers. Kauṭilya describes four such tests, i.e., *dharmopadhā* or test of piety, *arthopadhā* or test of material gain, *kāmopadhā* or test of lust, and *bhayopadhā* or test of fear. The department where an officer was to be posted and his promotion to a higher post depended, to a great extent, on his successfully coming out of these tests.[3]

II. ADMINISTRATION

Our work furnishes very meagre information about contemporary administrative organisation of Kashmir. A few interesting details gleaned from casual references may, however, be discussed here.

Monarchy

Monarchy was the order of the day. While there are numerous references to kings, no other form of government is even distantly alluded to. Royal policies, we are told, are aimed at averting calamities (*nītaya iva bhūmi-bhṛtāṁ suparihṛt-ānartha-saṁyogāḥ*, 316). The king administered his kingdom from the

1. Tripathi's commentary on *K* 988.
2. *Arthaśāstra*, vii.1; *HDS*, iii, pp. 222ff.
3. *Arthaśāstra* i.10.

capital (*kaṭaka*)[1] where some high officers of the state also resided permanently (60), evidently to assist the king in the discharge of his administrative responsibilities. We get a fair idea of the duties and interests of royalty from a stanza which refers to non-retreat from war, knowledge of staṭecraft, interest in good sayings (*subhāṣitas*) and indulgence in hunting as the traditional learning of the princely class.[2] This is illustrated by the example of prinçe Samarabhaṭa who was equally capable of appreciating the minute technicalities involved in the performance of a drama (939-47) and of describing various advantages and pleasures of hunting (950-57).

Kings were normally polygamous (795, 915). The queens lived in the royal harem (*avarodha* 912, *antaḥpura* 915) which was evidently situated at the capital town. The chief queen (*nṛpa-mahiṣī*) was the most respected among them and was in virtual control of the harem in all internal matters. A number of attendants was attached to the harem (*ceṭī* 910, 913, *parijana* 911). Mention is made of the garden for the girls-folk of the harem (*kulaputrikārāma*,[3] 789) which must have been located within the precincts of the royal palace.

Bureaucracy : Princes and their Entourage

The governance of a state is beyond the capabilities of a single individual, of howsoever high a calibre he may happen to be. The king was, therefore, assisted by a bureaucracy comprising a large number of officers of varying ranks. That the princes of royal blood occupied a high position in the body

1. For the use of *kaṭaka* in the sense of capital see Kahla plates of Kalacuri Soḍhadeva, line 29, *CII*, iv, p. 389.

2. सङ्ग्रामादनपसृतिः प्रेक्षाभिज्ञा सुभाषिताभिरुचिः ।
श्वाच्छोदनाभियोगः कुलविद्या राजपुत्राणाम् ॥

K 949.

But *contra Arthaśāstra*, viii.3.38, where hunting is mentioned as one of the vices springing from lust.

3. The *kula-putras* are mentioned repeatedly by Bāṇa. *Kula-putra*, as pointed out by V.S. Agrawala (*Harṣa-carita : A Cultural Study*, p. 93, note 2), denoted such of the princes as, being regarded by the king and the queen as their own sons, lived in the royal palace. Whether *kula-putrikā* meant such a princess cannot be determined in the absence of necessary information.

politic of the state and were appointed to high government offices is evidenced by the case of prince Samarabhaṭa, son of king Siṁhabhaṭa, who governed the province of Devarāṣṭra on behalf of his father (737) and, as such, had to deal with matters relating to vehicles, conveyances, infantry, village administration and the grievances of government employees (930, 932-38). They had power to grant land and offer monetary rewards (931, 960). They had their own paraphernalia of officers some of whom accompanied them wherever they went. Thus when prince Samarabhaṭa visited Vārāṇasī, he was reportedly accompanied by a small contingent of reliable officers (*parimit-āpta-parivāra*, 738), particular mention being made of *niyogins* (756), the minister (*saciva*, 811, 862, 961) who, besides performing his official duties, acted as his friend and guide, the minstrel (*vaitālika*, 761) who eulogised him on appropriate occasions (761-87) besides amusing him by singing stanzas of his choice (789-92) and officers attached to the finance department who received orders about monetary gifts (960). This reminds one of the Gupta period when there is evidence to show that the crown-prince had his own *kumārāmātyas* and military officers like the emperor himself.[1] It is interesting to note in this connection that Bhaṭṭotpala, a native of Kashmir, writing somewhat later, describes the *yuvarāja* as a partner of the king in the enjoyment of the kingdom.[2] When the prince went out in public his heralds cleared the road for his passage (755) and when he made his appearance in a popular gathering truncheon-bearing grim policemen controlled the throng (*niṣṭhura-yāṣṭika-niyamite loke*, 756). The prevalence of this practice earlier is vouched for by literary evidence, indigenous as well as foreign. Thus, while describing Mantragupta's procession by the king's highway, Daṇḍin states that people gave him way in fear of a beating from the staffs of ferocious policemen.[3] Bāṇa also refers to this practice repeatedly. As Harṣa marched at the head of his army for a conquest of the quarters thousands

1. *ASI*, *AR*, 1903-4, pp. 107-8, nos. 1, 6, 8, 12.

2. *Yuvarājo=rdha-bhāg rājā*, on *Bṛhat-saṁhitā*, xxx.19; *yuvarājo=rdha-bhogī rājā*, on *ib.*, xxxiv.10; *yuvarājaḥ prasiddho=rdha-rājya-bhāk*, on *ib.*, lxxii.4. Vide my *India as seen in the Bṛhat-saṁhitā of Varāhamihira* p. 470.

3. *Daśa-kumāra-carita* (Nirṇaya Sagara Press, Bombay 1928), p. 247.

of staff-bearing ushers were busy driving away multitude of people and thus clearing the way for the emperor.[1] That this privilege was sometimes enjoyed by some other high dignitaries of the state also is exemplified by the case of Skandagupta, the chief of elephant forces.[2] It was kept in abeyance during the period of mourning.[3] Its vogue at a much earlier date is indicated by a statement of Megasthenes, Seleucus' envoy at the court of Candragupta Maurya. Referring to the hunting procession of the emperor, Megasthenes says, "The road is marked off with ropes, and it is death, for men and women alike, to pass within the ropes."[4] The prince was always protected by trusted body-guards (*śarīra-rakṣa*) carrying swords (758) and attended by such other personal servants as betel-box bearer (*tāmbūla-karaṅka-bhṛt*, 759).

Pratihāra

Of the officers mentioned by Dāmodaragupta, *pratihāra* or the chief of palace guards, appears to have been an important functionary of the state. Being in immediate attendance on the king, he received royal commands and conveyed them to concerned officers (934). According to Kalhaṇa, *mahāpratihārāpīḍa* or the office of high chamberlain was one of the five new offices introduced by king Lalitāditya Muktāpīḍa over and above the eighteen offices already existing in Kashmir.[5] That this high office was sometimes held by members of the royal family is evidenced by the fact that king Jayāpīḍa had installed queen Kalyāṇadevī in the dignity of *mahāpratihārāpīḍa*.[6]

Nagara-prabhu

The *nagara-prabhu* or city-prefect was evidently the chief officer entrusted with the administration of a town. From the

1. *Harṣa-carita* (edited by A. Führer, BSS, 1909), p. 281.
2. *Ibid.*, p. 265.
3. *Ibid.*, p. 238.
4. J. W. McCrindle, *Ancient India as described by Megasthenes and Arrian* (Calcutta 1926), p. 71.
5. *RT*, iv. 141-42.
6. *Ibid.*, iv. 485.

mention of *nagara-prabhu* in connection with Abu, which was not a capital city, it follows that there was a separate *nagara-prabhu* for each town of some importance. He is obviously the same as the *nagarādhikṛta*,[1] *nagarādhipa*[2] or *nagarādhipati*[3] referred to by Kalhaṇa. He may be further identified with Kauṭilya's *nāgarika*.[4] There is reason to believe that he was included among the eighteen high state officials (*tīrthas*) mentioned in the *Mahābhārata*.[5] The office of the *nagara-prabhu* or *nagarādhyakṣa* dates back to the pre-Karkoṭa period, for there is reason to believe that the eighteen offices (*karma-sthānas*) reportedly introduced by Jalauka in Kashmir[6] were the same as the *tīrthas* mentioned above. He appears to have been charged with the enforcement of state laws and fined those found guilty of violating them. That he also acted as a civil judge in small causes, sometimes with the help of the jury, is indicated by verse 401 wherein a strumpet complains that she was forcibly carried by the *nagara-prabhu* before the people (i.e., jury) for judgment on the charge of demanding more fees.[7] The *Rāja-taraṅgiṇī* gives us a fuller idea of his responsibilities and powers which corroborate and supplement the information furnished by Dāmodaragupta. The *nagarādhipa* was charged with administrative, revenue, judicial and military functions in connection with the municipal administration. Thus Kalhaṇa narrates how king Yaśaskara (939-948 A.D.) amassed riches through four *nagarādhikṛtas*, who helped themselves in turn to money, and were hanging about each other's back.[8] Another *nagarādhipati*, Bhuyya, is credited with encouraging queen Diddā in her pious activities.[9] His role as the censor of morals, which has been

1. *Ibid.*, iv.81; vi.70; vii.1542; viii.3334.
2. *Ibid.*, vii. 580; viii.814.
3. *Ibid.*, vi.296.
4. *Arthaśāstra*, ii.36.
5. II.v.38. Cf. Rāmāyaṇa, II. c. 36.
6. *RT*, i.120.
7. प्रियसखि लोकसमक्षं नगरप्रभुणा हठेन नीताऽस्मि ।
   एवं तु नो कदाचिद्द्विगुणार्थंप्रार्थने कृतो न्यायः ॥
8. *RT*, vi.70.
9. *Ibid.*, vi. 296.

noticed on the basis of the *Kuṭṭanī-mata*, is found adumbrated in the *Rāja-taraṅgiṇī*, which states how city-prefects levied fines on the householders in the case of immoral conduct on the part of a married woman[1] and punished persons on the allegation that they had carnal intercourse with dancing-girls who had been received into households as wedded wives.[2] Another town-prefect, Vijayasiṁha, is said to have destroyed all thieves.[3] Nāga, the city-prefect of king Harṣa (1089-1101 A.D.), led a troop of horsemen against Sussala and Uccala.[4] King Sussala (1112-1120 A.D.) ordered his town-prefect, Janaka, to crush a rebellion of his soldiers in the city.[5]

Śaulkikādhyakṣa and Haṭṭapati

The *śaulkikādhyakṣa* and *haṭṭapati* were two other officers connected with the task of revenue collection. The *śaulkikas*, according to Kalhaṇa[6] and Kṣemendra,[7] were posted on the frontier routes and realised customs duties over commodities coming and going through the watch-stations. The *śaulkikādhyakṣa*, therefore, appears to have been the chief of the customs office (531). The *śaulkika* is referred to in some epigraphic records also.[8] *Haṭṭapati* (540), literally the 'lord of the market'[9], was evidently in charge of the collection of the state's share of the sale-proceeds of goods from shop-keepers in the market. He obviously belonged to the office of *aṭṭapati-bhāga* which, Kalhaṇa informs us, was one of the two new departments created by the Utpala king Śaṅkaravarman (883-902 A.D.).[10] However, our reference clearly indicates that the office of *haṭṭapati* was in existence even during the Karkoṭa period and that it may have been abolished in the intervening period and restored by Śaṅkara-

1. *RT*, viii. 3336.
2. *Ibid.*, viii. 3338.
3. *Ibid.*, vi. 580.
4. *Ibid.*, vii. 1542.
5. *Ibid.*, viii. 814.
6. *Ibid.*, vii. 2010.
7. *Samaya-mātṛkā*, ii. 102.
8. D. C. Sircar, *Indian Epigraphy*, pp. 363, 366, 368, etc.
9. D.C. Sircar (*ibid.*, p. 373) renders the designation as 'superintendent of markets' and P. V. Kane (*HDS*, iii, p. 976) as 'market-master'.
10. *RT*, v. 167; S. C. Ray, *Early History and Culture of Kashmir*, p. 127.

varman or that the latter may have reorganised it. The *haṭṭa-pati* is mentioned in the Ramganj plate of *Mahāmāṇḍalika* Īśvaraghoṣa, a ruler of Ḍhekkari in North Bengal who flourished about the 12th century A.D.[1]

Niyogin, from *niyoga*, an 'office', was also an important officer whose functions cannot be exactly determined. Some officers of this category were in constant attendance over the king and rendered him personal service such as providing him a seat (756). They were also entrusted with the execution of royal commands including disbursement of lands to government employees (937). The *niyogin* seems to be the same as *niyogastha*, *niyoga-niyukta*, *naiyogika*, *niyukta* and *niyuktaka* mentioned in inscriptions of different dates.[2] We have also a vague reference to an officer belonging to the finance department (*dhana-niyukta*) who received royal orders about donations (960). There is also an allusion to revenue from a village (*grām-otpatti*) and a village officer (537), but our text gives us no information about rural administration. The *yāṣṭikas* (756) were very much like our police constables and like them had earned reputation for notoriety and rough dealing.

Allotment of Land to Government Officers

The practice of allotting lands as emoluments to government officers had been in vogue in India from very ancient times. Manu (vii.119), for example, enjoins that an officer in charge of ten villages should enjoy one *kula* (of land), that in charge of twenty villages, five *kulas*, the superintendent of a hundred villages, a village, and that of a thousand villages, a town. The *Mahābhārata* (Śāntiparva 87.7-8) also recommends the grant of a village to the superintendent of a hundred villages and that of a *śākhānagara* to the officer in charge of a thousand villages. Kauṭilya (ii.1.7) states that the king should grant lands to his officers, but without the right of sale or mortgage. Yuan Chwang also observes, "Ministers of state and common officials all have their portion of land and are maintained by cities assigned to them".[3] The prevalence of this practice in Kashmir during

1. N. G. Majumdar, *Inscriptions of Bengal*, iii, p. 153; D.C. Sircar, *Indian Epigraphy*, p. 373.
2. *Ibid.*, pp. 356, 363; *Indian Epigraphical Glossary*, p. 221.
3. Watters, *On Yuan Chwang's Travels in India*, i, pp. 176-77.

the Karkoṭa period is vouched for by our poem which refers to the allotment of a village (931) and of many *halas* of land (937) to government employees. In course of time these officers grew into landed aristocrats and enjoyed the title of *Ṭhakkura* (931) which, as appears from the *Rāja-taraṅgiṇī*, was applied to small nobility, probably Rajputs, and corresponds to the present *Ṭhākur*, a title borne by the chief cultivating class in the hill territories to the south of Kashmir.[1]

The order of land grant was always given in writing (931). According to Kalhaṇa, land grants were executed by an official called *paṭṭopādhyāya* belonging to the *akṣapaṭala* or Accounts Office.[2]

Government employees were, however, not quite happy with their lot and often voiced their grievances. The king was at great pains to satisfy them; sometimes he made empty promises, sometimes reminded them of their old, close relationship, sometimes threatened them and placed the blame on the concerned officers (932-938).

Corruption of Officials

As we have seen above,[3] the post-Jayāpīḍa and pre-Utpala period in the history of Kashmir was marked by almost complete anarchy when government officers derelicted from their duty, corruption ramped high in administration and prostitutes, not kings, ruled for all practical purposes. The *Kuṭṭanī-mata* confirms this impression by drawing pointed attention to embezzlement prevailing in government and wastage of public money on prostitutes. Thus, Dāmodaragupta refers to a *śaulkikādhyakṣa* who never bothered about royal interference and had unlimited income which he spent on whores (531). A *haṭṭapati* is also spoken of as depositing hardly one-fourth of the total amount collected by him in the state exchequer, the remaining amount being enjoyed by a courtesan (540). A village chief is said to have ordered the payment of all the revenue from the village to a prostitute (537). Sons of royal officers also emulated the latter and exhausted themselves on strumpets. The entire

1. *RT*, M.A. Stein's translation, i, p. 292, n.290.
2. *RT*, v.397-98.
3. *Supra*, pp. 28-30.

story of the *Kuṭṭanī-mata* revolves round one such person, Cintāmaṇi, the son of Bhaṭṭa, a high government officer. Royal favourites also misused their position and influence in a similar manner.[1] To crown all this, even kings, who were expected to set an example before the subjects, expended their huge wealth and energy on wenches and were ultimately reduced to the status of paupers. The second story centring round prince Samarabhaṭa is symbolic of this state of affairs.

Mahādraṅga or Mahodraṅga

Reference must be made here to the term *mahā-draṅga* or *mah-odraṅga*, literally 'the great *draṅga* or *udraṅga*'.[2] The word *udraṅga* is used frequently in copper-plate inscriptions in connection with land-grants and has been variously explained as 'the share of the produce collected usually by the king',[3] 'the fixed tax', 'the land tax', 'the principal tax', or 'the tax on the permanent tenants', which may have in some regions been paid in grains.[4] The *Śāśvata-kośa* explains *udraṅga* by *uddhāra* and *udgrantha* (*udgraha*?) which, coupled with the context in which it has been employed in copper-plate charters, has been taken to support the above meanings.[5] The term *draṅga* is of common occurrence in the *Rāja-taraṅgiṇī* and the later Chronicles, and M.A. Stein takes it to signify everywhere a watch-station established near mountain passes for the double purpose of guarding the approaches to the Valley and of collecting customs revenue. In the latter signification it may be identified with the *śulka-*

1. *K*, 538, 542. The reading *nṛpa-vallabha* in verse 537 of Kaul's edition appears preferable to *bhaṭṭ-ādhipa* in verse 538 of Tripathi's edition.

2. अभ्यन्तरव्ययार्थं प्रविलब्धो यो मया महा(v.l. हो)द्रङ्गः ।
तत्राऽपि तेऽनुबन्धो नो जाने किं करोमीति ॥

K 936.

2. This is the reading given by Kaul (verse 935 of his edition). Tripathi prefers the reading *na vilabdho* in place of *pravilabdho* and *mahodraṅgaḥ* in place of *mahā-draṅgaḥ*.

3. *CII*, iii, pp. 97-8, note 6.

4. D.C. Sircar, *Indian Epigraphy*, pp. 360, 393; *Indian Epigraphical Glossary*, p. 349.

5. *CII*, iii, pp. 97-8, note 6; *Indian Epigraphy*, p. 393. The word *udraṅga* is no doubt noted in Zachariae's edition of the *Śāśvata-kośa*, pp. xxix, 260, but I am unable to locate it in the text.

sthāna or customs-station, while the former meaning is supported by the commentary on the *Maṅkha-kośa* which gives *draṅga* as equivalent of *gulma* and *rakṣā-sthāna*.[1] However, most of Sanskrit lexicographers take *draṅga* in the sense of a town or city,[2] and according to the *Vācaspati-kośa* quoted in the commentary on the *Abhidhāna-cintāmaṇi udraṅga*, which is the same as *draṅga*, denoted a township smaller than *karvaṭa* and bigger than *pattana*.[3] In a late mediaeval inscription the word *draṅga* is actually employed in the sense of a town,[4] and the term *udraṅga* prefixed by *mahat* (*mahodraṅga*) appears to have the sense of 'a big town' in the Alina copper-plate inscription of the Maitraka chief Śīlāditya VII, dated (Gupta-Valabhī) year 447.[5] A consideration of the context in the *Kuṭṭanī-mata* also would show that *mahā-* (or *—o*) *draṅga* stands for 'a large township' and, by implication, 'income therefrom', the other possible meanings 'a big principal tax' and 'a big watch-station' being completely unintelligible. In the light of these facts despite what Stein has said it is not unlikely that in the *Rāja-taraṅgiṇī* also the word *draṅga* is sometimes used in the sense of 'a township'.

Wars and Weaponry

Wars were of frequent occurrence in ancient India. Non-retreat from the battle-field was regarded as the family convention (*kula-vidyā*) of the princes (946). Of the weapons of

1. On *Maṅkha-kośa* 574; M.A. Stein, *RT*, ii, pp. 291-92.

2. *Halāyudha-kośa*, 285; *Haima*, iv.37; *Vācaspatya*, v, p. 3775; *Śabda-kalpa-druma*, ii p. 758;. Monier-Williams, *Sanskrit-English Dictionary*, s.v. *draṅga*; V.S. Apte's *Sanskrit-English Dictionary*, s.v. *draṅga*. G. Bühler also takes *draṅga* to mean 'a township' and renders the words *drāṅgika* and *draṅgika* occurring in Maitraka inscriptions by 'heads of town's. Vide *IA*, iv, p. 105, line 15; p. 175, line 6; v, p. 205, line 14.

3. कर्वटादधमो द्रङ्गः पत्तनादुत्तमश्च सः ।
उद्रङ्गश्च निवेशश्च स एव द्रङ्ग इत्यपि ॥

Cited by T.M. Tripathi on *K* 938.

4. D.R. Bhandarkar, *List of Inscriptions of Northern India*, No. 810, where we have a reference to an officer in charge of the town (*draṅga*) of Vairāṭa.

5. *CII*, iii, No. 39, line 46 where the Maitraka king Kharagraha II is said to have ceaselessly made grants of *mah-odraṅgas*, etc. Here *udraṅga* can by no stretch of imagination be taken in any other sense.

war, offensive and defensive, our poet mentions the bow (*dhanuṣ* 108, 969; *cāpa* 122; *kodaṇḍa* 289) including its extremity (*aṭanī* 969), arrows (*śara* 122, 185, 681, 710; *bāṇa* 122, 188, 969; *iṣu* 289, 976; 1006; *mārgaṇa* 953, *sāyaka* 262) and quiver for them (*bāṇadhi* 122; *bāṇa-tūṇa* 188; *śara-pūrṇa-tūṇa* 681), spear (*bhallī* 260) capable of piercing an armour,[1] sword (*khaḍga* 69, 705, 742, 758; *kṛpāṇa* 758) which was tied on the waist (69), dagger (*asidhenu* 742), a wheel-like missile (*cakraka* 758), a mechanical device for hurling stones (559) and mail (*varma* 260, *sannahana* 289). There is also a reference to the drawing of the weapons out of their sheaths (*kośa-haraṇam*=*astreṣu*, 189).

Ethics of War

A bard is represented to have praised prince Samarabhaṭa for having spared the lives of enemies who have given up fighting (768). This is obviously a reference to ancient Indian ethics of warfare according to which a soldier was not to strike one merely looking on without actually taking part in the fight, nor one whose weapons are broken, nor one who is afflicted with sorrow, nor one who is in fear, nor one who has turned to flee.[2]

At yet another place Sugata is said to be averse to war (778).

1. However, these references occur in erotic contexts.
2. *Manu-smṛti*, vii. 9; *HDS*, iii, p. 210.

CHAPTER III

RELIGIOUS CONDITIONS

Connected with pornography as the *Kuṭṭanī-mata* undoubtedly is, it sheds but little light on the religious tenets of the period. But the little information it supplies tallies full well with what we know from other sources such as the *Rāja-taraṅgiṇī* and the *Nīlamata-purāṇa*. The evidence at our disposal leaves no doubt that Brāhmaṇical Hinduism and Buddhism were flourishing side by side. The situation was, thus, similar to what the Chinese pilgrim Yuan Chwang had witnessed about one century and a half earlier,[1] and what was true of the religious history of Kashmir from time immemorial. But this interval was marked by a decided decline in the popularity of Buddhism in Kashmir as in other parts of India. And this coincided with the ascendance of Brāhmaṇism to a pre-eminent position. This state of affairs is fully represented in our text which only sparingly alludes to Buddhism,[2] while it is replete with references to various tenets of Brāhmaṇical Hinduism. As regards the latter, a sort of polytheism was prevalent, the worship of Śiva and Viṣṇu being far more popular than that of other deities. The number of references to these two gods far exceeds others. Casual references to religious beliefs and practices are found scattered throughout the work. With these introductory remarks, we may now proceed to analyse the evidence afforded by the poem.

I. ŚAIVISM

Śiva—His Various Names and Iconography

Śiva worship as a popular faith had been prevalent in Kashmir from a remote age. The great popularity that it enjoyed in the late eighth and early ninth century A.D. is vouched for by Kalhaṇa's references to pious Śaiva establish-

1. The Chinese traveller states, "They (the people of Kashmir) were fond of learning and had a faith which embraced orthodoxy and heterodoxy (that is, Buddhism and other religions). The Buddhist monasteries were about 100 in number, and there were above 5,000 Buddhist brethern". Wu-k'ung, who lived in Kashmir some time above a century later, gives the number of Buddhist monasteries at his time as 300. Vide T. Watters, *On Yuan Chwang's Travels in India*, i, pp. 261, 264.

2. There are altogether four references to Buddhism.

ments emanating from kings, inmates of the royal harem and others.[1]

Śiva was worshipped under various names of which mention is made of Īśvara (18, 1004), Paśupati (5, 635), Ugra (769), Hara (119, 487, 756, 1041), Śambhu (131, 241), Śarva (195, 978), Vṛṣabhadhvaja (738, 778), Bharga (918), Nīlalohita (971), Tripurāntaka (749, 486, 1005) or Tripuraripu (194). Reference is also made to various traits of his iconography, viz., his body besmeared with ashes (5, 131), the half lunar orb adorning his forehead[2], snakes wrapped on his wrists,[3] and his bull mount.[4] The Ardhanārīśvara or Ardhagaurīśvara motif, wherein the left half of his body is occupied by his consort Pārvatī, appears to have been very popular.[5] It is said that Śiva has accommodated Gaurī in the half of his body as though separation from his beloved was unbearable to him even for a moment.[6] The androgynous form is alluded to in another verse also which, while describing a beautiful courtesan, states that if she happens to fall within the sight of Śiva, she may altogether wipe out his existence from the three worlds as she would

1. Lalitāditya Muktāpīḍa's mother Narendraprabhā built a Śiva temple called Narendreśvara after her own name (*RT*, iv. 38), while Lalitāditya himself erected a lofty stone temple for Śiva Jyeṣṭharudra (*ibid.*, iv.190). His minister Mitraśarman installed a Śiva-liṅga called Mitreśvara (*ibid.*, iv.209). Āca, the chamberlain of Dāmodaragupta's patron Jayāpīḍa, had a shrine of Śiva Āceśvara constructed (*ibid.*, iv.513).

2. *Śaśadhara-khaṇḍa-vibhūṣita-deha*, *K* 4; *Śambhu-śirasi śaśi-lekhā*, *K* 131; *śiśira-kara-kānta-mauli*, *K* 241; *sthānaṁ bhavati sa paśupatir=apasaṁśayam=ardha-candra=lābhasya*, *K* 635; *mūrdhani somam*, *K* 978; *bāl-aiv-ārjava-rahitā sphurat-īśvaram=etya candra-lekh-eva*, *K* 1004.

3. *Sad-bhujaṅga-parivāra*, *K* 5; *Bhog-īndra-vibhūṣana*, *K* 109; *koṭaka-sthita-pavana-bhojana*, *K* 241.

4. *Nyak-kṛta vṛṣa iti Śarve*, *K* 195. Cf. the name Vṛṣabhadhvaja noted above.

5. उपहसति गिरिसुताया लावण्यं येन सततलग्नेन ।
न द्रवतामुपनीतं भोगीन्द्रविभूषणस्य देहार्धम् ॥

K 109.

Cf. *RT*, i.2 which invokes the Ardhanārīśvara form of Śiva.

6. मन्येऽभीष्टवियोगं निमेषमपि दुःसहं समवधार्य ।
हरिणा वक्षसि लक्ष्मीर्विधृता गौरी हरेण देहार्धे ॥

K 487.

occupy his right half, the left half being already reserved for Pārvatī.[1]

Śaiva Mythology

Casual allusions to various aspects of Śaivite mythology are also noticed. The legend of the destruction of the demon Tripura by him is implied in the meaningful names like Tripurāntaka and Tripuraripu, which have been noted above. Another Paurāṇic legend which finds mention in our work is his destruction of the demon Andhakāsura. At one place we are told that Śiva killed Andhaka who had bowed down before him,[2] while another verse avers that after killing Andhaka Śiva kept his body over his *triśūla*.[3] One of the most famous Śaiva legends is the burning of Kāma, the Indian god of love, by Śiva and is frequently alluded to by our poet.[4] A feeling of surprise is expressed if the god Vṛṣadhvaja does not eat poison (*Vṛṣa-dhvaj=opi na viṣāditā-yuktah*, 778). This is evidently an allusion to the well-known Paurāṇic legend of the churning of the ocean (*samudra-manthana*) in which Śiva also participated and, at the request of the gods, drank the deadly poison emitted by Vāsuki in consequence of which his neck became blue and he came to be known as Nīlakaṇṭha, "the blue-necked". This legend is narrated at length in the *Mahābhārata* and the Purāṇas.[5]

1. यदि पतति सा कथञ्चिद् वीक्षणविषये हरस्य तदवश्यम् ।
त्रिभुवनमशिवं कुरुते वामेतरदेहभागमासाद्य ॥
K 119

2. भवतो भवतो धैर्यं, तेन हि भिन्नोऽन्धको रिपुः प्रणतः ।
K 768.

3. उपरिगता शूलानामन्धासुरगात्रलेखेव ॥
K 19.

Cf. *Matsya-purāṇa*, 179.

4. दह्यमानस्मरनिर्गतधूम, *K* 44; पशुपतिनयनहुताशनभस्मित, *ibid.*, 202; हरहुङ्कृतिदग्धदेहसंक्षोभ, *idid.*, 277; भर्गविलोचनपावकदाह, *ibid.*, 918; दग्धेऽपि वपुषि भीतिं न विमुञ्चति नीललोहितसमुत्थाम् *ibid.*, 971; त्रिपुरान्तकनयनदाहदग्ध, *ibid.*, 1005; दग्धोऽपि पुनर्दग्धो नूनमनङ्गो हरेण, *ibid.*, 1041.

5. *Mahābhārata*, Ādi, Ch. 18; *Matsya-purāṇa*, Chs. 248-250.

Śiva and Gaurī

Śiva is said to have been attended by the demigods known as Vidyādharas (241). Of the members of his family, mention is made of his consort Gaurī (109, 166), the daughter of the snow-peaked mountain Himālaya (*prāleya-nag-ādhirāja-tanayā*, 18; *giri-sutā*, 109), and his son Skanda-Kārttikeya.[1] Women worshipped Gaurī for long, happy wedded life (*saubhāgya*, 166). A number of vows (*vratas*) were observed by people, especially women, with the object of securing *saubhāgya* and are described in the Purāṇas and Dharmaśāstra literature. One such *vrata* was Gaurī-tṛtīyā which was to be celebrated on the third of the bright half of Nabhasya, Vaiśākha or Mārgaśīrṣa.[2] Other vows of a similar nature were Gaurī-caturthī, Gaurī-tapovrata, Gaurī-vivāha, Gaurī-vrata, and Gaurī-Gaṇeśa-caturthī.[3] The present-day Gaṇagaur popularly celebrated by women in Rajasthan and Malwa also deserves to be noted in this context. The goddess Pārvatī was specially associated with Kashmir. According to the tradition recorded in the *Nīlamata* and the *Rājataraṅgiṇī*, during the first six Manvantaras Kashmir was filled with water and formed the Lake of Satī (*Satī-saras*).[4] Further, Kashmir was regarded as the very body of Umā who assumed the form of the Vitastā (Jhelum) which is the main river of the Valley.[5]

Kārttikeya

Śiva's son Kārttikeya, variously referred to as Śarajanman (117), Guha (241), Mahāsena (486) and Kumāra (1014), also appears to have been popularly adored. The Paurāṇic legend that he observed the vow of life-long celibacy appears to have specially attracted our poet. He praises Mahāsena of excellent vow as the only one whose heart is not touched even slightly by a woman's love[6] and as one beyond the reach of

1. *K* 117, 241, 486, 1014.
2. *Matsya*, Ch. 62.
3. *HDS*, v, p. 296.
4. *Nīlamata*, vv. 12-13, 43-45, 165-166, 171-174, 198-217. *RT*, i. 25.
5. *Nīlamata*. vv. 26, 247-252; *RT*, i. 29.
6. वर्ण्यः सद्व्रत एकस्त्रिपुरान्तकनन्दनो महासेनः ।
   हृदयं यस्य न स्पृष्टं मनागपि वामलोचनाप्रेम्णा ॥ *K* 486

Cupid's acts.[1] In another stanza, Mālatī's messenger, while describing the bewitching beauty of her mistress to Cintāmaṇi, is represented to have stated that Śarajanman is able to observe celibacy only because he had no occasion to look at her beauty.[2] It may be mentioned here that the *Nīlamata* describes certain religious festivals wherein worship was offered, among others, to Skanda.[3]

Vārāṇasī as a Centre of Śaivism

Vārāṇasī was, as now, regarded as particularly sacred to Śiva and was a stronghold of Śaivism. About one century and a half earlier Yuan Chwang found there over 100 Deva (Śiva) temples and above 10000 professed adherents of the sects, the majority being devotees of Śiva. He also found a *t'u-shi* (bell-metal ?) image of Deva (Śiva) nearly 100 feet high which was life-like in its awe-inspiring majesty.[4] It was popularly believed that one who died at Vārāṇasī attained liberation, a belief that is still current. Our poet refers to this notion when he states that in Vārāṇasī even those who had abandoned themselves to the enjoyment of mundane pleasures, not to speak of the pious people, became united with Śiva.[5] This reminds one of the assertion of the *Matsya-purāṇa* (180. 71) that even a person whose mind is addicted to pleasures of sense and who has given up devotion to dharma is not reborn (i.e., is freed from the cycle of births and deaths) if only he happens to die at Vārāṇasī, and that the Brāhmaṇas, Kṣatriyas, Vaiśyas, Śūdras, persons of mixed castes, insects, ants, birds and beasts, when they die in course of time at Avimukta (Vārāṇasī), all find happiness being endowed with a crescent of the moon on their heads, a third eye on their foreheads and a bull on the flagstaff (*ibid.*, 181.

1. न कुमारो मारकर्मणोऽस्बाह्य:
K 1014.
2. जघनभरालसयाता नायाता सा विलोचनप्रसरम् ।
तिष्ठति तेन मनोहर शरजन्मा ब्रह्मचर्येण ।। *K* 117.
3. Vv. 381, 435, 6c4, 647-649, 995.
4. T. Watters, *op. cit.*, ii, p. 47.
5. अनुभवतामपि यस्यामुपभोगान् कामतः शरीरवताम् ।
शशधरखण्डविभूषितदेहलयः किल न दुष्प्रापः ॥ *K* 4.

17-21).[1] It was with the object of paying a visit to the god Vṛṣabhadhvaja (Śiva) that prince Samarabhaṭa had gone to Vārāṇasī. The shrine of Vṛṣadhvaja is referred to in the *Mahābhārata* (Vanaparva, 84.78)[2] which states that by worshipping Vṛṣadhvaja and bathing in Kapilahrada at Vārāṇasī one attains religious merit equal to that accruing from the performance of the Rājasūya. It is also mentioned as one of the *liṅgas* and Śaiva shrines of Vārāṇasī in the *Liṅga-purāṇa* (xcii. 70, 106), while the Kāśī-khaṇḍa of the *Skānda Purāṇa* (Pūrvārdha, ch. 10, v. 94)) speaks of Vṛṣabhadhvaja as one of the *liṅgas* at Kāśī. It is interesting to note in this connection that our author does not mention Viśveśvara who is now regarded as the tutelary deity of Vārāṇasī. In fact, there is overwhelming literary and archaeological evidence to show that Viśveśvara did not attain this status until about the beginning of the thirteenth century A.D. The *Matsya-purāṇa* (cxxi. 28-29) enumerates eight main Śiva-*liṅgas* of Vārāṇasī, the most important being Avimukteśvara; the list, however, does not include Viśveśvara.[3] Likewise, Viśveśvara is conspicuously absent in the list of the seven shrines, viz., (i) Pītakeśvara, (ii) Avimukteśvara, (iii) Kalaśesvara, (iv) Gabhastīśvara, (v) Lolārka, (vi) Yogeśvara and (vii) Devadevasvāmin, which are known from the numerous religious sealings found at Rajghat, representing the ancient site of Vārāṇasī, to have flourished from *circa* fourth to the ninth century A.D.[4] Of these, the largest number of sealings, eight, dating from the fifth-sixth to the ninth century A.D. belong to Avimukteśvara, thereby indicating its continuing importance during this long period. The Banaras Inscription of Pantha belonging to the beginning of the eighth century A.D. also refers to Avimukta.[5] Some other inscriptions of the eleventh and twelfth centuries also refer to Avimukta as the most famous

1. Vide also *Matsya-purāṇa*, 184. 36; *HDS*, iv, pp. 629-30.

2. Critical edition, Vanaparva, 82. 69-70.

3. Viśveśvaradeva, however, occurs as another name of Avimukteśvara. Vide *Matsya-purāṇa*, clxxxii. 17. This may be at the root of the later identification of Avimukteśvara and Viśveśvara.

4. V. S. Pathak, Religious Sealings from Rajghat, *JNSI*, xix, pp 168-179. For another list, see Motichandra, *Kāśī kā Itihāsa*, pp 96-97.

5. *EI*, ix, p. 60, text line 2.

liṅga at Vārāṇasī.[1] After the twelfth century A.D., however, Avimukta sank into insignificance and his place as the presiding deity of Vārāṇasī was usurped by Viśveśvara. The earliest references to Viśveśvara, it is instructive to note, are found in some Gāhaḍavāla[2] and Sena[3] inscriptions dating from the thirteenth century A.D.[4]

The *Kuṭṭanī-mata* refers to some important shrines of Vārāṇasī. The reference to Vṛṣabhadhvaja indicates that it continued to be an important shrine of Vārāṇasī till at least the eighth-ninth century A.D. Besides Vṛṣabhadhvaja, Dāmodaragupta shows acquaintance with two other shrines of this hallowed city. One of these shrines called Gambhīreśvara is not known from any other source.[5] As regards the second shrine, the editors of the *Kuṭṭanī-mata* have adopted the reading *Kamaleśvara* in preference to the other variant found in manuscripts, viz., *Kalaśeśvara*.[6] However, while nothing whatsoever is known about Kamaleśvara from any other source, a seal inscribed with the name of Kalaśeśvara has been discovered at Rajghat. In the light of this and the literary evidence to be cited later on we prefer the reading *Kalaśeśvara*. The seal in question is oval in shape and measures ·9"x·7", the field being divided by a line in the middle. The upper field contains the figure of Gaṇeśa seated in *paryaṅkāsana* with the trunk turned towards right, while the lower half bears the inscription *śrī-Kalaśeśvara* in characters of about the seventh century A.D. (Fig. 1)[7] Kalaśeśvara was an associate *liṅga* in the temple of Śveteśvara. According to a story narrated in the *Liṅga-purāṇa* as quoted in Bhaṭṭa Lakṣmīdhara's *Kṛtya-kalpataru*, the sage Śveta installed a *liṅga* known as Śveteśvara after his own name. It was so sacred that

1. *Ibid.*, xxv, pp. 179, 185.
2. *JASB*, xxxi, p. 123.
3. Bhandarkar's *List of Inscriptions of Northern India*, No. 1692.
4. For a full discussion of this question vide V.S. Pathak in *JNSI*, xix, pp. 174-175; Motichandra, *Kāśī kā Itihāsa*, pp. 96, 145.
5. *K* 743. Gambhāreśvara is a variant. Jagannath Pathak's statement that it may still be standing on the Scindia Ghat at Vārāṇasī (vide his edition of *K*, p. 155, fn.1) does not admit of verification.
6. *K* 736 of Tripathi's edition and 735 of Kaul's edition.
7. *JNSI*, xix, p. 175, Pl. II.12.

one who came in its presence assumed the form of Ganeśa. Once when he was worshipping god Śiva, Kāla, the god of death, caught hold of him and when requested to wait for a while till the completion of the worship derisively ridiculed him and expressed his helplessness. Thereupon, Śveta completely surrendered to the god who, in order to save his devotee, came out of Śveta's water-pot (*kalaśa*), assumed the form of Gaṇeśa and burnt Kāla with the fire emanating from his eyes and disappeared there. Since then Kāla became bodyless (*videha*) and none can see him while he is busy destroying the people. As god Śiva emerged there out of Śveta's water-pot on his own, it came to be known as Kalaśeśvara.[1] Dr. V.S. Pathak, who published the seal, thinks that the story seems to have started from the *aṅka* (emblem) of Gaṇapati on the seal.[2] However, it appears more probable that the story widely circulated at the time of the seal and that the figure of Gaṇeśa was engraved upon it only to illustrate the legend. Our reference indicates the continuing popularity of the shrine of Kalaśeśvara in the late eighth-early ninth century A.D. Mañjarī, the heroine of the second story of the *Kuṭṭanī-mata*, is said to have been an attendant of Kalaśeśvara (*Kalaśeśvara-pāda-mūla-Mañjaryā*, 736).[3] It may be added here that Kalaśeśvara is referred to in the

1. *Kṛtya-kalpataru*, vol. viii : Tīrtha-vivecana-kāṇḍa (G.O.S., No. XCVIII), pp. 99-101. It way be pointed out, however, that although Ch. 30 of the *Liṅga-purāṇa* (Venkateshwar Press edition) narrates the anecdote of Śveta's victory over death by Śiva's favour, there is no reference there either to Śiva's emergence from *kalaśa* or the Kalaśeśvara *liṅga*.

2. *JNSI*. xix, p. 176.

3. Tripathi finds it difficult to explain the expression *Kamaleśvara-pāda-mūla Mañjaryā Pravarācārya-duhitrā*. He and, following him, others take it to mean that Mañjarī was apparently a daughter of Pravarācārya but was really begotten by a person named Kamaleśvara. This, however, does not appear to be correct. In numerous inscriptions the word *pāda-mūla* is found used in the sense of 'an attendant', 'a servant', and the context leaves no room for doubt that a temple attendant is meant. Vide Khalimpur Plate of Dharmapāla, line 51, *EI*, iv, p. 250; Pandukeśvara Plate of Lalitaśūra, line 20, *IA*, xxv, p. 180; Nilgunda Plates of Cālukya Vikramāditya VI, line 75, *EI*, xii, p. 155. The word also occurs in this sense in Kannada and Tamil epigraphs (*ibid.*, p. 283, text line 244; *SII*, iii, pp. 138 and 250). In a Mandar Hill inscription of (Gupta) year 30-349 A.D. one Viṣṇudatta is described as the *pāda-mūla* of the god Virajoguhāsvāmin (*EI*, xxxvi, p. 305). Its derivative *pāda-mūlika* is also used to denote an attendant or servant in both inscriptions (*ibid.*, xviii, p. 156, text line 2) and literature. In the Jātakas this word by

Padma-purāṇa and the Kāśī-khaṇḍa of the *Skānda Purāṇa*[2] also.

Śiva and Kubera

Śiva and Kubera were believed to be closely related. If Kubera avoided Śiva's company, it was a matter of surprise.[3] The existence of friendly relations between the two deities is alluded to by Daṇḍin[4] and Kṣemendra[5] also. The antiquity of this association can be traced back to at least the second century B.C. as indicated by the occurrence of the dual form *Śiva-Vaiśravaṇau* in Patañjali's *Mahābhāṣya* (on Pāṇinī vi. 3.26), which further informs us that it was a post-Vedic development.[6] The mythical stories of the origin of their friendship and Śiva's help to Kubera on several occasions are narrated in the epics and the Purāṇas.[7]

Śaiva Sects

Of the several Śaiva sects that are known to have flourished during our period, mention is made of the Pāśupata system only

itself or in combination with some other word is found frequently employed in this sense. Vide F. Kielhorn, Pādamūla Pādamūlika, *IA*, xxvii (1898), p. 252; T.W. Rhys Davids and William Stede, *Pali-English Dictionary*, s.v. *pāda-mūlika*. In the Sasbahu inscription of Mahīpāla the word *pāda-kula* is used in the same sense (*IA*, xv, p. 89, v. 74). In Tamil inscriptions we have *pādamūlattār* in the sense of 'a temple attendant'. Cf. D.C. Sircar, *Indian Epigraphical Glossary*, p. 224. And as we have shown above, the correct reading is *Kalaśeśvara*, not *Kamaleśvara*. Mañjarī is thus intended to be represented as the daughter of one Pravarācārya and an attendant of Kalaśeśvara. For a full discussion on this verse vide my paper, The Reading and Interpretation of a Verse in the Kuṭṭanī-mata in the Light of Archaeological and Purāṇic Evidence, *Purāṇa*, xiii, pp. 60-66.

1. Svarga-khaṇḍa, ch. 37, v. 7 (Venkateshwar Press edition).
2. Pūrvārdha, ch. 10, v. 86.
3. अटता धात्रीमखिलामिदमाश्चर्यं मया परं दृष्टम् ।
   धनदोपि नयननन्दन परिहरसि यदुग्रसंपर्कम् ॥
   K. 769
4. *Daśakumāra-carita*, iv. p. 172.
5. *Samaya-mātṛkā*, iv. 26.
6. ब्रह्मप्रजापती शिव-वैश्रवणौ, स्कन्दविशाखौ - द्वन्द्व इत्यनुवर्तमाने पुनर्द्वन्द्वग्रहणस्यैतत् प्रयोजनं - लोकवेदार्थो द्वन्द्वस्तत्र यथा स्यात् । कश्च लोकवेदार्थो द्वन्द्वः ? वेदे ये सहवापनिर्दिष्टाः न चैते वेदे सहवापनिर्दिष्टाः ।
   On Pāṇini, vi.3.26, viii.1.25.
7. *Mahābhārata*, Śalyaparva, 47.29; Śāntiparva, Ch. 289; *Padma-purāṇa*, Svarga-khaṇḍa, Ch. 16.

(539, 753). The prevalence and popularity of the Pāśupata school in Kashmir is indicated by numerous references in the *Rāja-taraṅgiṇī.*[1] At one place we have a reference to a Pāśupatācārya named Bhāva-Śuddha (539). Here *Bhāva* is an honorific title assumed by Śaiva *ācāryas*,[2] Śuddha alone being the personal name. The title *Bhāva* appears to have been widely popular among the Pāśupatas during this and subsequent period. If our poet is to be relied upon, the standard of sexual morality among the Pāśupatas in the period under study was not very high, for we read at two places of the attachment of the Pāśupata teachers to prostitutes.

An important development in the religious history of Kashmir during the period was the foundation of monistic Śaivism or what is popularly called Kashmir Śaivism.[3] Saṅgamāditya, the fourth ancestor of Somānanda, the founder of the Pratyabhijñā school, and Atrigupta, an ancestor of Abhinavagupta, the greatest authority on Pratyabhijñā, had settled in Kashmir about the middle of the eighth century A.D. and probably tried to popularise monistic Śaiva Tantras. Vasugupta, the founder of the Spanda branch of Kashmir Śaivism, was probably a contemporary of Dāmodaragupta and may have just systematised the philosophical ideas of the monistic Tantras in his *Śiva Sūtras* when Dāmodaragupta composed the *Kuṭṭanīmata.*[3] Absence of any reference to or indication of monistic Śaivism in our poem may not be without interest. It probably indicates that the monistic Śaiva philosophy being rather abstruse had not yet attracted the masses who stuck to popular forms of Śaivism.

II. VAIṢṆAVISM

Vaiṣṇavism enjoyed as much popularity as, if not more than, Śaivism in Kashmir during our period. It was the family

1. *RT,* i.17-18; iii.267, 460; v.404.
2. E.g. Bhāva-Sarvajña, the author of the *Nyāya-bhūṣaṇa*, and Bhāva-Vidyeśvara, commentator of the *Sapta-padārthī.*
3. For an account of pre-Abhinavagupta history of Kashmir Śaivism see K.C. Pandey, *Abhinavagupta, An Historical and Philosophical Study*, pp.82ff.

religion of the Karkoṭas who vied with each other in endowing Vaiṣṇava foundations.[1] Their zealous patronage must have substantially contributed to the great increase in its popularity.

Viṣṇu—His Names and Iconography

By the time of Dāmodaragupta Vaiṣṇavism had fully developed as a sectarian system. The different currents emanating from the solar god Viṣṇu, the cosmic god Nārāyaṇa and the historical god Vāsudeva-Kṛṣṇa had fused together to form an integrated whole without leaving any trace of their individuality. This fact is illustrated by the ascription of the attributes and achievements of one god to the other. Thus the episodes concerning Hiraṇyakaśipu and Bali are found connected with Kṛṣṇa-Hṛṣīkeśa (315, 774). Similarly, the goddess Lakṣmī, traditionally the divine consort of Viṣṇu, is associated with Keśava (979).

The god is referred to under various names, viz., Hari (33, 204, 258, 487), Nārāyaṇa (993), Keśava (979), Govinda (860), Hṛṣīkeśa (774), Puruṣottama (772), Mahāpuruṣa[2] (1011), and Kṛṣṇa (315).

The *Kaustubha* gem (33, 195) and *vanamālā* (135), a garland reaching the knees, which adorned his breast (993), are the only iconographic features of Viṣṇu mentioned in our poem. *Kaustubha* was as much a cognizance of Viṣṇu[3] as horses of the

1. Durlabhavardhana, the founder of the Karkoṭa dynasty, built a shrine of Viṣṇu Durlabhasvāmin (*RT*, iv.6) and his son Malhaṇa had a shrine of Viṣṇu Malhaṇasvāmin erected (*ib.*, iv.4). Candrāpīḍa, son of Durlabhaka, constructed a shrine of Tribhuvanasvāmin (*ib.*, iv. 55ff.); his *guru* Mihiradatta built the temple of Viṣṇu Gambhīrasvāmin (*ib.*, iv. 80), and one of his officers, Calitaka, that of Calitakasvāmin (*ib.*, iv.81). For other Vaiṣṇava temples built by the Karkoṭa kings see *RT*, iv.188, 193, 194-199, 201-2, 208, 275, 276, etc.

The *Nīlamata* describes certain festivals dedicated to the worship of Viṣṇu which also indicate the popularity of Vaiṣṇavism in Kashmir. Vide *Nīlamata-purāṇa* edited by Kanjilal & Zadoo, Appendix A, Nos. 10, 17, 30, 33, 39, 43, 49.

2. For the use of the name Mahāpuruṣa for Viṣṇu, see Pattan Plates of Vākāṭaka Pravarasena II, V.V. Mirashi, *Inscriptions of the Vākāṭakas*, *CII*, v, p. 60, text line 22; *Bhāgavata-purāṇa*, ii,1, 10; v.4, 6, 15, 16-7; etc.

3. In *K* 195, Viṣṇu (in Vāmana incarnation) is called *Kaustubhābharaṇa*.

Sun god, the elephant (Airāvata) of Indra and wealth of Kubera (33).

Viṣṇu and Lakṣmī

The inseparable union of Viṣṇu with his consort Śrī-Lakṣmī was taken for granted. Lakṣmī is not infrequently represented as having her station on the breast of Viṣṇu (118, 204, 979). It is stated that as though unable to bear separation from his beloved even temporarily, Viṣṇu has stationed Lakṣmī on his breast (487). A lady constantly remaining in the mind of her husband is compared to the goddess Lakṣmī never leaving the breast of Viṣṇu (168). A damsel not united with a suitable man is likened to lightning without clouds, moon-light without the moon, Rati without Kāma, and goddess Śrī fallen from the breast of Viṣṇu (258). It was a commonplace to describe the excessive beauty of a man or woman with reference to the position of Lakṣmī on the breast of Viṣṇu. For example, while describing the physical features of Sundarasena it is stated that seeing his expansive breast resembling a slab of gold Lakṣmī found her position on Hari's breast uncomfortable.[1] Likewise, while narrating the charms of Mañjarī, prince Samarabhaṭa is represented to have said that if Keśava were to see her, Lakṣmī cannot give up the fear of her fall from Viṣṇu's breast.[2] The description of Lakṣmī as the daughter of the ocean (Saindhavī 979) alludes to the myth of her origin from the ocean as it was being churned by the gods and titans.[3]

1. कलधौतफलकशोभां बिभ्राणं यस्य पृथुतरं वक्षः ।
दृष्ट्वा चिराय लक्ष्मीर्हरिहृदये दुःस्थितिं मेने ॥
K 204.

2. केशव इह सन्निहितः सापि मनोहारिरूपसंपन्ना ।
तद्वक्षश्च्यवनभुवं कथमुज्झति सैन्धवी शङ्काम् ॥
K. 979.

This is the reading of Kaul's edition (verse 978). Tripathi's reading *tad=vakṣaḥ śry=avana-bhuvaṁ* lands him into imaginary and hair-splitting interpretations.

यदि कथमपि मधुमथनः पश्यति तामसमबाणसर्वस्वम् ।
तदसारभारभूतामिव लक्ष्मीमुरसि विनिहितां मनुते ॥
K 118.

3. Cf. *Mahābhārata*, Ādiparva, 18.35.

Paurāṇic Legends

Some of the Paurāṇic legends relating to Viṣṇu are alluded to. The destruction of the demons Mura, Madhu, Naraka and Kaṁsa is implied in the meaningful designations Murāri (773) or Muraripu (991), Madhumathana (118), Narakavairin (168) and Kaṁsāsuravairin (135). The lotus growing from the navel of the enemy of Mura (*Mura-ripu-nābhi-saroruha*, 991) is also mentioned. The legend of Govinda's amorous sports with cowherdesses, numbering sixteen thousand, had been fully developed by our poet's time.[1] At one place we read that even though divine damsels were under his authority and he was the foremost among the clever people, yet he was attached to cowherdesses.[2] Yet another stanza describes him as of universal form (*viśvarūpa*), for, though one, he resides in the hearts of many a woman.[3] This is obviously an allusion to the Viśvarūpa-darśanādhyāya of the *Bhagavadgītā* (Ch. 11) wherein Kṛṣṇa is said to have manifested his Universal Form to Arjuna.

Avatāras of Viṣṇu

Of the incarnations (*avatāras*) of Viṣṇu, implicit allusion is made only to the Man-Lion (Narasiṁha) and the Dwarf (Vāmana) ones. The hostility between Kṛṣṇa (i.e. Viṣṇu in the Man-Lion form) and Hiraṇyakaśipu was firmly established in the popular mind and it was impossible for one to have a liking for both of them at the same time (315). The episode of Viṣṇu (Hṛṣīkeśa) begging of the demon king Bali at the time of the sacrifice is clearly mentioned (774). Consequently

1. किं वहसि वृथा गर्वं प्रियोऽहमिति योषितां नराधीश ।
काङ्क्षन्ति स्म मुरारिं षोडशगोपीसहस्राणि ।।
K 773.

2. अप्सरसः किं न वशे ऽदग्ध्यवतां च किं न धौरेयः ।
येन चकारासक्तिं गोविन्दो गोपदारेषु ।।
K 860.

3. हृदयेषु कामिनीनामेकोऽनेकेषु वससि येन त्वम् ।
जनकः कुसुमास्त्रभृतः पुरुषोत्तम तेन विश्वरूपोऽसि ।।
K 772.

Viṣṇu was called a beggar (195). We have references to Rāma, son of Daśaratha, also, but he is not described as an incarnation.

Vaiṣṇava Deities

Among the Vaiṣṇava deities we find mention of only Baladeva, the bearer of the ploughshare (Halin), noted for his inebriety (136), and Pradyumna, a manifestation of Kāma born as a son of Vāsudeva-Kṛṣṇa (305, 772).

Vaiṣṇava Ascetics

Dāmodaragupta affords us a penetrating insight into the lives of the Vaiṣṇava ascetics also. He describes them as carrying a seat and a staff and donned in brown (*kaṣāya*) clothes, observing the vow of silence and looking on sides and driving the people away lest they should pollute them by their touch. It is said that they followed Vaiṣṇavite scriptures (*Hari-śāsana*) and were respected by all the Vaiṣṇavas.[1] In the *Mṛcchakaṭika* also we get the description of a Vaiṣṇava ascetic of Ujjayinī who carried a staff and a water-pot (*kuṇḍikā*). In Śūdraka's *Padma-prābhṛtaka* also there is found a reference to a class of Vaiṣṇavas known as Caukṣa who laid too much emphasis on avoiding other's touch.[2] This point is also stressed in the *Pāda-tāḍitaka* of Śyāmilaka who further adds that they carried a staff and a *kuṇḍikā* and used to present lemons to their teachers and the deity.[3] The *Bṛhat-saṁhitā* (lxxxvi. 43) of Varāhamihira also contains a reference to the Cokṣas.[4] The Caukṣas

1. योऽयं गृहीतबृसिकः कुशकर्णो विधृतदण्डकाषायः ।
लोकस्पर्शशिङ्की कृतापसारो विलोकयन् पार्श्वौं ॥
कुर्वाणो मौनव्रतमुत्पादितसकलवैष्णवप्रीतिः (श्रद्धः) ।
हरिशासनं प्रपन्नस्त्रिपुरान्तकदर्शनापदेशेन ॥
स्त्रैणं पश्यति युक्त्या साकांक्षं वर्जितान्यजनदृष्टिः ।
कुमुदिनि मम हृदयगतं भवितव्यं व्याजलिङ्गिनाऽनेन ॥
K 748-750.

2. *Caturbhāṇī* (edited by Motichandra and V. S. Agrawala), pp. 21-22.
3. *Ibid.*, pp. 163-65.
4. Ajay Mitra Shastri, *India as seen in the Bṛhatsaṁhitā of Varāhasmihira*, p. 555-56. Utpala explains *Cokṣa* as a wicked person (*cokṣo duṣṭa it iprasidhaḥ*) which is wrong. This probably indicates that the Caukṣas had earned a bad reputation because of their notoriety.

are also mentioned in Bharata's *Nāṭya-śāstra*.[1] It seems that the Vaiṣṇava ascetics described by our author were the same as the Caukṣas. It is interesting to note in this connection that these ascetics had a liberal religious attitude and showed respect to non-Vaiṣṇavite deities also. Both our author and the *Padma-prābhṛtaka* represent these ascetics as worshipping Śiva.[2]

The above also indicates the existence of cordial relations between the followers of the two principal Brāhmaṇical systems of the time. And this is as must be expected. For in Kashmir both Śiva and Viṣṇu are known to have been popularly worshipped without any trace of sectarian animosity. There were festivals on which both the deities were worshipped.[3] The Karkoṭas had adopted Vaiṣṇavism as their family religion, yet they generously endowed many Śaiva foundations.[4] Thus Narendraprabhā, queen of Durlabhaka, built the shrine of Śiva Narendreśvara, while Lalitāditya Muktāpīḍa erected stone a lofty temple of Jyeṣṭharudra[5] and presented eleven crores to the shrine of Śiva Bhūteśa on the successful termination of his victorious campaigns.[6]

The above description of Vaiṣṇava ascetic is found in connection with Vārāṇasī which shows that although the city was a stronghold of Śaivism, Vaiṣṇavism also had a good following. This is corroborated by archaeological evidence. Near Bakariya Kund at Vārāṇasī has been found a Gupta sculpture depicting Kṛṣṇa lifting the Govardhana mountain thereby indicating the presence of a large temple of Kṛṣṇa on the spot. Rajghat has yielded many seals bearing Vaiṣṇavite personal names in Gupta characters, while one seal actually contains the replica of a Vaiṣṇava temple of the Gupta age.[7] The

1. *Nāṭya-śāstra*, xvii. 38. Abhinavagupta explains *Cokṣa* as a sect of the Bhāgavatas, also called Ekāyana :—

चोक्षा भागवतविशेषा ये एकायना इति प्रसिद्धाः ।

2. For some interesting information about the Caukṣas, see Chandrabali Pandey, Mṛcchakaṭika kā Parivrājaka, *Naī Dhārā* (Hindi), October 1952, pp. 3-4; Motichandra & V.S. Agrawala, *Caturbhāṇī*, p. 21.
3. Kanjilal & Zadoo, *Nīlamata-purāṇa*, Appendix A, p.3, No. 10.
4. *RT*, iv. 38.
5. *Ibid.*, iv. 190.
6. *Ibid.*, iv. 189. Vide also *ibid.*, iv.209, 214.
7. Motichandra, *Kāśī kā Itihāsa*, p. 99.

Sarnath Stone Inscription of Prakaṭāditya belonging to the end of the seventh century A.D. records the construction by him of a temple of the god Viṣṇu, under the name Muradviṣ, and some provision for its repairs.[1]

III. OTHER DEITIES

The Hindus of our period were not very sectarian in spirit. They evinced a sort of religious eclecticism which characterised Indian life from time immemorial and worshipped numerous gods and goddesses irrespective of the sect to which they might have belonged. And this feature finds full expression in our poem which casually refers to a number of gods and goddesses.

Brahmā

Brahmā (977), also called Viśvasṛj (108, 263, 975), Vidhi (105, 114), Dhātṛ (120, 489, 976) Vidhātṛ (259), Viriñca (177), Ātmabhū (963) and Vedhas (244), along with Viṣṇu and Śiva constitutes the famous trinity of Hindu gods. He is particularly noted for his control of organs of sense (194), placid demeanour (*śāntātman* 975) and devotion to study, evidently of the Vedas (977). While narrating Mañjarī's charms, prince Samarabhaṭa is represented to have told his minister that if Brahmā, not to speak of others, were to see that jewel among women, the essence of the world, he would lose his concentration in study and become despondent. Creation is represented as his major function. Most of the references to Brahmā are in connection with the creation of feminine beauty. Viśvakarman, the divine architect, is said to have carried out his orders. The Paurāṇic legend of his birth from the lotus growing from Viṣṇu's navel is hinted at in his descriptive epithets *kamala-janman* (876) and *Hari-nābhi-paṅkaja-bhū* (194). The story of the creation by Brahmā of the peerless divine damsel Tilottamā for the destruction of the demon-brothers Sunda and Upasunda, sons of Nikumbha, which is described in detail in the *Mahābhārata* (Ādiparva, Chs. 210-211), *Kathā-sarit-sāgara* (xv. 135-40) and other works,[2] is also mentioned (*Sund-Opasunda-nāśaḥ phalam=Ātmabhuvas=Tilottamā-sṛṣṭeḥ,* 963).

1. *CII*, iii, pp. 285-286.
2. Vide my *India is seen in the Bṛhatsaṁhitā of Varāhamihira*, p. 135.

Indra

Indra (994), also referred to as Puruhūta (193, 1032) and Purandara (176), was regarded as the lord of heaven (*Nākādhipati* 121, 484) and of the gods (*amarendra* 33). The abode of Indra (*Purandara-sthāna*) was considered to be an exemplary town and when a city was to be described as astoundingly beautiful it was said that it excelled even Indra's city (176). Pāṭaliputra is thus described, while Vārāṇasī is said to be another Amarāvatī in this world created by Brahmā inasmuch as like the latter which is beautified by the Nandana garden, inhabited by gods and patrolled by divine army the former also could boast of beautiful parks, scholars (*vibudhavatī*) and the river Gaṅgā (*nākavāhinī-juṣṭā*, 17). He has a thousand eyes; while describing Mālatī's matchless beauty it is said that Indra's thousand eyes are fruitless if he cannot see her (121). He is said to have been sanctified by the performance of a hundred sacrifices (*makha-śata-pūta* 193). This is evidently an allusion to the popular notion that one attains the rank of Indra by performing a hundred *Aśvamedha* sacrifices. It is vividly illustrated by Kālidāsa who describes how Indra obstructed the completion of the hundredth *Aśvamedha* of the Ikṣvāku king Dilīpa lest he should become a rival to him.[1] The elephant mount, which is his cognizance, is alluded to in his descriptive epithet *gaja-nātha* (33). We have also a reference to the outraging by Indra of Ahalyā's modesty. While describing men's natural attraction to others' wives it is said that even though heavenly courtesans carry out his behests with folded hands, yet Indra, being attracted by others' wives, had illicit intercourse with Ahalyā.[2] Of Indra's retinue, mention is made of his consort, Śacī (*Sacī-pati* 859), and his son Jayanta. As for the latter, it is said that he did not have immeasurable virtues to his credit (*na Jayanto = ananta-guṇaḥ*, 1014). As pointed out by Tripathi, this is probably an allusion to the legend that

1. *Raghu.-vaṁśa*, Canto iii.
2. शिरसा रचिताञ्जलयो दधति निदेशं त्रिविष्टपे गणिकाः ।
परदाररसाकृष्टस्तथापि भेजे शचीपतिरहल्याम् ॥
K 859.

having assumed the form of a crow Jayanta struck Sītā's bosom with his beak when she was at Citrakūṭa.[1]

Sūrya

The god Sun, referred to as Hari (33), Pataṅga (244) and Caṇḍabhās (250), had seven horses yoked to his chariot (250). Horses were as important an emblem of Sūrya as the Kaustubha was of Viṣṇu and elephant of Indra (33). Referring to the height of the Arbuda mountain, the poet rhetorically states that it appears as if the god Brahmā knowing the sky-passage of the horses of the Sun to be without any resting place has created the mountain for their rest.[2]

Kubera

Kubera (179), also called Dhanada (769), Dhanapati (1027) and Draviṇapati (33), was regarded as the lord of riches, and his city, Alakā, was an exemplar of prosperity (179). Reference has already been made to his friendship with Śiva.[3] He is said to have been divested of his greatness by the demon king Rāvaṇa,[4] an allusion to the well-known epic legend that the latter, strengthened by a boon of Brahmā, defeated the former, drove him out of Laṅkā and seized his Puṣpaka *vimāna*.[5]

We also get some interesting references to Kubera's son Nalakūbara. He was famed for his handsomeness and for being loved by beautiful ladies (1027). The stories concerning his love affairs with the divine damsel Rambhā, an exemplar of feminine beauty, enjoyed wide popularity.[6] At one place we read of Rambhā, overcome by passion, going to meet Nalakūbara (1000). The story of Rambhā going to keep an appointment with Nalakūbara and being intercepted and molested

1. *Rāmāyaṇa*, Sundarakāṇḍa, Ch. 28, verses 12ff.

2. अवगम्य निरवलम्बनमम्बरमार्गं पतङ्गतुरगाणाम् ।
अयमवनिधरो मन्ये विश्रान्त्यै वेधसा विहितः ॥

K. 244.

3. *Supra*, p. 67.

4. *Hṛta-Dhanapati-māhātmyā pravṛttir=iva rakṣasāṁ patyuḥ*, *K* 1004.

5. *Rāmāyaṇa*, Uttarakāṇḍa, Ch. 15; *Mahābhārata*, Vanaparva 275.32-35.

6. Nalakūbara's affair with Rambhā is alluded to by Subandhu also. Vide *Vāsavadattā* (edited with an introduction, Engl. tr. and notes by Louis H. Gray), pp. 73, 90, 159, 167.

by Rāvaṇa who was then encamped on the Kailāsa mountain is narrated at length in the *Rāmāyaṇa* (Uttarakāṇḍa, Ch. 26) and the *Mahābhārata* (Vanaparva, 280.59-60). At another place (1013) he is described as miserable or unfortunate (*varāka*). This, as suggested by Tripathi, may have a reference to the legend of his being transformed into an *arjuna* tree in Gokula in consequence of a curse of Nārada which is recounted in detail in the *Bhāgavata* (x.10).

Agni

Agni, called Hutavaha (489) and Hutāśana (491) and styled *bhagavat* (489), is referred to in connection with funeral.

Yama

Yama, referred to as Antaka (479), was a *lokapāla*, the regent of the southern quarter (488). He is represented as the lord of the dead (*pareta-nātha* 565), and it was believed that the dead go to his abode.

Viśvakarman

Viśvakarman, the divine architect, is mentioned in connection with the planning and layout of the city of Pāṭaliputra. On looking at the beautiful city it came to one's mind as if it was laid out as an exemplar (*varṇaka*) of his craftsmanship by Viśvakarman when asked by Brahmā to display his skill in laying out a model of township for the three worlds.[1]

Bṛhaspati

Bṛhaspati, referred to as Guru (193), was traditionally regarded as the repository of learning (*vidyā-vasati*, 193) and the lord of speech (*vacasām adhīśa*, 201). When a person was to be described as a great scholar he was compared to Bṛhaspati (193). His son, Kaca, is also mentioned.

Kāma

Kāma (577), the Indian god of love, is referred to under

1. त्रिभुवनपुरनिष्पादनकौशलमिव पृच्छतो विरिञ्चस्य ।
दर्शयितुं निजशिल्पं वर्णकमिव विश्वकर्मणा रचितम् ॥

K 177.

various names like Smara ((44, 52), Madana (908, 917), Kandarpa (543, 925), Manmatha (258, 919), Māra (732), etc. His body was burnt by Śiva[1] in consequence of which he came to be known as 'bodyless' (*atanu* 108, 330; *anaṅga* 100, 1041; *aśarīra* 95; *vyaṅga* 976; *vidhvasta-śarīra* 266). He is born of remembrances (976) or of mind and is consequently called *saṅkalpabhava* (1), *saṅkalpaja* (52), *manobhava* (918), *manojanman* (122) and *hṛcchaya* (916). Being self-born, he is called *ananya-bhava* (1007) and *ātmajanman* (995). Being the husband of Rati,[2] he was also known as *Ratikānta* (46) and *Ratiramaṇa* (1013). Kāma and Rati were so very inseparable from one another that a beloved separated from her lover was compared to Rati without her consort (258). His bow and arrows being supposed to have been composed of flowers (108, 976), he is also styled *kusumacāpa* (97, 122, 202, 267), *kusumabāṇa* (144), *kusumaśarapāṇi* (908), *kusumapraharaṇa* (962), *kusu-māstra* (772, 1005) and *kusumāyudha* (886, 1022). The spring season being dear to him, he is called *priyasurabhi* (61) and *kusumākara-vallabha* (135). His arrows are five in number (484, *daśārdhabāṇa* 969) which being uneven, he is also styled "uneven-arrowed" (*asamabāṇa* 118, *asamasāyaka* 1026). His flag was marked with the figure of a crocodile (*makara*) or fish (*mīna*) which was his cognizance (*makaraketana* 46, 590, 989; *makaraketu* 106; *makaradhvaja* 88, 116; *mīnaketu*[3] 989). It is interesting to note in this connection that a *makara* (or *mīna*) *dhvaja* dating from the first or second century B.C. has been discovered at Besnagar. The circumstantial evidence indicates that the capital in question represents Pradyumna who was regarded as a manifestation of Kāma. The *Harivaṁśa* (Viṣṇu-parva, 106.46ff.) relates at length how Kāma, after being burnt by Śiva, incarnated himself as a son of Kṛṣṇa born of Rukmiṇī.[4] It is for this reason that Kṛṣṇa is represented as the father of the "floral weapon bearer", i.e., Kāma (772). The legend of the

1. 44, 202, 277, 918, 971, 1005, 1041.
2. 1, 202, 258, 577, 908, 1013.
3. Tripathi gives *mīnaketu* as a variant, the reading adopted by him being *makaraketu*. Kaul (verse 988) adopts the reading *mīnaketu* and gives no variant.
4. Also cf. *Mahābhārata*, Anuśāsanaparva, 148.20-21.

destruction of the demon Śambara by Kāma incarnated as Pradyumna and the reunion of the latter with his former consort Māyāvatī, which is narrated in detail in the Purāṇas,[1] is alluded to in the epithet *Śambaradhvaṁsin* applied to him (971).

While dilating the performance of the first act of the *Ratnāvalī*, Dāmodaragupta gives a vivid description of a festival called Kusumāyudhaparva or Kandarpamahamahotsava which was performed in honour of Kāma (886-925)). The antiquity of this festival is vouched for by Vātsyāyana who refers to it under the name Suvasantaka (*Kāmasūtra*, i.4.42). It was celebrated on the 13th of the bright half of Caitra when Kāma was supposed to have been re-born as Pradyumna.[2] The popularity of this festival in Kashmir is indicated by the *Nīlamata* (655-658) which recommends its observance. The worship of an image or painting of the god of love was its central item. It was marked by an outburst of joyous feelings when men and women putting all restrictions and distinctions aside indulged in merry-making, throwing scented coloured powder and water on one another, singing songs, dancing sometimes to the accompaniment of musical instruments, playing dice and uttering obscene words, collectively called *carcarī*[3] (886). Participants in the festival included men and women, young and old, high and low ranks.

Hanumat

Hanumān occurs as a personal name (409) which may indicate the popularity of the legends appertaining him.

Goddesses

As for the goddesses, mention has already been made of Gaurī, Lakṣmī and Śacī. The only other goddess named by our poet is Sarasvatī, the Indian goddess of learning. Pāṭaliputra is said to be the permanent habitat (*kula-gṛha*) of Sarasvatī,

1. *Harivaṁśa*, Viṣṇuparva, chs. 104-107; *Śiva-purāṇa*, Dharmasaṁhitā, viii.43-6. Cf. *Mahābhārata*, Anuśāsanaparva, 14.28.

2. *HDS*, v, part i. p. 369. For some other festivals connected with Kāma worship vide *ibid.*, pp. 257-58, 281, 310-11, 368; Tripathi's gloss on *K* 886.

3. For various meanings of *carcarī*, see Tripathi's commentary on *K* C For a full discussion, vide *infra*, h. IV. 68.8

implying thereby the fame of the city as a well-known centre of learning (176).

Nectar (*pīyūṣa*) is said to be the food of the deities (992).

Besides worshipping all and sundry gods and goddesses, every family had its own tutelary deity (*iṣṭa-devatā* 143, *kula-devatā* 187). A happy occurrence was supposed to be due to the favour of the family deity.

IV. OTHER OBJECTS OF WORSHIP

From time immemorial India has been the cradle of the people following diverse religious beliefs. But in course of time these varying religious tenets crystallised into some major systems which tried to assimilate as many of the popular beliefs as possible. The different major religious orders vied with one another to augment their strength and popularity by incorporating within their own fold the adherents of various cults which had maintained an independent existence from olden times. Buddhism, Jainism and Brāhmaṇical Hinduism all did the same. They assigned these cult-objects a subordinate place in their respective pantheons. This is illustrated by the absorption in them of diverse elements like the cults centring round the Apsarases, Yakṣas, Gandharvas, Vidyādharas, elephants, snakes, etc. These are now as important an element of Hinduism as any other. This was a *fait accompli* long prior to the time of our poet.

Devayonis

The belief in the existence of semi-divine spirits or *devayonis*[1] in India is of a high antiquity. Of them, the Apsarases, Gandharvas, Vidyādharas, Kimpuruṣas and Bhūtas are named by Dāmodaragupta. The Apsarases (860, 876) or divine damsels were regarded as heavenly courtesans (*gaṇikā* 859, *deva-gaṇikā* 1000) and are described as waiting upon the gods like Indra and Govinda with folded hands and ever-ready to carry out their behests (859-860). They were believed to be skilled in dramatic performances (876). Three of the Apsarases, Tilottamā, Rambhā and Urvaśī, are mentioned by name.

1. For a list of demi-gods vide *Amara-kośa*, i.1.11

Tilottamā, as we have seen above, is said to have been created by Brahmā for the destruction of the demons Sunda and Upasunda. Rambhā was regarded as an expert dancer and an exemplar of feminine beauty. While describing the proficiency of an earthly dancer it had become axiomatic to say that she excelled even Rambhā (86). Likewise, a lady of matchless beauty was often compared to Rambhā (116, 699). Reference has already been made to her affairs with Nalakūbara. Urvaśī, is said to have been attached to Purūravas (1000).

The Gandharvas, it was believed, inhabit the Himalayas (180), while the Vidyādharas are associated with the Arbuda mountain (241). The Kimpuruṣas are represented as having their abode on the Meru mountain (316). They were of two kinds, horse-faced and human-bodied and human-faced and horse-bodied, both of which are frequently represented in early Indian sculpture. We have a reference to the possession of a person by the Bhūta who, it was believed, could make one act even against one's own interests (725).

Sages and their Consorts

Mention must also be made in this connection of the sages and their consorts who, too, commanded popular veneration. Sages such as Manu, etc. are said to be knowers of the three times, past, present and future (719). Nārada, son of Brahmā, was traditionally regarded as an expert musician (876). Tradition remembers him as the inventer of the lyre, the musical instrument *par excellence* of India. In the famous Allahabad pillar inscription of Samudragupta also mention is made of Nārada's mastery in music.[1] The sages Bharata, Kohala and Mātaṅga are mentioned in connection with dramatic performance (876-877). The sage Kapila had a great reputation for his concentration and self-control (115, 1040). An allusion is made to the epic legend of his reducing Sagara's sons to ashes (195). A paronomasiatic stanza refers to the *munis* Hārīta, Śuka, Vyāsa and Bharadvāja (247). The wife of the Great Sage (*mahāmuni-dayitā*) was noted as a model of chastity (203). She may be either Vasiṣṭha's wife Arundhatī or Atri's wife

1. *CII*, iii, p. 8, line 27.

Anasūyā who are regarded as the greatest Hindu models oɪ feminine chastity.

Nāga Cult

The Nāga cult appears to have enjoyed wide popularity in Kashmir. According to the tradition recorded in the *Nīlamata* the Nāgas apprehending the extinction of their race from the wrath of Garuḍa found, through Viṣṇu's favour, a sheltering place in the lake known as Satīsaras which later turned into the valley of Kashmir[2] and had Nīla anointed as their sovereign. Kashmir was believed to have been attended by a number of Nāgas headed by Nīla who was regarded as the protector of the land.[3] The *Nīlamata* ordains the celebration of a number of festivals dedicated to the worship of Nīlanāga.[4] These traditions are not referred to by our author who contents himself by alluding to some legends concerning Śeṣanāga. Regarded as the lord of serpents, Śeṣa was believed to be thousand-mouthed (125). He is described as possessed of beautiful gems, many (i.e. thousand) hoods, the bearer of a heavy burden (of the earth which he was supposed to support) and as an abode of stability.[5]

Elephants of Quarters

People also believed in the existence of the elephants of the quarters (*āśā-karin*) who were entrusted with the task of bearing the earth (246).

Demonology

The popular respect for the gods, goddesses and semi-divine spirits was spontaneous, while the demonaic spirits were propitiated with the object of forestalling the calamities which

1. Verses 51 ff. See also Appendix, verses 73 ff.
2. Also cf. *RT*, i.31
3. *Ibid.*, i. 28, 30; *Nīlamata*, 1049-1115. For an alphabetical list of the chief Nāgas of Kashmir, see *ibid.*, Appendix B.
4. *Ibid.*, Appendix A, Serial Nos. 7, 32, 46. Also cf. no. 57 (1st day of Kārttika) when Nāgas were worshipped together with the Gandharvas, Piśācas and Brāhmaṇas.
5. सन्मणिरनेकभोगो गुरुभारसहः स्थिरात्मतास्थानम्
   नरदेव चित्रमेतद् यदशेषगुणैस्त्वमाश्लिष्टः ।
   K 779.

they were otherwise supposed to bring. The demonesses (*yātudhāna-jāyāḥ* 250) were believed to be flesh-eaters. The female ghouls (*ḍākinī*) are said to be fond of drinking blood (*ḍākinya iva ca rakta-vyākarṣaṇa-kauśal-opetāḥ*, 317). The *ḍākinīs* were associated with the Mother Goddess cult at least from the Gupta period as evidenced by the Gangdhar stone inscription of Viśvavarman, dated Mālava-Vikrama year 481.[1] Mention is also made of Miṣṭaka, a commander of the army of the Dānavas (253). The demon king Rāvaṇa is referred to in connection with the *Rāmāyaṇa* episodes (786, 861, 1004). References to the demons Tripura, Andhaka, Madhu, Hiraṇyakaśipu, Bali, Sunda, Upasunda and Śambara have already been studied in connection with the gods who are said to have destroyed them.

Asura-vivara

It was believed that the *Asura-vivara* or the habitat of the Asuras in the nether world abounded in beautiful women, and the city of Pāṭaliputra which also included a large population of beautiful ladies among its inhabitants is compared to it (180). This motif, important as it is from the point of view of contemporary religious history, is not infrequently referred to in literature. In the *Viṣṇu-purāṇa*, Nārada is said to have exclaimed, "What can be compared to Pātāla where the lovely daughters of the Daityas and Dānavas wander about fascinating even the most austere".[2] Bāṇabhaṭṭa, who had a penetrating insight into various facets of contemporary life, has referred to this motif several times both in the *Harṣa-carita* and the *Kādambarī*. In the IVth book of the *Harṣa-carita*, while referring to thousands of the ladies of the feudatories of Prabhākaravardhana assembled to celebrate Harṣa's birth, Bāṇa says that it looked as if the *Asura-vivaras* had been opened out.[3] People appear to have been very anxious to obtain pretty women and riches of the *Asura-vivara* and resorted to various Tantric practices for this purpose. Lohitākṣa, a friend of Bāṇa,[4] and the Draviḍian priest of the

1. *CII*, iii, no. 17.
2. *Viṣṇu-purāṇa*, Engl. tr. by H.H. Wilson, p. 204.
3. *Harṣa-carita*, iv, p. 186.
4. *Asura-vivara-vyasanin*, *ibid.*, i, p. 67.

Caṇḍikā temple which Candrāpīḍa visited on his way to Ujjayinī[1] are said to have been addicted to such rites. We learn from Bāṇa that people had to pass through some deep dark ditch in order to reach the *Asura-vivara*. Describing the Śaiva saint Bhairavācārya who had covered himself with a black blanket, Bāṇa states that it appeared as if he were practising entry into the dark nether world (*pātāl-āndhakār-āvāsa*) for reaching the *Asura-vivara*.[2] Daṇḍin describes how a Brahmin named Mātaṅga, protected by prince Rājavāhana, entered the nether world (*rasātala*) through a hole and obtained wealth and a beautiful Asura damsel.[3] Both Bāṇa and Daṇḍin seem to connect this practice with Śaivism.[4] According to Bāṇa, those officiating at the Tantric rites in question were known as *Vātika*.[5] This belief was sometimes exploited for political purposes. Thus, in the *Harṣa-carita* we read how the ministers of the king of Mekala carried away a king of Magadha, who was addicted to the *Asura-vivara*, by an underground passage resounding with the alluring music of the anklets of numberless pretty ladies[6]. The popularity of this practice in Kashmir is vouchsafed by Kalhaṇa who tells us how King Raṇāditya went to the cave of the demon Namuci passing through the water of the river Candrabhāgā (Chenab), obtained sovereignty over the nether world and partook and made his subjects partake in the love of the Daitya women.[7] It is interesting to note in this connection that according to the *Kathā-sarit-sāgara* one of the entrances into the Pātāla was made by Maya in Kashmir.[8] Rogues and cheats often took advantage of this belief and harassed the people. Kṣemendra in his *Samaya-mātṛkā* describes how a deceptive prostitute threw away men addicted to the *Asura-*

1. *Lagn-Āsura-vivara-praveśa-piśācena, Kādambarī*, Pūrvabhāga, p. 461.
2. *Harṣa-carita*, iii, p. 154.
3. *Daśa-kumāra-carita*, Pūrvapīṭhikā, ii, pp. 28-29.
4. Bāṇa refers to it in connection wth a Śaiva saint, while Daṇḍin represents Mātaṅga to have been instructed by Śiva about his entry into the nether world.
5. *Harṣa-carita*, iii, p. 148.
6. *Ibid.*, vi, pp. 269-270.
7. *RT*, iii. 468-473.
8. Tawny, *The Ocean of Story*, ii, p. 197.

vivara and anxious for the women of the nether world into deep wells.[1]

V. RELIGIOUS PRACTICES

The Paurāṇic Hinduism prevailing in our period was characterised by a synthesis of the Vedic sacrificial ritual and the rites and practices appertaining the various originally independent cults that had now been amalgamated in Brāhmaṇical Hinduism. Temples played an important part in this synthetic religion. To some extent this commingling is reflected in our text which refers to both the sacrifices and the temple ritual.

Sacrificial Ritual

The allusions to sacrifices are of a general character and do not go beyond indicating the popularity of sacrificial ritual. At one place we read of Dharma, afraid of the Kali age, concealing itself with a blanket that is the smoke rising from the sacrificial fire,[2] while elsewhere we come across persons whose faces are washed by the tears occasioned by the smoke of the three kinds of fire, viz., *gārhapatya*, *āhavanīya* and *dakṣiṇāgni* (416). In the families maintaining Vedic traditions, boys received training in cutting sacrificial fuel (*samidh*) from their very childhood (420; also cf. 200). Sacrifices were performed with the *vaṣaṭ* formula pronounced aloud and thus filling the ears (417). The Brāhmaṇas pronounced the Vedic *mantras* and ate the remnants of the sacrificial oblation (*puroḍāśa* 414). The Śrauta sacrifices involving animal-killing were current as may be inferred from a reference to the sacrificial posts (*kratu-yūpa*). On account of these posts the city of Pāṭaliputra is compared to Harinagara (180).

1. बिलसिद्धिघृतश्रद्धागृहीताभरणाम्बरान् ।
सा चिक्षेपान्धकूपेषु पातालललनोत्सुकान् ॥
Samaya-matṛkā, ii.100.

2. कलिकालोदितभीत्या क्रतुहुतवहधूमकम्बलावरणः ।
तिष्ठन् निभृतोऽपि वृषश्चरितैरनुमीयते यत्र ॥
K 182.

Temples

Temples had come to play an increasingly important role in the socio-religious life of the people. The extant literary and epigraphic evidence attests the brisk temple-building activity in the early mediaeval period when people were trying to cover each and every inch of available space with temples dedicated to various gods and goddesses. During this period the temple was not only a place of religious worship, but it also served as a venue of colourful social activities. Abu and Vārāṇasī were adorned with a number of temples. The temples of Vārāṇasī were very lofty and the banners flying from their spires (*śikhara*) rendered the sky variegated (6). Vārāṇasī, being a stronghold of Śaivism, had numberless Śaiva shrines. The Śaiva temples often bore names composed of the name of the founder or donor forming the first part and the word *īśvara* being its terminal portion. Gambhīreśvara was one such temple (743). Sometimes the initial portion of the name was connected with some episode in its history. Kalaśeśvara was such a temple.[1]

The association of *deva-dāsīs* or dancing girls with the temple, which originated at a much earlier date, had now become a regular feature of temple organisation. The institution had its beginnings in the necessity to provide for music, dance and dramatic performances before the deity. Another factor responsible for it may have been the desire of the votaries to provide the gods installed in the earthly shrines with the same luxuries as were available to them in their heavenly abode. One such luxury available to them were the divine damsels or Apsarases; in their earthly abode also they were provided with them in the form of *deva-dāsīs*. Gambhīreśvaradāsī was evidently a dancing girl attached to the temple of Śiva Gambhīreśvara (743). As we have shown above, Mañjarī was also a *pāda-mūla* or temple-attendant belonging to the shrine of Śiva Kalaśeśvara. About this time the custom had become deep-rooted in Kashmir. Our author informs us that the occupation had become hereditary being followed by generation after generation.[2] Kalhaṇa tells

1. See *supra*, pp. 65-67.

2. Cf. *K* 663 which states how a courtesan gave up the temple service which had come down to her hereditarily for the sake of her lover.

us how Lalitāditya Muktāpīḍa chanced to see two *deva-dāsīs* who told him that their descent made dancing and singing before the deity incumbent upon them and that the custom, handed down by tradition, had become fixed in their family.[1] Even regularly wedded wives could be given away as dancing girls to temples.[2] More often than not these *deva-dāsīs* were a source of corruption. We learn from Kalhaṇa that temple maids could be taken away by kings for illicit love,[3] and Dāmodaragupta leaves the impression that they were in no way better than ordinary courtesans. One of the *deva-dāsis*, Mañjarī, is represented as gratifying a prince's lust for the sake of wealth, while another temple-maid is said to have been in illicit love with an ordinary man.

Apart from the *deva-dāsīs*, ordinary prostitutes also appear to have given performance before the deity from time to time. This explains the presence, among others, of courtesans in the crowd that surrounded prince Samarabhaṭa immediately after he had finished his worship at the temple of Vṛṣabhadhvaja (757).[4]

The temple was also used as venue of dance and dramatic performance for popular recreation. The first act of the *Ratnāvalī* is said to have been enacted within the premises of the Vṛṣabhadhvaja temple at Vārāṇasī.[5]

The temple also served as a rest house where travellers could spend their nights (224).

Deva-yātrā

The custom of *deva-yātrā* or the carrying of the images of gods in procession on certain occasions was popular. Men and women, irrespective of their social gradation, freely participat-

1. *RT*, iv. 265-274.
2. *Ibid.*, iv. 36.
3. *Ibid.* Also cf. Jayāpīḍa's marriage with Kamalā who used to perform in a Kārttikeya temple at Puṇḍravardhana. See *supra*, p. 28.
4. The *Kathā-sarit-sāgara* and the *Bṛhat-kathā-mañjarī* also associate prostitutes with temples. Vide *supra*, pp. 24-26.
5. Bhavabhūti's dramas were played on the occasion of the *yātrā* of Kālapriyanātha, i.e., Sūrya image installed at Kalpi, evidently in the premises of the temple.

ed in them, thus getting an opportunity to establish new contacts which often resulted in clandestine love (869). These processions are referred to as *ghaṭā* by Vātsyāyana[1] and as *sura-yātrā* or *daivata-yātrā* by Varāhamihira.[2] Such processions are still current.

People invoked a god or goddess with the object of averting a calamity or illness of a beloved with the promise of worship and offerings (*baly-upahāra*) on the accomplishment of the desire. Non-fulfilment of this promise after securing the object was believed to bring in distress to the persons concerned (612-613). This practice is called *upayācitaka* by Varāhamihira.[3] Such practices are still prevalent.

Śrāddha

Śrāddha feasts were popular then as now. There is a reference to the hunting of rhinoceros in the rites directed to the manes (*pitṛ-tarpaṇa-prasaṅge khaḍga-grahaṇam*, 198). It is interesting to note in this connection that Dharmaśāstra texts dating from very ancient times attach great significance to rhinoceros in the context of the *śrāddha* ceremony. While the flesh of other animals served to the Brāhmaṇas at the *śrāddha* feast was believed to give manes only temporary gratification, the flesh of rhinoceros is said to result in their inexhaustible permanent satisfaction. The *Āpastamba-dharmasūtra* (ii.7.17.1), for example, tells us that the gratification of the *pitṛs* emanating from the flesh of rhinoceros served to the Brāhmaṇas seated on rhinoceros skin is endless. The same view is expressed in the *Baudhāyana-gṛhyasūtra* (ii.11.53, 65), the *Viṣṇu-purāṇa* (iii.16.3), the *Matsya-purāṇa* (17.31-36), the *Viṣṇudharmottara-purāṇa* (i.141. 50-51), the *Padma-purāṇa* (Sṛṣṭikhaṇḍa, 9.158), the *Kūrma-purāṇa* (ii.20.43), the *Skānda Purāṇa* (Kāśīkhaṇḍa, iv. 14-20), the *Agni-purāṇa* (163.32-33), the *Manu-smṛti* (3.272), the *Yājña-valkya-smṛti* (1.260-61) and a host of other texts.[4] Sanctity was also attached to the use of vessels made of the bones of rhino-

1. *Kāma-sūtra*, i.4.26, 33.
2. Ajay Mitra Shastri, *India as seen in the Bṛhat-saṁhitā of Varāhamihira*, p. 180.
3. *Ibid.*, p. 187.
4. Cf. *HDS*, iv, pp. 422ff.

-ceros for serving food at the *śrāddha* feast.[1] This tradition was, thus, so deep-rooted that there is nothing surprising if at some *śrāddha* feasts at least the flesh of rhinoceros was actually served. The scene of rhinoceros hunt represented on the Rhinoceros-slayer type gold coins of the Gupta emperor Kumāragupta I may have been connected with this religious requirement as suggested by S.V. Sohoni.[2] The rhinoceros still plays an important role in connection with the *śrāddha*. "In Nepal", says S.H. Prater, "the flesh and blood of the rhinoceros is considered highly acceptable to the manes. High caste Hindus and most Gurkhas offer libation of the animal's blood after entering its disembowelled body." The horns of rhinoceros are also used. According to Prater, "On ordinary Śrāddha days the libation of water and milk is poured from a cup carved from its (i.e. rhino's) horn."[3] The evidence of our work indicates the use of rhinoceros (probably its flesh and utensils fashioned from its bones) in the *śrāddha* ceremony in the 8th-9th centuries A.D.

Japa

The *japa* or continuous muttering of some fixed sacred formulae had become an important item of contemporary religious life.[4] We have a reference to the movement of lips at the time of *japa* (*japatām = ev-ādhara-sphuraṇam*, 200). These formulae usually comprised names of one's favourite deity and their repetition was believed to fulfil one's cherished desire (*japati samīhita-siddhyai*, 1017). Certain numbers were believed to possess mysterious sanctity, and special reference is made to a *mahāstotra* consisting of twelve names (*dvādaśa-nāmaka mahā-stotra*, 1017). Number 12 appears to have been regarded as particularly sacred, and we have several extant examples of sacred formulae comprising twelve syllables or names. The twelve-syllabled formula *Oṁ namo bhagavate Vāsudevāya* used in worshipping Vāsudeva and twelve-named *Saṅkaṭa-nāśana-stotra* of Gaṇapati may be cited as well-known examples. It is interest-

1. *Baudhāyana-gṛhyasūtra*, ii.11.65; *Viṣṇu-dharmottara-purāṇa*, i.140.40.
2. *JNSI*, xviii, pp. 178ff. But *contra ibid.*, xxv, pp. 29ff.
3. *The Book of Indian Animals*, p. 192.
4. The antiquity of the practice of *japa* has been traced to the *Ṛgveda* (8.11.5). Vide Usha R. Bhise, The Importance of Nāman in the Ṛgveda, *Summaries of Papers, AIOC*, Silver Jubilee Session, 1969, pp. 2-3.

ing to note in this connection that several manuscripts of a work called *Śiva-dvādaśa-nāma-stotra* containing invocation of god Śiva under his twelve names[1] are preserved in the Government Oriental Manuscripts Library, Madras.[2] Varāhamihira also refers to the worship of god Viṣṇu under his twelve different names on the 12th day of the several months which resulted in the worshipper's union with the Lord and cessation of the chain of births and deaths.[3]

Pilgrimage

The *tīrtha-yātrā* or pilgrimage to places regarded as sanctified by the divine presence or by some important religious episode was believed to yield immeasurable religious merit. Important centres of pilgrimage were scattered throughout the length and breadth of the country, and there was scarcely any region where there were no pilgrimage centres. Bringing the people of the different parts of the country together, this institution fostered the cause of national integration in a unique manner at a time characterised by the absence of swift means of communication eliminating the distance factor. This institution still plays a significant role in the religious life of a great majority of the people of India. Whereas Vedic sacrifices were confined to certain sections of the people, the institution of pilgrimage was open to all. Even a courtesan could go on a pilgrimage (545).[4]

Vārāṇasī was very early recognised as a great centre of pilgrimage as it is even now. The reason for this probably was its association with the god Śiva and the liberal patronage extended by the rich. A large number of people, rich and

1. शिवो रुद्रः पशुपतिर्नीलकण्ठो महेश्वरः ।
हरिकेशो विरूपाक्षः पिनाकी त्रिपुरान्तकः ॥
शम्भुः शूली महादेवो नामान्येतान्यनुक्रमात् ।
चतुर्थ्यन्तं समुच्चार्य दद्यात् पुष्पाञ्जलिं प्रभोः ॥

2. *Descriptive Catalogue of Sanskrit Manuscripts in the Government Oriental Manuscripts Library*, Madras, Vol. iv, 2nd Part, No. 2418, pp. 1696-97; Vol. xvii, Nos. 1259-1261, pp. 6646-47.

3. *Bṛhat-saṁhitā*, civ. 14-16; Ajay Mitra Shastri, *India as seen in the Bṛhat-saṁhitā of Varāhamihira*, pp. 187-88.

4. Kṣemendra also describes in his *Samaya-mātṛkā* the pilgrimage of a courtesan.

poor and high and low, belonging to places, far and near, thronged the city for the purpose of pilgrimage. Prince Samarabhaṭa had been to Vārāṇasī from the distant Devarāṣṭra on such a mission. It is probable that Dāmodaragupta had also personally come to Vārāṇasī on such a pilgrimage and stayed there long enough to get himself acquainted with the minutest details of its contemporary life which he has recorded in his work.

Arbuda or Mt. Abu appears to have been another important centre of pilgrimage during our period. It was also frequented by visitors from far off places like Pāṭaliputra. It was adorned with shrines dedicated to different deities, stepped wells, parks, ponds and rivers and was resorted to by saints for observing penance and meditation. It appears to have been particularly sacred to Śiva.[1] It is pertinent to note in this connection that according to extant archaeological evidence prior to becoming famous as a sacred city of the Jainas after the construction of the Vimala-vasahī in A.D. 1030 Abu was a flourishing Brāhmaṇical Śaivite site. The area just behind Vimala-vasahī is the site of the Kanyākumārī and Rasio Valam shrines along with a Viṣṇu temple. A little to the west of these shrines there are remains of an older Śaiva shrine and an older brick temple with later repairs in stone. The Viṣṇu temple contains post-Gupta (6th-7th century) sculptures of three Mātṛkās, the Śeṣaśāyī Viṣṇu of the Gupta age and a sculpture of Sūrya. The Kanyākumārī or Śrīmātā shrine has in it another Mātṛkā figure of the Gupta period and a sculpture of standing Pārvatī assignable to the 9th or 10th century A.D. Thus it was a Hindu centre with Śaiva and Vaiṣṇava temples dating from the late Gupta period to early eleventh century A.D.

Disposal of the Dead

We get very meagre information on this point. However, cremation was the usual mode of disposing off the dead body (480). The funeral pyre was prepared from wood (490).

1. Verse 241 compares the Arbuda mountain to Śambhu, while in verse 249 we have a reference to devotees of Śiva inhabiting Abu.

2. Muni Jayanta Vijaya, *Holy Abu*, Translated into English with an Introduction by U. P. Shah and a Foreword by V.S. Agrawala, pp. x-xi.

Asceticism

Asceticism played a very significant role in the religious life of India from very ancient times. Almost all the different religious orders, which were otherwise opposed to each other, laid great stress on asceticism. Non-Brāhmaṇical sects like Jainism and Buddhism went to the extent of regarding ascetic life as *sine qua non* to attain final deliverance. Dāmodaragupta has frequently drawn upon this motif in his poem under study. In the Brāhmaṇical order asceticism (*pravrajyā*, 478; *saṁnyasana*, 496) formed the fourth or last stage (*antyāśrama*, 495) in the life of a man. It was believed to be a means of emancipation from the world (*saṁsāra-mukty-upāya*, 492) and of the destruction of ignorance (*avidyā-prahāṇa-saṁsiddhi*, 495), the root cause of all sufferings. Ascetics carried a staff which became a sign manual of their life (13). Formal taking of the staff formed an important item of the ceremony marking the initiation into the ascetic life which is consequently referred to as the vow of carrying a staff (*daṇḍa-grahaṇa-vrata*, 492). Self-restraint was basic to the ascetic life (53). Ascetics lived in the forest, and we have a reference to a forest inhabited by sages performing penance, endowed with the stability of mind and steadfast in the observance of their duties (497). The resort of saints was noted for its peace and tranquillity (180). Many of the entrants to the ascetic order were persons disappointed with their life. Such was the case with Sundarasena. To such people this constantly changing world appeared to be a resort of sufferings only (494). As the ascetics were supposed to be free from all selfish interest, they were expected to develop an attitude of equality towards the old and the young, the ailing and the strong-bodied, and the high-born and the lowly (93) and not to vent any discrimination in respect of animals and human beings (999). This evidently refers to the concept of *sama-darśin* so beautifully enunciated in the *Bhagavad-gītā*, 5.18. It is said that those who know the Supreme Soul (*Paramātman*) concentrate their mind on the Puruṣa alone (996, 1011).

Some interesting ascetic practices are also referred to. One such practice is the *pañca-tapas* or performing penance amidst five fires. A love-lorn lady afflicted by the cuckooing of a cuckoo, cool fragrant breeze, flowers, cupid and bees is compared to one performing the fivefold penance (299). It is a very severe austere practice wherein one has to sit in the midst of fire burning ablaze on the four sides and under the sun. Such a penance was reportedly performed by Pārvatī for securing Śiva as her husband.[1] Mention is also made of a penance observed by a woman for winning the affection of her beloved (*Śubhaṅkaraṇaṁ tapaḥ*, 166) the exact nature of which cannot be determined. It may, however, refer to the type of penance performed by Pārvatī as described by Kālidāsa in his *Kumāra-saṁbhava* (v).

VI. BELIEFS AND SUPERSTITIONS

People had faith in the efficacy of magical formulae (*mantra*). These *mantras*, it was believed, could attain many things which were beyond the access of ordinary means. The belief that by the pronunciation of certain incantations serpents could be called out of their habitat (48) persists to this day. There were in existence certain magical formulae (*mantra-vidhi*, 559; *vaśīkaraṇa-yoga*, 543) which, it was thought, enabled one to win over one's beloved.

The belief in rebirth and the fructification of actions was a time-honoured concept which was admitted by most of the religious systems of ancient India, both Brāhmaṇical and non-Brāhmaṇical. Thus, a happy occurrence was believed to be due to the meritorious acts of earlier lives (91, 459), while an unhappy event was regarded as the result of the accumulated sins of previous births (423, 440, 826).

The movements of planets (*graha-gati*) were believed to influence the course of human life. Thus a good or bad occurrence was deemed to have been caused as much by the favourable or unfavourable disposition of planets as by one's own good or bad acts (826). In the Dharmaśāstra and astrological texts detailed rules are given for the performance of *graha-śāntis* or *graha-yāgas* for getting the effects of the unfavourable disposition of planets neutralised. Such beliefs and propitiatory rites are still current.

1. *Kumāra-sambhava*, v. 23.

The nether world (*pātāla-tala*) was believed to be a resort of serpents (179).

The moon was regarded as the lord of vegetation (245).

The semblance of the shadow-like object in the orb of the moon was believed to be due to the shadow of Rāhu, son of Siṁhikā (110), who was held responsible also for the lunar eclipse (190).

People also believed in fate (*daiva*) which was taken to determine much of human life (820).

That one goes to the other world, heaven or hell, after death was also an article of faith. We are told that it could not be determined in advance whether one would go to heaven or hell (820).

People performed penance with the object of attaining the position of a god (*suratāpti*, 966).

VII. PURPOSE OF RELIGION

Attainment of peace is said to be the main object of religion. That which does not result in peace is not a real religion (*ko dharmo nir=upaśamaḥ*, 723).

VIII. PURUṢĀRTHAS

According to Brāhmaṇical standpoint, the goal of human existence was the attainment of four *puruṣārthas* (*puruṣārtha-catuṣṭaya*, 1055), viz., *dharma* or right conduct, *artha* or economic interests, *kāma* or satisfaction of bodily, emotional and artistic urges, and *mokṣa* or liberation. Of these the last could be attained only by the select few who were spiritually advanced, the common man being concerned with the first three only (652-53).[1] The attainment of each one of these three without hindrance to others was, of course, the ideal. But different schools of thinkers vented their preference for one or other of them according to their predilections. The Dharmaśāstra writers, for

1. Verse 652 refers to the attainment of *dharmo*, *artha* and *kāma* by a prostitute by gratifying the sexual urge of a pauper, contact with a rich man, and intercourse with a man of equal sexual potency respectively. Verse 653 condemns one whose acts do not result in the fulfilment of either *dharma* or *artha* or *kāma*. Cf. Verse 1031 which also mentions *puruṣārthas*.

instance, stressed *dharma* while the *Arthaśāstra* of Kauṭilya regards *artha* as supreme.[2] Our author is reticent on this point.

IX. BUDDHISM

As noted above, Buddhism, though somewhat on the road of decadence, flourished side by side with Brāhmaṇical Hinduism and was still a force to be reckoned with. Our author makes some interesting references to Buddha and Buddhism which shed welcome light on the condition of Buddhism and its relations with other sects during the period under study.

The Buddha is referred to as a *ratna* or jewel, the essence of the universe (781),[4] which evidently points to the well-known Buddhist concept of the Three Jewels or *triratna* comprising the Buddha, Dharma and Saṅgha.

Non-violence was an article of faith with the Buddhists, and surprise is expressed if the Buddha is not opposed to warfare.[5]

We have an interesting allusion to the Vijñānavāda school of Buddhism. An adherent of this philosophy is styled a non-dualist (*advayavādin*) who did not believe in the universal or generality (*jāti*), empirical self or ego (*ātman*) and external objects (*artha-jñāna*).[6] It is well-known that the Vijñānavāda or Yogācāra school of Mahāyāna Buddhism did not accept the existence of anything except *vijñāna* or *citta*, i.e., pure consciousness and was thus a monistic system. According to it, all *dharmas* except consciousness are unreal; consciousness alone is taught by the Buddha as an established truth. Every phenomenal thing, being governed by the cause-effect relationship,

1. *Gautama-dharmasūtra*, ix.46-47; *Āpastamba-dharmasūtra*, ii.8.20.22-23; *Manu-smṛti*, ii. 224; iv.176; *HDS*, ii., pp. 8-9.

2. *Arthaśāstra*, i.7.3-7.

3. Verse 1055, however, mentions sexual gratification as the essence of the four *puruṣārthas*. But this certainly does not represent the author's view.

4. This stanza describes Buddha as an *advayavādin*, obviously in conformity with the Vijñānavāda school. Cf. *Amara-kośa*, i.1.14, which gives *advayavādin* as a name of the Buddha.

5. सुगतोऽपि नाजिविमुखः, *K* 778.

6. यस्य न जातिर्नात्मा नार्थज्ञानं न मानसे प्रशमः ।
भवसि भवसाररत्नं तेनाद्वयवादिना सदृशः ।। *K* 781

is of necessity momentary. The reality transcends all categories and is free from momentariness. The subject-object duality must be overcome in order to attain oneness with pure consciousness.

During the period under review there appears to have prevailed great rivalry between Buddhism and Brāhmaṇical Hinduism. Dāmodaragupta draws our attention to the incompatibility of the faith in the Sugata, i.e., Buddha, and an appreciation of the *śākhās* of the Vedas.[1] This is in strong contrast with the religious conditions of the earlier period the keynote of which was the prevalence of harmonious relations among various faiths. The *Nila-mata*, belonging to the 6th or 7th century A.D., brings in relief the cordiality existing between Buddhism and Hinduism. It describes the Buddha as an incarnation of Viṣṇu, prescribes the celebration of his birthday in accordance with the instructions of the Śākyas, i.e., Buddhists who were also to be honoured with a variety of gifts.[2] Kings of Kashmir also gave the benefit of their patronage to both Hinduism and Buddhism. Thus, queen Anaṅgalekhā constructed the Anaṅgabhavana Vihāra,[3] and king Lalitāditya had a number of *caityas* and *vihāras* built and Buddha images made.[1] This situation underwent a great change with the coming into prominence of the monistic Śaiva philosophy and a period of rivalry between Buddhism and Brāhmaṇical Hinduism ensued. Buddhists had now to remain content with a comparatively less significant position. It is worth noting in this connection that the town of Avantipura founded by king Avantivarman in the latter half of the ninth century A.D. has not yielded even a single Buddhistic object.[5]

1. अभिमतसुगतावस्थितिरभिनन्दितचरणयुगलरचना च ।

K 266.

The same idea is found in Subandhu's *Vāsavadattā*, p. 194:—

कश्चिद् बौद्धसिद्धान्त इव क्षपितश्रुतिवचनदर्शनोऽभवत् ।

It is not improbable that Dāmodaragupta borrowed it from Subandhu.

2. *Nila-mata*, vv. 684-690; Ved Kumari, *The Nīlamata Purāṇo, A Cultural and Literary Study of a Kāśmīrī Purāṇa*, p. 175.

3. *RT*, iv. 3.

4. *Ibid.*, iv. 188, 200, 203, 204, 210, 211, 215, 258-264.

5. For an account of the remains at Avantipura. vide R.C. Kak, *Ancient Monuments of Kashmir*, pp. 118-125; *A Handbook of the Archaeological and Numismatic Sections of the Sri Pratap Singh Museum, Srinagar*, pp. 47-57.

X. JAINISM

Except doubtful references to the *Nagnas* (367) or *Nagnācāryas* (562), viz., nude Digambara Jaina ascetics, we have no information about Jainism. A Nagnācārya named Narasiṁha is said to have been in love with a courtesan and to have immolated himself in the flames of fire to be followed by his beloved.

CHAPTER IV

SOCIAL LIFE

I. SOCIAL ORGANISATION

Varṇa System

The information that we get from our work about the structure of the society obtaining in Kashmir during the early mediaeval period is very fragmentary indeed. However, there is no doubt that, as in the rest of India, in Kashmir also social organisation was mainly based on the age-old institutions of Varṇas and Āśramas (*Varṇ-āśrama-dharma*). Dāmodaragupta evinces familiarity with the Varṇa system (310, 780), though he does not explicitly refer to the four Varṇas as such anywhere in his work. He was a Brāhmaṇa himself as are some of the characters of his poem. We shall, therefore, not be unjustified in expecting more information about this section of the society. The Brāhmaṇas, variously referred to as Vipra (181, 393, 785), Dvija (14), Dvijanman (193) and Agrajanman (412), undoubtedly occupied the uppermost position on the social ladder. In keeping with ancient Indian tradition,[1] they are styled gods on earth (*bhūmi-deva*, 199; *vasudhā-deva*, 763). It was a religious duty to respect them (763, 785). They are described as observing their six traditional duties,[2] viz., study, teaching, performing sacrifices for self, officiating at other people's sacrifices, making gifts and accepting gifts.[3] They abstained from taking intoxicating drinks.[4] This last statement is vouched for by independent literary and epigraphical evidences. The Jodhpur inscription of Pratihāra Bāuka tells us that the sons of Haricandra born of his Kṣatriya wife Bhadrā became drinkers of wine,[5] implying thereby that Brāhmaṇas did not drink wine. Arab travellers of the ninth century A.D. also looked upon abstention from taking wine as a distinct characteristic of the Brāhmaṇas.[6]

1. *Viṣṇu-dharmasūtra*, xix.20-22; *Manu-smṛti*, ix.317; *Parāśara-smṛti*, vi.52-3, etc. Vide also *HDS*, ii (i), pp. 134-36.

2. *Ṣaṭ-karmaṇy-āyatāḥ*, 249 (*ṣaṭ-karmāṇo-yatā* is another reading); *ṣaṭ-karma-vibhūṣaṇam*, 417.

3. For a detailed discussion of these duties, see *HDS*, ii (i), pp. 105ff.

4. *Dvija-nilayeṣv-apraśannatvam*, 14.

5. *Rājñī Bhadrā ca yān sūte te bhūtā madhu-pāyinaḥ*, verse 8, *EI*, xviii, p. 95.

6. Elliot, *History of India as told by its own Historians*, i, p. 9, cited by R.C. Majumdar in *EI*, xviii, p. 98, fn. 1.

The Jaina author Somadeva Sūri (10th century A.D.) in his *Yaśastilaka-campū* regards the habit of drinking wine prevalent among the Brāhmaṇas of Vaṅgī-maṇḍala as due to the defect of the reigning king.[1] Some Brāhmaṇas, evidently of an advanced age, took to a life of austerity with the object of securing heaven; they gave up worldly attachments, violence and cruelty, observed self-restraint, lived a peaceful life given to the performance of meritorious acts and lived on wind and fruits (248-49).

An idea of the ideals that a Brāhmaṇa was expected to keep before him may be had from the description of Brāhmaṇa Purandara of Pāṭaliputra (193-200) and from his missive to his son Sundarasena who had gone astray (411-24). Purandara is described as performing a number of sacrifices, an abode of learning, away from lust, observing truth and restraint, steadfast in the observance of his prescribed duties, avoiding destruction of life and intercourse with other people's wives (193-96). His lineage was reputed for its spotlessly good conduct, its adherence to the prescribed rites like offering oblations to the departed ancestors, discussions on the Vedas, and observance of *japa* and sacrifices; the boys of the family took to the life of a Brahmacārin wearing girdle; its inmates never wielded weapons; there were no family feuds resulting into partition (197-200); it was spotless; its members were known for their straightforward conduct and for abstention from the destruction of life; they were free from back-biting (412-13).

The letter sent by Purandara to his son alludes to the austere life of an ideal Brāhmaṇa: his mouth was purified by the drinking of *soma* juice; he recited the Vedic *mantras*; he cut the *kuśa* grass for use in religious rites, sometimes resulting into injury to his fingers; he maintained the three sacred fires—*gārhapatya*, *āhavanīya* and *dakṣiṇāgni*, the smoke of which brought tears in the eyes; the sound of *vaṣaṭ* at the time of offering oblations to gods was his ear-ornament; he performed his six-fold duty; in boyhood he studied from a teacher whom he respected and did service; he wore deer-skin while observing a vow; he cut sacrificial fuel; in his youth he settled as a householder, and in old age left his family to the care of his son(s) and himself strove for the attainment of heaven (414-24).

1. K. K. Handiqui, *Yaśastilaka and Indian Culture*, p. 99.

The above was, however, only an ideal which could have been practised only by a few, not by all. A vast majority of the Brāhmaṇas, like others, must have led an ordinary life given to the enjoyment of mundane pleasures. Instances of Brāhmaṇas visiting brothels were not unknown.[1] And it was in order to rescue Sundarasena from the clutches of a courtesan that the above letter is said to have been written.

Some of the Brāhmaṇas also joined administrative services and occupied high positions. Dāmodaragupta himself, as we learn from Kalhaṇa, was the chief minister (*dhī-saciva*) of king Jayāpīḍa.[2] While describing Purandara it is said that none in his family took to the use of weapons (198). But Kalhaṇa furnishes a number of examples of Brāhmaṇas adopting military careers.[3]

It was the duty of the king to keep the members of the different castes firm in the observance of their respective duties. The order of the precedence of the different Varṇas was fixed by tradition. The lower castes appear to have been looked down upon. At one place the last Varṇa (i.e., Śūdra) is stated to be mean by nature and its rise to a superior position in the social scale is spoken of with contempt (780).

It is true that we have no mention of the intermediate Varṇas, viz., Kṣatriya and Vaiśya. But this does not warrant the view of some scholars that in early Kashmir 'there was no such caste as Kṣatriya, Vaiśya or Śūdra'.[4] As we have just seen, Dāmodaragupta refers to the *jaghanya-varṇa*, i.e., Śūdra. Elsewhere, he states that a prostitute has no preference for a particular caste in the matter of carnal intercourse but favours particular colours only for the purpose of toilet.[5] The prevalence of the system of four Varṇas in Kashmir is also indicated by the *Nīla-mata* and the *Rāja-taraṅgiṇī*. The former work describes at length the duties of the four castes,[6] while the latter not only

1. *K*, 37, 38, 393.
2. *RT*, iv. 490.
3. S. C. Ray, *Early History and Culture of Kashmir*, pp. 84-85.
4. *Ibid.*, p. 86.
5. वर्णविशेषापेक्षा प्रसाधने नो रतिप्रसङ्गेषु, *K* 310.
6. Ved Kumari, *op. cit.*, pp. 77-87.

shows a general acquaintance with the institution of Varṇa[1] but contains specific references to the Kṣatriyas[2] and the Vaiśyas[3] in connection with the ancient history of Kashmir. The fact, therefore, seems to be that as in other parts of the country so in Kashmir the system of the customary four castes formed the foundation stone of the Hindu social organisation.

Āśramas

According to the traditional Hindu standpoint, the span of human life was divided into four stages called *Āśrama*, viz., those of a *Brahmacārin* or student, *Gṛhastha* or householder, *Vānaprastha* or forest-anchorite, and *Saṁnyāsin* or wandering ascetic. There is sufficient evidence to indicate Dāmodaragupta's acquaintance with this institution. The *Brahmacārin*, called *baṭuka*, wore a girdle which sometimes gave way (198). The householder is referred to as *geha-pati* (224), *gṛha-svāmin* (225) and *gṛha-bhartṛ* (817). We get no reference to the forest-anchorite, though some vague descriptions of austere practices may allude to them. The order of the wandering ascetic is called the last *āśrama* (*anty-āśrama*, 495). He always carried a staff with him (13, 492). The object of this *āśrama* was to secure liberation (492) and effect the removal of ignorance (495). Sometimes this *āśrama* was resorted to by people disgusted with worldly life. We have allusions to the austere practices followed by these mendicants.[4]

Ancient Indian writers were divided about the order in which one was to follow the different *āśramas*. According to one view, the four *āśramas* were to be resorted to one after another in the serial order; neither one can drop one or more of these stages nor reverse their order. Another school allowed option after *brahmacarya*, viz., one can enter the last stage immediately after finishing one's study or after the householder's life.[5] Dāmodaragupta seems to have favoured the second view,

1. *RT*, iv. 111.
2. *Ibid.*, viii. 3031, 3063-69, 3077, 3230.
3. *Ibid.*, vii. 207.
4. See *supra*, pp. 92-3.
5. These viewpoints were called *samuccaya* and *vikalpa* respectively. For a full discussion of these, see *HDS*, ii (i), pp. 424-25.

for he describes Sundarasena as becoming an ascetic immediately after studentship.[1]

II. FAMILY

Family is the smallest unit of social organisation. To a great extent, one's behavioral pattern and happiness or otherwise of life are determined by the environment of the family. This is particularly true of ancient India where scriptural law considered a person more as a constituent member of a family than as a free individual.

Relations

We get references to a number of family relations such as a son,[2] daughter,[3] mother,[4] father,[5] brother,[6] sister[7], husband,[8] wife,[9] son-in-law,[10] brother-in-law[11] and mother-in-law.[12] The oldest male member of the family was regarded as its chief.[13]

The birth of a son was an occasion of joy (146).

Joint family system was the prevailing order of the day. Even after marriage man continued to live in the same house with his parents and brothers (583-84). Sometimes, however, bonds of affection and mutual love became loose and family feuds arose after marriage, resulting into partition of family property (199). This was not unoften due to misbehaviour on the part of brothers and partisan attitude of the mother as also lack of adjustment on the part of the wife in her new family (583-84).

1. While there is mention of Sundarasena's studentship (418, 421), there is no allusion to his married life.
2. *K* 146, 201, 220, 240, 430-32.
3. *Ibid.*, 146.
4. *Ibid.*, 142, 151, 220, 222, 432.
5. *Ibid.*, 234, 429, 431, 584.
6. *Ibid.*, 220, 583.
7. *Ibid.*, 220.
8. *Ibid.*, 187, 226, 227, 508-510, 509, 821, 822.
9. *Ibid.*, 185, 196, 203, 222, 226, 496, 584.
10. *Ibid.*, 146.
11. *Ibid.*, 583.
12. *Ibid.*, 584.
13. *Ibid.*, 224, 225, 817.

III. MARRIAGE AND POSITION OF WOMEN

Marriage

Marriage ceremony is referred to as *pariṇaya* (792) and *Pāṇi-grahaṇa* (167). The latter implies the grasping by the bridegroom of the bride's hand which forms an important item of the sacrament of marriage.

Polygamy

Polygamy was prevalent, especially among well-to-do sections of society. The poet describes the pitiable condition of a polygamous man (*bahujāni*), one of whose wives is angered at her violation, another is indifferent because of the nonfulfilment of her demand, another is sad as she has been denied a seat closeby, the fourth maintains a distance because of mutual quarrel, and the fifth, who is newly wedded, is too shy to behave with him freely.[1]

At another place Mālatī is said to have failed in meeting her lover in a rainy night as he was busy with his wives (599, 601). In yet another verse we read of thousands of women interested in the same man (770).

Wife

Dāmodaragupta gives a graphic picture of an ideal wife: a wife born of a noble family is the abode of all worldly pleasures; she follows her husband like reflection; she feels grieved in her husband's grief; she is happy when her husband is happy; when he is worried, she is also worried; but when he gets enraged, she is only timid; she never speaks ill against him and always follows his mind; she also gives him full sexual pleasure; those are fortunate indeed who have such a wife (440-45). In short, an ideal wife was expected to follow her husband both in happi-

1. एका खण्डनकुपिता विरसान्या प्रणयभङ्गवैलक्ष्यात् ।
काचिन्निकटतरासनमप्राप्य बिभर्ति निर्वेदम् ॥
अन्या कलहान्तरिता नवपरिणयलज्जयापरा सहिता ।
रमणीगणमध्यगतः स्मरातुरः किं करोतु बहुजानिः ॥
K 791-92.

ness and sorrow. She rendered personal service to her husband. Even if the bonds of mutual love had slackened, she continued to live with her husband as a matter of propriety (510). The husband exercised full control over his wife and kept a close watch over her movements (818-19).

The lot of a housewife, particularly in rural areas, was an unenviable one. Hers was a life of toil and hard work with little comfort. Dāmodaragupta gives us a beautiful word-picture of her life: when she was tired after the hard work of the day and her body wet with sweat, in the evening she went to a nearby well to fetch water; she helped her husband in agricultural operations such as harvesting also; she went to dense fields at some distance to pick up cotton fruits; she unhusked paddy with the help of a pestle (863-74).

Sometimes the wife found it difficult to adjust herself in the new environment of her husband's family. She found only defects in her newly adopted family and talked highly of her parents' family. She held her brothers-in-law guilty of misbehaviour and accused mother-in-law of a partisan attitude and incited her husband for separation. She even insulted her husband who went all out to please her by any means.[1] The vicious practice of polygamy, to which reference has been made above, must also have contributed to the disharmony between the husband and the wife. Another factor responsible for it was the insulting attitude of the husband and the hot temperament of the elders making it difficult for the wife to stay in the same house (509). As usual, the blame for separation was laid on the wife, though in fact all the non-cooperative and unreceptive members of the family were responsible for it.

Veil

Current social etiquette required women of respectable families to put on a veil (*avaguṇṭhana*) on face while coming out

1. सूचयति पृथक्करणं, भ्रातॄणां वक्ति विषमशीलत्वम् ।
विवृणोति गृहविसंस्थामभिनन्दति पितृकुलस्य गुणवत्ताम् ॥
अन्यसुतपक्षपातं कथयति मातुस्तिरस्करोति पतिम् ।
पार्श्वनिमग्नां जायां मानयति विमुच्य कार्मुकं मदनः ॥
K 583-84.

in public . The veil, as well as humility, low voice and slow movements, was regarded as a characteristic of a woman of good moral character (848). Sometimes a piece of knitted cloth (*vadan-āvṛti-jālikā*) was used for this purpose. While describing the play of dice on the festival in honour of the god of love in which women of all sorts participated, knitted veil alone is said to have distinguished respectable ladies (*āryā*) from ordinary women (*anāryā*).[1] Kṣemendra describes how a mischievous courtesan, passing as a daughter of a high royal officer, covered her face up to half the nose with a piece of cloth.[2] The *Padma-prābhṛtaka*[3] and the *Dhūrta-viṭa-saṁvāda*[4] also describe a *kulavadhū* as wearing a veil, called *avaguṇṭhana* and *lajjā-paṭa* respectively. In Bāṇa also we come across references to the use by respectable women of a net-work of cloth to cover their faces.[5] Though rather rarely, we find, representation of women with veil in early Indian painting (Pl. XVI[31]) and plastic art.[6]

Freedom of Movement

Women were allowed considerable freedom of movement. Even ladies of aristocratic families, who normally preferred to remain away from public gaze, came out of their houses on festive occasions and participated in the festivities freely as did other women who were not so confined to their houses (889). They played dice with other women (895) and, when engrossed in the festivities, did not shirk from using obscene words in public (894).

Religious observances like the procession of divine images (*deva-yātrā*) also gave women an occasion to come into contact with men (869).

Female Education

We have ample evidence to indicate that women during our period received a good deal of literary education and train-

1. तुल्यव्यापारगिरां ललनानां देवनप्रसक्तानाम् ।
आर्यानार्यविगमं वदनावृतिजालिका कुरुते ॥
K 895.
2. *Samaya-mātṛkā*, ii. 54.
3. *Caturbhāṇī*, p. 41.
4. *Ibid.*, p. 74, verse 13.
5. V. S. Agrawala, *Harṣa-carita : Eka Sāṁskṛtika Adhyayana*, pp. 23, 56.
6. *Ancient India*, No. 4, figurine nos. 170-74.

ing in practical and fine arts. The literary works represented to have been studied by them included the *Kāmasūtra* of Vātsyāyana and similar texts of Madanodaya, Dattaka and Rājaputra, Bharata's *Nāṭya-śāstra* and the writings of Viśākhila and Dantila. They also attained proficiency in arbori-horticulture, painting, needle-work, wood work, metal-work, dietetics, music and dance (123-25). Although all these references appertain courtesans, there can be no doubt that ladies in aristocratic and cultured families also must have been given similar literary training. Bilhaṇa, it is interesting to note, mentions with justifiable pride the fact that women of Kashmir could speak Sanskrit and Prakrit fluently.[1]

Anumaraṇa

The practice of the self-immolation of the widowed wife on the funeral pyre of her deceased husband (*anumaraṇa*) appears to have enjoyed great popularity. Dāmodaragupta describes it as a duty of women (*strī-dharma*, 492). The wide-spread currency of this custom is indicated by the numerous examples of courtesans who are said to have followed their lovers on funerary pyre (560, 561, 562).[2] Kalhaṇa also has recorded several instances of queens,[3] ladies of aristocratic families[4] and even courtesans[5] immolating themselves along with the dead bodies of their husbands and lovers.

Female Morality

The standard of female morality, as that of the male one, in the 9th century A.D. was by no means high. Prostitution, about which more will be said in the sequel, was very much rampant. Although no concrete instance of sexual immorality on the part of married women is recorded by our poet, there can be no doubt about its existence. When Samarabhaṭa

1. *Vikramāṅkadeva-carita*, xviii.6.

2. Verses 559 and 565 also give examples of courtesans who, unable to live without their lovers, breathed their last. These, too, may have been cases of the practice of *suttee*.

3. *RT*, v. 226; vi. 107; vii. 103, 477-80, etc.

4. *Ibid.*, viii. 445, 2334.

5. *Ibid.*, vii. 724, 859.

showed his inclination towards Mañjarī, the minister who had accompanied him to Vārāṇasī is represented to have eulogised sexual relations with other men's wives (811-61). In support of his contention he is said to have quoted profusely from Hindu mythology. The bold defence of illicit intercourse with other women by itself is a clear indication of the wide-spread prevalence of this vice. The female go-betweens (*dūtīs*) played a key role in uniting the two parties (839). A woman's indulgence in unlawful sexual connection with a man other than her husband led to her own ill-fame as well as of her family and even made her very life doubtful, besides barring her entry into the heaven (833, 508). Such a woman was looked down upon by her own relatives who rebuked her, and her former friends avoided her company. People laughed at her when she put on a veil on her face, made a show of humility, conversed in a low voice and moved gently—all characteristics of a respectable woman (848-50). This moral laxity sometimes resulted from the repeated insults hurled by the husband, hot temper of the elders and other household difficulties, marriage of persons not suited to one another and lack of mutual harmony (509, 813-22).

IV. PROSTITUTION

As we have seen above,[1] prostitution played a significant role in the contemporary history of Kashmir. Dāmodaragupta, who occupied the high office of *dhī-saciva* under king Jayāpīḍa Vinayāditya, had an opportunity to watch it from close quarters, and as such we may naturally expect him to exhibit a close acquaintance with the intricacies of this profession. Our hopes are not belied, and the poet presents us with the whole secret of this trade and illustrates it into niceties of details. In fact, in the whole range of Sanskṛit literature there is no other work which can excel it in this regard. A perusal of the *Kuṭṭanī-mata* gives us an insight into prostitutes' mode of behaviour, their proficiency in literature and fine arts, their greed for money and practices and customs connected with the craft.

1. See *supra*, pp. 28-30.

The Attitude of the Society

Although prostitution was tolerated as an inescapable social evil, the society looked down upon prostitutes (546) and condemned men indulgent to them in unmistakable terms. One's addiction to strumpets was regarded as a result of one's evil deeds in a previous life (440). This contemptuous attitude was mainly due to the proverbial deceptive character of the prostitutes (485) and the injury they hurled on the current notions of social morality. There could be no greater shock to a father than to know that his son had become a victim of this vice. The high degree of contempt in which this institution was held is indicated by Guṇapālita's long lecture on the unreliability of the strumpets and Purandara's rebuking errand to his son Sundarasena (301-24, 411-24). It may be repeated in this connection that the main object of the poem was to acquaint the readers with the cheating devices of the courtesans and save them from succumbing to their (hetairai's) apparent charms (1059).[1]

Literary and Artistic Accomplishments

However, if notwithstanding this unequivocal condemnation and disownment the hetairai had a flourishing business, it was because of certain attractive features of this institution. Prostitution was primarily an urban institution with all the niceties of the glittering town life attached to it.[2] As against ordinary women of rustic habits, courtesans were ladies of refined manners and pleasant etiquettes. They were free and frank in their behaviour and were able to entertain men by various diversions like garden-parties (665-84) and water-sports (685-91). They were witty and expert talkers (143-48, 165-72, 863-74) and keen observers of human psychology. They were repositories of fine arts like music (357), dance (346, 355) and theatrical performance (794ff.) and attained proficiency in the traditional sixty-four arts specially meant for them (499). They received liberal training specially in the literary and

1. See *supra*, pp. 37-8.

2. *K* 863 which styles a courtesan (*gaṇikā*) *nāgarikā* and contrasts her to a village woman.

practical lore connected with their profession. An idea of the curriculum can be had from verses 123-25 which describe Mālatī's accomplishments. It included erotic texts of Vātsyāyana, Madanodaya, Dattaka, Viṭa, Rājaputra and others, the *Nāṭya-śāstra* of Bharata, Viśākhila's treatise on art, Dantila's writing, practical arts like arbori-horticulture (*vṛkṣ-āyurveda*), needle-work, wood-work, metal-work and cookery, and fine arts like painting, cut-work in leaves (*patra-ccheda*), music - vocal and instrumental, and dance.

As custodians of fine arts, they undoubtedly rendered a great service to the society by keeping ancient traditions alive. If Dāmodaragupta is to be relied upon, they specially cultivated the art of acting, although, it must be noted, they regarded it only as a secondary means of livelihood (801). Consequently they could not achieve the desired skill in stage-craft (794-99).[1] Some of them, however, took greater interest in their assignment and did their job well.[2] As an example, our poet gives a graphic account of the performance by courtesans of the First Act of the *Ratnāvalī* of Harṣavardhana (881-928).

The hetairai did gratify the sexual instincts of men seeking after pleasures. But it was mainly by virtue of these refinements that people of the aristocratic sections of the society were attracted towards them. Besides freely supplying sexual needs, they also provided diversions to people of free nature who were disgruntled with their wives who were confined to the premises of the household and were too shy to respond freely to their demands (441-445).

Nomenclature

The hetairai are referred to by various words like *veśyā*,[3] *kṣudrā*,[4] *rūpājīvā*,[5] *vāravadhū*,[6] *vāra-yoṣit*,[7] *paṇya-vadhū*,[8]

1. This must have been true of other arts as well.
2. Mañjarī is said to have excelled in imitating Sāgarikā, daughter of the king of Siṁhala (*K* 803). She was able to differentiate on stage the *karuṇa* and *vipralambha śṛṅgāra* sentiments (8[illegible]9).
3. *K* 485, 498, 560, 642, 646, 656, etc.
4. *Ibid.*, 317, 440, 797.
5. *Ibid.*, 458.
6. *Ibid.*, 811, 972.
7. *Ibid.*, 565.
8. *Ibid.*, 94, 499.

paṇya-strī,[1] *prakaṭa-rāmā*,[2] *pradhāna-nārī*,[3] *gaṇikā*,[4] *dāsī*,[5] *vilāsinī*,[6] *ceṭikā*,[7] *veśa-vilāsavatī*,[8] *vāra-strī*,[9] *vāra-ramaṇī*,[10] *śūlā*,[11] *aniyata-puṁsā*,[12] *rati-śilpa-jīvikā*[13] and *veśa-yoṣit*.[14] Some of these terms are significant inasmuch as they throw light on some fundamental aspects of this profession. Thus, the words *rūp-ājīvā* and *rati-śilpa-jīvikā* point to the fact that physical charms were the principal means of their livelihood. *Aniyata-puṁsā* and words beginning with *vāra* show that a harlot was not confined to any single man but was accessible to all. *Paṇya-strī* and *paṇya-vadhū* indicate that she was something like an object of trade which could be had at a fixed payment. *Dāsī* and *ceṭikā* suggest that in the estimation of people their social status was no better than that of female slaves or manual servants. Their low social position is also suggested by the word *kṣudrā*. Other words indicate their luxurious life and their residence in a particular area of a town.

Two Kinds

Two kinds of harlots can be easily distinguished. There were some hetairai of a higher status who were not easily accessible to all and sundry and confined to a single rich client so long as all his wealth was not exhausted. Mālatī and Mañjarī belonged to this category. Others were ordinary whores at whose houses there was always a crowd of customers and who were easily available to all those who could afford to pay their fees.[15] The harlots whose conversation was overheard by

1. *K.*, 511.
2. *Ibid.*, 645.
3. *Ibid.*, 546.
4. *Ibid.*, 559, 566, 655, 657, 859, 863, 1045.
5. *Ibid.*, 562, 641, 658, 794.
6. *Ibid.*, 503, 561.
7. *Ibid.*, 812.
8. *Ibid.*, 95.
9. *Ibid.*, 5.
10. *Ibid.*, 92.
11. *Ibid.*, 19, 68, 796.
12. *Ibid.*, 644.
13. *Ibid.*, 637.
14. *Ibid.*, 20. Moti Chandra (*The World of Courtesans*, p. 24) thinks that the institution of *gaṇikā* was started by the ganas from whom others borrowed it.
15. एकः क्रीणात्यद्य प्रातर्भविता तथाऽपरः क्रेता ।
    अन्यवशे क्षणमेकं न विक्रयः शाश्वतोऽस्ति वेश्यानाम् ॥
    K., 646.

Sundarasena and Samarabhaṭa on their way to the courtesan Hāralatā at Abu and the temple of Śiva Vṛṣabhadhvaja at Vārāṇasī respectively were evidently of this class.

Ordinarily, men who hankered after harlots went to the latter's houses. Sometimes, however, we find courtesans themselves going to meet their clients. The latter practice was resorted to when the customer happened to belong to a royal family as evidenced by the instance of Mañjarī and Samarabhaṭa (1046).

Lure of Money

From harlots' point of view pecuniary gain was the sole motive of their profession. Prostitution of the body was a means of their livelihood. For them love was a craft (*ratiśilpa*) enabling them to secure a livelihood (637) and body a tradeable commodity.[1] The whole corpus of trickeries elaborately described in the manuals dealing with this institution and vividly illustrated in our poem was adopted by this class of women with the object of eking out their livelihood and amassing wealth in order that they might lead a prosperous life. They were well aware of the fact that they could not maintain themselves by any means other than trading their physique to satiate the sexual urge of licentious men. This idea is beautifully presented in a stanza which tells us that a prostitute is incapable in her childhood and old age and that if she happens to fall in genuine love in youth she can do nothing but beg.[2]

A hetaira always cared for immediate gain without bothering about the past or future (644). She could be easily approached if only one had wealth (638). Her feigned love and other accessory acts were coeval with wealth (303).[3]

1. Verse 41 refers to Mālatī's complaint that even by spreading the commercial commodity in the form of her body she was unable to get a desired lover, while verse 641 describes a courtesan as living by selling her body.

2. बाल्ये तावदयोग्या पश्चादपि वृद्धभावपरिभूता ।
तारुण्ये रागहृता यदि गणिका भ्रमतु तद् भिक्षाम् ॥

K 544.

3. Also cf. *ibid.*, 305, 315, 318, 322.

We have a good deal of information about the various devices employed by harlots to squeeze the wealth of their paramours. Once a man fell into the clutches of a strumpet. She made a show of great attachment as if she loved him genuinely. She gave him full sexual satisfaction and aroused his jealousy and passions to the climax (149-74, 498-527) and then proceeded to divest him gradually of all his belongings. The tricks resorted to for this purpose included the following:—

i) An artificial quarrel with her mother in which the latter rebuked her for having discarded a number of rich and generous aspirants of her love for the sake of the present client and asked back her own belongings threatening to leave her and go on a pilgrimage (528-545) and the hetaira professed true selfless love for her present lover (546-56).

ii) Concocting the story that when, for some reason, the lover failed to come on a rainy night the courtesan went to meet him and was relieved of her ornaments by thieves on way (586-604).

iii) At the behest of the harlot a trader came to her in the presence of her lover and asked her to return the money she had borrowed from him (605-10).

iv) Expression of anxiety for not having been able, for want of necessary means, to make offerings to the goddess which she had promised when her lover was indisposed (611-13).

v) The burning of the house from which all the valuables have already been removed and declaring complete destruction (614).

Having thus squeezed all the wealth of her lover and having ascertained by various means that he had been completely impoverished the courtesan resorted to various devices to drive him out. These included offering him a separate seat, laxity in the observance of normal courtesies, conversation full of jealousy and laughter, heart-burning jokes, praising his rivals as endowed with greater qualities and entertaining more love for her, accusing him of talkativeness, interrupting his speech, condemning his behaviour, avoiding his company under some pretext, not keeping time, lying sideways while on the bed, pretending sleep, expressing anxiety when made to face him, protesting against touching private parts of the body, showing indifference to his queries, shaking the face when he wants to kiss her, shrinking the body at the time of embrace, intolerance of striking, biting with teeth and scratching with nails, dislike of long coitus, asking him to sleep when he wants a coitus, passing ironical remarks when he is tired after sexual intercourse, laughing at him when he exhibits his skill, inquiring of watchman about time with the desire for the end of the night, getting down from the cot with quickness and coming out of the bedroom shouting aloud 'it is dawn, it is dawn', and making the maid condemn one-sided love and the hankering of the poor after courtesans whose sole consideration is monetary gain (616-60). If in spite of all this he did not leave her then she told him that though she still loved him by heart, she could not disobey her mother and, therefore, he should leave the place for a few days in order to enjoy her company again thereafter (661-63). And when she was free from him she proceeded to ensnare again a lover who had formerly been discarded by her but had of late regained his former prosperity. She succeeded in accomplishing the impossible by reminding him of their earlier companionship and enjoyment of picnics and water-sports and attributing their separation to a misunderstanding brought about by a villain. She discarded him again after extorting all his wealth (664-733).[1]

In all this a hetaira was guided by stark utilitarianism. Her logic was a very practical one. Her conduct is illustrated by the following three similes : (i) Even as the bees abandon a honeycomb from which honey has been drunk and where nothing but wax remains so also she discards a man impoverished

1. This exposition of the knacks of the craft is based on Vātsyāyana's *Kāma-sūtra*, vi.2.37 (artificial quarrel), vi.3.10 (borrowing money for him), vi.3.7 (theft of ornaments), vi.3.8 (burning the house), vi.3.18 (selling her own ornaments for the lover), vi.3.4 (purchasing articles from a trader on loan in the presence of the lover). However, there can be no doubt that these tricks must have been frequently resorted to by harlots and that the works on Kāmaśāstra have borrowed these matters from actual life.

It may be noted here that the *Vasudeva-hiṇḍī* also mentions feigned illness and the burning of the house as being resorted to by courtesans for realising money. Vide A. P. Jamkhedkar; *Cultural History from the Vasudeva-hiṇḍi* (an unpublished Ph.D. thesis), pp. 215-16.

but at the same time overwhelmed by passion.[1] (ii) Like people who throw a snare covered with flesh, capture a plump fish, cook it with spices, eat its flesh and reject its skin and bones, she too ensnares a man with the help of her smile, side-long glances and sweet tongue, polishes him observing courtesies, appropriates all his wealth and gives him up when he is just a bundle of skin and bones, i.e. poor.[2] (iii) Just as people throw away a mango after chewing it so does a harlot leave a man after extorting all his wealth (733).

These squeezing habits of the hetairai must have presented a strange sight of the erstwhile affluent men rendered penniless. It is said that those who fall in love with harlots have to extend their hands for begging (324). At another place we read of men whose wealth was extorted by courtesans and who, covered with tattered garments, were compelled to eat in free feeding houses (34, 39). Above all, we have the example of prince Samarabhaṭa who is said to have been rendered completely impoverished by Mañjarī.

All this, of course, does not mean that hetairai were completely immune from the natural urge of genuine love. Although extremely scarce, instances of courtesans falling in selfless love with men of their hearts' liking were not altogether unknown. The example of Hāralatā, which reminds us of the courtesan Vasantasenā in Bhāsa's *Cārudatta* and Śūdraka's *Mṛcchakaṭika*, was one such. Some other examples are also reported (559-66). But these were, by the very nature of facts, exceptions.

1. पीडितमधु मधुजालं तुच्छीभूतं च मन्मथग्रस्तम् ।
मुञ्चन्ति मदनशेषं क्षुद्राश्च प्रकटरामाश्च ॥
K 645

2. स्वशरीरामिषदिग्धं वक्रस्मितदृष्टिपातवाग्वडिशम् ।
प्रक्षिप्याकृष्य जडं स्फुरणेन विवर्जितं सुपरिपुष्टम् ॥
हस्तद्वयान्तरागतमुपचारपरिव्ययेन संस्कृत्य ।
भुक्त्वा यावन्मांसं त्यक्ष्यसि चर्मास्थिशेषितं मत्स्यम् ॥
Ibid., 734-35

Cf. the following statement in the *Vasudeva-hiṇḍī* :—As a fruitless tree is deserted by birds, and the rivers and ponds, when dry, by goose, so also a person, when bankrupt, is worthy to be left by the courtesans. Jamakhedkar, *op. cit.*, p. 214.

Fees

The fees charged by the hetairai were known as *mūlya* (333, 352), *bhāṭī* (336, 342, 363) and *grahaṇaka* (364). Fee paid in gold is referred to as *kanaka-bhāṭī* (363). The fees had to be paid in advance (363-64). Every harlot had her fees fixed. Sometimes, however, the competition among the clients led to a rise in fees (336, 534). Fraud by either party in this respect was of common occurrence. There is, for example, a reference to a prostitute accepting fees from many and indulging in sexual act with one (338). Another stanza mentions the case of a strumpet who realised fee from one person but allowed another man to have sexual intercourse with her (342). Likewise, we hear of some clients who had their carnal desires satiated but did not pay fees afterwards (333) or otherwise deceived prostitutes (332). While we have references to courtesans being tried and fined for such offences by governmental or social agencies (401, 342), there is no means to know if the clients were also similarly punished for fraud on their part. Perhaps they were not, for once a customer left the residence of a courtesan it would be difficult to locate him unless he came for the second time.

Initiation

A harlot was called *dārikā* before she launched on her profession (368). The initiation of a maiden as a hetaira was an occasion to be celebrated. The man who had the first sexual intercourse with the initiate had to pay a very heavy fee which was within the reach of the rich alone (350). This was an age-old custom and is referred to in other works also. The custom is reported to have been current among the prostitutes of Vārāṇasi till recently.

Brothels

Normally a courtesan worked singly and independently; but there appear to have existed some brothels, possibly with more than one inmate, under the charge of a man. The keeper of a brothel was called *śūlā-pāla* (68, 796). He looked after arrangements of theatrical performances given by harlots belonging to his establishment (68). He exercised strict control over the inmates of his brothel. A verse refers to his not allowing a harlot to act on the stage saying she was passing through the menses (796). We learn from an epigraph of the eleventh century hailing from Rajasthan that the *śūla-pālas*[1] accompanied courtesans, possibly inmates of their respective establishments, to give musical and dance performances on the occasion of the *yātrās* of various deities.[2]

The Bawd

No account of prostitution will be complete without a reference to the mother, real or adopted, who was a *sine qua non* of the establishment of a hetaira. She was variously called *mātṛ*,[3] *jananī*,[4] *kuṭṭanī*,[5] and *śambhalī*.[6] She was normally an elderly lady with a fund of experience to her credit and as such served as friend, philosopher and guide to prostitutes. Some of these women, who had been successful courtesans in their youth and had thereby developed deep insight into the nature of men and things, were highly respected in their community, and a number of harlots flocked to them for instructions into the intricacies of the profession. Vikarālā is described as one such lady (27-30). She was to courtesans even as a teacher is to his pupils. Mālatī saluted her with her head touching the earth, took her seat when offered by Vikarālā, and rose from the seat and put her queries before her with folded hands (31-32). The courtesans were aware that their success in the profession depended, in a large measure, on the mothers (33-39). Men

1. the same as our *śūlā-pāla*.

2. Nadol inscription of Cāhamāna Jojalladeva, dated V. 1147, *EI*, xi, p. 28. Monier Williams (*Sanskrit-English Dictionary*, s.v. *śūla*, p. 1086) is right in taking *śūlapāla* (more correct form *śūlā-pāla*) to mean 'the keeper of a brothel' or 'frequenter of brothels'. The former meaning seems to be more probable, for the word *pāla* does not go well with a frequenter of brothels. Although the *śūlā-pālas* may have accompanied the prostitutes on musical instruments while singing or dancing, there is nothing to support the meaning 'associates of courtezans', suggested by D. R. Bhandarkar (*EI*, xi, p. 28).

3. *K* 345, 350, 359, 365, 528, 556, 604.

4. *Ibid.*, 555.

5. *Ibid.*, 2, 334, 337, 368.

6. It is a variant for *kuṭṭanī*, *ibid.*, 2.

were over-awed by the bawds and knew well that the first step to success in winning over the beloved was the willing consent of the bawd. That is why she was day and night surrounded by the clients who sought her favour by offering her rich presents (25, 30). She was of help to courtesans in ways beyond number. She procured rich customers for her ward and tried to keep them ensnared until all the wealth was squeezed. It was she who received the customers first and tried to please them by pleasant speech. As an example reference may be made to the way Mālatī's mother is asked to address her new customer, Cintāmaṇi. "Today", said she, "have the blessings borne fruit; today are the deities pleased, that you, the ornament of auspiciousness, have adorned my house by your presence." "Fie at the people happy at the birth of a son; daughters are really praiseworthy by dint of whom sons-in-law like you are obtained." "You know us well, you appreciate merits and you accord us respect though, yet, O you pleasant to my heart, I would say (a few words) because of affection for my daughter. Mālatī has genuine love for you ; may I request you to act in such a manner as she has not to suffer the pangs of separation from you" (143, 146-48). She got rid of men after they had exhausted all their wealth (334). When there were more than one customer for a courtesan and they fought among themselves, she pacified them (337). She exercised a great deal of control over her ward and for that reason was often blamed by unwanted clients who were made to cherish the fond belief that though their beloved loved them, it was only because of the bawd that she was helpless (345). The fees were also fixed and received by her (350, 363, 364). And when all the wealth of a client was exhausted she helped her ward in devising various tricks for ousting him. She went to the extent of indulging in a feigned quarrel with her ward for this purpose. And when all these tricks proved ineffective, the harlot got rid of him by laying the whole blame for it on the bawd (662).[1] The importance of the bawd can be gauged by a reference to the *Samaya-mātṛkā* of the Kashmiri poet Kṣemendra (11th century) who gives a vivid description of the pitiable condition of a prostitute with-

1. The *Ubhayābhisārikā*, verse 26, states that just as kings accuse ministers for their own misdeeds so also courtesans put their own blame on mothers.

out the mother. We are told that a hetaira without a bawd is never free from men and that the rogues never leave the house of a courtesan without the mother even as a cat does not leave the oven in the winter.[1] He equates a courtesan without a bawd to a ground strewn with flowers without thorns and the royal fortune without a minister.[2] He, therefore, counsels the courtesans to be never without mother; if one does not have a real mother, one should find out a shrewd lady and adopt her as mother.[3]

The role of the mother has been emphasised in a number of ancient texts. We learn from Kauṭilya that a courtesan who lost her beauty was appointed a mother and that a courtesan handing over her ornaments to the keeping of any one else but the mother was subjected to a fine of four *paṇas* and a quarter.[4] If a courtesan ran away or died, the mother provided a substitute.[5] Vātsyāyana refers to the natural (*mātṛ*) as well as the artificial (*mātṛkā*) mother[6] and states that a courtesan should always remain under her control and never violate her orders. She should feign quarrel with the mother showing attachment to the lover and do nothing without her consent. The mother could compel a harlot to unite with a man even against her desire.[7] The *Dhūrta-viṭa-saṁvāda* of Īśvaradatta informs us that visitors of courtesans avoided their mothers even as people avoid rivers infested with dangerous animals.[8] The *Ubhayābhisārikā* states that a hetaira could be engaged by the mother with a man not liked by her.[9] It describes the mother as the very death to the lovers and as a source of enmity and quarrel among the young men.[10] For lovers of courtesans the mothers were like calamities that could not be warded off and were skilled in squeezing the wealth of the lovers.[11] Even as the kings

1. *Samaya-mātṛkā*, i. 42-43.
2. *Ibid.*, i. 45.
3. *Ibid.*, i. 49.
4. *Artha-śāstra*, ii, 27. 5, 11, 17.
5. *Ibid.*, ii.27.2.
6. *Kāma-sūtra*, vi. 2. 3.
7. *Ibid.*, vi. 2, 3, 4, 5, 37, 38, 42.
8. *Dhūrta-viṭa-saṁvāda*, verse 50, *Caturbhāṇī*, p. 100.
9. *Ibid.*, pp. 127-28 & verse 13.
10. *Ibid.*, p. 133, verse 19.
11. *Ibid.*, p. 135.

attribute their own misdeeds to the ministers so also a harlot blames the mother for her own misdeeds.[1] Daṇḍin describes at length how the mother strove for the physical and mental development of her ward, trained her in various arts and worked for her professional success.[2]

The Female Messenger (*Dūtī*)

Another indispensable aid to a harlot was a sharp, ready-witted and skilled message-girl (*dūtī*). It was through these go-betweens that desired customers were to be approached. Vikarālā advises Mālatī to send to her prospective client, Cintāmaṇi, a clever, bold *dūtī* capable of gauging others' feelings and endowed with sarcastic speech (89). Hāralatā and Mañjarī are also said to have sent such messengers to convey their love-sickness to Sundarasena and Samarabhaṭa respectively (283, 989). The skill with which they carried out their undertaking is amply illustrated by the speech attributed to them. They first presented flowers and betels to the prospective lovers, gave a graphic account of the physical charms and lovelorn condition of their mistresses, enticed them by words arousing their passions to a high pitch, and if they found that their speech did not bear the desired fruit, they resorted to sarcasm.[3]

The Clientale

It would be interesting to know something about the social background of the visitors of the harlots. The customers generally belonged to the richer sections of the society which could afford the luxury. They included princes (335, 367, 400, 736ff.), favourites of the king (542), government officials like the *śaulkikādhyakṣa* (531), the *haṭṭa-pati* (540) and the village chief (537), and businessmen (746). The sons of high government officials (37, 59, 538) and the only spoiled son of an old ailing rich man[4] (532) were easy victims to this vice. Sons of rich state dignitaries without any responsibility, particularly those who stayed

1. *Caturbhāṇī*, p. 140, v. 26.

2. *Daśa-kumāra-carita*, Uttara-pīṭhikā, ii, pp. 78ff. For a full account of the role of the mother see Ludwik Sternbach in *Bhāratīya Vidyā*, v, pp. 114-42.

3. *K* 91-137, 286-300, 991-1041.

4. Cf. *Samaya-mātṛkā*, v. 63.

away from their parents and were masters of their own affairs, were preferred by harlots as they would succumb to temptations more easily. Cintāmaṇi is represented as such a client (59-60). Some eunuchs also visited prostitutes in order to propagate their manliness (541).[1] Cases of incapable but dissatisfied old men (394), Brāhmaṇas (38, 393) and religious teachers (539, 753) visiting hetairai were also not unknown.[2] Some villagers were also attracted by the glittering city life and paid visits to courtesans. But, being unacquainted with the urban institution of prostitution, they had to return disappointed and were derisively laughed at by harlots. A villager, it is said, seeing the eyes of his beloved closed in the ecstasy of the moment of supreme joy took her to be dead and ran away out of fear (397-99). It may thus be concluded that the clients hailed from all the different strata of the society, but mostly they belonged to the aristocracy.

The Viṭas

Mention must also be made in this connection of a class of people known as *viṭa* (333, 339, 342, 368, 755). The *viṭa* figures frequently in Sanskrit plays and is described at length in the texts on dramaturgy and erotics. According to Bharata, he was to be skilled in pleasing prostitutes, sweet, courteous, poet, proficient in argumentation, bold and shrewd.[3] Vātsyāyana defines a *viṭa* as a man who has exhausted his wealth in enjoyment, is endowed with good qualities, is married and is respected among harlots and in *goṣṭhīs* and earns his livelihood thereby.[4] He acted like the minister of peace and war between the city-bred lovers (*nāgarakas*) and hetairai. He often played the role of a messenger and helped the two lovers to come together.[5] The close association of the *viṭas* with harlots is obvious from these and other references.[6]

1. *Samaya-mātṛkā*, v. 65.
2. Cf. *Kāma-sūtra*, vi.1.10, which names easily approachable clients of harlots. They included, among others, the rich, state officers, those who acquire wealth without much effort, having uninterrupted income, eunuchs desirous to publicise their manliness, favourites of kings and ministers, disobedient to the elders, careless about money, an only son and religious mendicants.
3. *Nāṭya-śāstra*, xxxv.55.
4. *Kāma-sūtra*, i.4.45.
5. *Ibid.*, i.4.47; i.5.37; ii.10.48.
6. For a reference to a work entitled *Viṭa-śāstra* (Breviary of Rakes), see *Bṛhat-Kathā-śloka-saṅgraha*, Ch. X.

The *Kuṭṭanī-mata* contains several references to *viṭas* who are represented there as frequenting the colonies of prostitutes and more often than not involved in quarrels and other unsavoury acts. They did not pay prostitutes their fees and when seen were taken to task by the latter (333). They walked before courtesans singing and making faces (339), and sometimes uniting a harlot with a rich lover enjoyed her company free of charge (340). Elderly *viṭas* mediated between hetairai and their clients in quarrels relating to payment of fees (342).In the accounts of Sundarasena's journey to Hāralatā's residence at Abu and that of Samarabhaṭa to the temple of Vṛṣabhadhvaja at Vārāṇasī we have interesting descriptions of the chat among prostitutes, bawds and *viṭas* which indicate great attachment of *viṭas* to harlots, their freedom and carelessness, and love of deriding others (331-68, 743-55).[1]

There is a reference to a courtesan charging fee from one and entering into sexual intercourse with another man and her being tried before the elderly *viṭas* and being fined double the amount of fee (342). This seems to indicate the existence of an organisation of some senior *viṭas* for trying the offending inmates of the profession and dealing with other complaints connected therewith. The *Pāda-tāḍitaka* of Śyāmilaka records an interesting episode which throws welcome light on this institution. A Brāhmaṇa, it is said, was struck on his head by a hetaira with her foot. The Brāhmaṇa was overtaken by remorse, and when the assembly (*pariṣad*) of learned Brāhmaṇas was unable to decide upon the atonement he should observe, the question was referred to an assembly of senior *viṭas*, for according to the established legal convention of ancient India, age-old customs of different regions, castes, families and *tīrthas* were regarded as authentic provided they were not opposed to the Vedas. The assembly met with all the attendant formalities in the *viṭa-maṇḍapa* and after a long discussion took decision in the matter. A list of all the chief *viṭas* was carefully drawn and they were formally invited, due care being taken to include each and every *viṭa* who mattered. Some high dignitaries like kings, state officers, etc., came in this category.[2] It would thus appear

1. These features are typically represented in a figure from Kumrahar excavations. See Pl. X. 16.
2. *Caturbhāṇī*, pp. 149ff.

that like other castes and occupational classes, courtesans and *viṭas* had age-old conventions peculiar to them which were recognised as authentic like law and had a legal right to settle the issues falling within their jurisdiction. For this purpose they had a regular council which held its meetings at a fixed place. The evidence supplied by the *Kuṭṭanī-mata* shows that in some form or other this institution existed at least down to the ninth century A.D. and played an important role in regulating prostitution in ancient Kashmir.

Another agency which exercised some control over prostitutes was government. We read of a courtesan being tried by the *nagara-prabhu* in the presence of the public for demanding double the amount of the prescribed fee (401).[1]

Colonies of Prostitutes

According to our evidence there were regular colonies of prostitutes (*veśa-sanniveśa*, 368) at Abu and Vārāṇasī. At the latter place it seems to have been situated very close to the temple of Vṛṣabhadhvaja. Sundarasena and Samarabhaṭa had to pass through these colonies while going to Hāralatā's habitat and the Vṛṣabhadhvaja temple respectively. Our author gives a vivid account of the conversations among *viṭas*, prostitutes and procuresses. Life in these colonies was very busy and business quite brisk. To these colonies flocked prostitutes from different parts of the country. We have a reference to a harlot from Kerala at Abu being visited by a southerner (402). It may be reasonably surmised that there must have existed regular colonies of harlots in every big city. The *Padma-prābhṛtaka* and *Pāda-tāḍitaka* prove the existence of such a colony at Ujjayinī[2] and the *Dhūrta-viṭa-saṁvāda* and *Ubhay-ābhisārikā* at Pāṭaliputra.[3] The cosmopolitan character of these colonies is indicated by the *Pāda-tāḍitaka* which mentions the presence at Ujjayinī of the courtesans hailing from Surāṣṭra, Pāṭaliputra, Kāśī,

1. Cf. *Samaya-mātṛkā*, i.16; ii. 48. Also cf. *RT*, viii. 3338 where it is stated that the *nagar-ādhipa* persisted in punishing many persons on the allegation that they had carnal intercourse with dancing girls who had been admitted into households as wedded wives.

2. Ujjayinī is the venue of the scenes of these monologues.

3. Pāṭaliputra is the venue of these plays;

Śūrpāraka (modern Sopara), Siṁhala, Śūrasena, Lāṭa, Draviḍa and Barbara and of the Yavana extraction.[1]

IV. IDEAL FEMALE FORM

It will not be quite out of context to refer here to the standards of feminine beauty in ancient India as seen in the work under study. Sanskrit poets derive great delight in describing feminine charms; they endow their heroines with ideal beauty and shower unstinted encomium over every limb and every possible movement of the body; they always conceived the lady as the very embodiment of ideal beauty. For the time being it appears as if there can be no lady on earth more beautiful and charming than the one being described at the moment ; this is true even when the poet has to describe more than one lady at different places in his work. While describing one lady he seems to forget that he has earlier in the same poem delineated another lady equally beautiful. Most of these descriptions, however, follow a set pattern established by a long tradition of erotics and rhetorics. But there is always to be noticed a touch of highly erotic feeling and passion. This is particularly true of erotic poetry where delineation of feminine charms is motivated solely by the desire to arouse passionate sexual urge. The *Kuṭṭanī-mata*, too, is an erotic poem and is inspired by the same objective.

Sanskrit poets are addicted to the youthful female form, descriptions of pre-youth and old age being rather rare. Dāmodaragupta describes physical charms of females at three different places in the poem: in the description of Mālatī by Vikarālā (44-57) and by the message girl (108-20) ; in the delineation of Hāralatā by the poet himself (257-65), and in that of Mañjarī by Samarabhaṭa (961-87). Besides, a number of casual allusions are scattered throughout the poem. It must be said, however, to the credit of our poet that while he had to follow the current notions about the ideal female form as a matter of course, his three descriptions are free from the boredom of conventional pattern. Though the ideal form of the different parts of the body was bound to be the same, the poet has, by

1. *Caturbhāṇī*, pp. 152 ff. Vide also Introduction, p. 30.

employing different similes, succeeded in introducing a great deal of variety which speaks volumes for his poetic talent.

A slightly bent (192), soft (988) and slim body (985) with a fair complexion like the lightning (258) or the beams of autumnal moon (265) was preferred. The poet admires dense hair (187); he has special preference for jet-black rows of curls (189) falling on the forehead which he compares to the shadow of Rāhu in the half-orb of the moon (110). In her braided hair he sees the wick of the smoke arising from the god of love when he was put aflame by Śiva (44). As for its jet black colour he feels compelled to compare it to the swarms of bees (110); her long braid decked with flowers is enough to inspire passion (964). Her broad long eyes (186) as tremulous as those of the deer (189, 964, 967, 981, 986) are capable of wounding the hearts of men by sharp deadly shafts of the glance (185). Her fast moving eyes can win over the whole world with damn ease (986). The lips must always be naturally red like the *bandhujīva* flower (113), the trembling ones being specially loved (986). The well-formed row of teeth is compared to a spurt of lightning (47), and the ear-lobes to the lotus flower (112, 981). The mouth, compared to the lotus flower (111, 264, 965) and the orb of the moon (111), with its playful movement (965), is a stimulus of love. So is the sportive movement of the slightly raised eyebrows, sweet smile and the graceful glances (45).

Coming lower down, like other Sanskrit poets, Dāmodaragupta is never tired of speaking of the breasts as spreading (49, 974), dense (187), high (265, 974) and plump (987). Slender waist (45, 51, 452, 968, 985) with folds (187) and the row of hair serving as a natural ornament (187, 985) is very much in favour. The row of hair is once compared to the string of the bow of Kāma (52). The navel must be deep (188).

The part below the waist which attracted the attention of Sanskrit poets most are the hips which must be broad (188), plump (987) and so heavy (53, 114, 266, 975) as to impede even the gait (117), and in fairness rivalling a rock of gold (53).

The thighs resembling the trunk of an elephant (53, 988) or the plantain staff (54, 116), and the fully rounded shanks looking like a golden creeper (55) are a source of pleasure to the poet. The soft soles with their reddish tinge indeed belittle the pomegranate and the *sthala-kamalinī* (56). Small hands and feet were particularly appreciated (186).[1] The upper arms should be as soft as lotus-stalk (50). The slow gait (192) impeded by the burden of the heavy hips (117) puts an elephant or swan to shame (57), while the tinkling speech excels the sound of the lyre (264) and the voice of the cuckoo (48).

This description appears more or less to be based on well-established artistic conventions. In ancient Indian sculpture and painting female figures are traditionally represented with expansive and raised bosoms, a slim waist, a deep navel, prominent hips and small feet while the softness and the warmth of flesh are also quite perceptible. Delicate folds on the belly are also sometimes emphasised while in some instances a slight swoop in the body is also noticed (Pl. XI. 17).

VI. PERSONAL NAMES AND TITLES

We get very little information about personal names and titles. But a few points may be gathered from some of the personal names occurring in the poem. They are as follows:-

(i) Sometimes the names of the father and the son ended with the same word, e.g., Nayadatta was the son of Sāgaradatta (36) while Śubhadeva was the son of Dīkṣita Bhavadeva (38).

(ii) *Sena*-ending names appear to have been popular both among males[2] and females.[3] Such names were borne by Brāhmaṇas also. e.g. Sundarasena.

(iii) Svāmin-ending names were popular among the Vaiṣṇavas, E.g., Keśavasvāmin (530), Prabhusvāmin (541).

(iv) As we have seen above,[4] *Bhāva* was assumed as an honorific title by the Śaiva teachers. Dāmodaragupta refers to a Pāśupatācārya named Śuddha who bore the title *Bhāva* (538).

1. Cf. the Hindi proverb, '*Sir baḍā saradāra kā, Paira baḍā gaṁvāra kā, Hātha baḍā hatyāre kā*' i.e.. a leader has a big head, a fool has a big foot, and a murderer has big hands.

2. *K* 538, 540, 745.

3. *Ibid.*, 36, 38, 320, 326, 337, 348, 350-51, 360, 366.

4. *Supra*, p. 68.

(v) Of the Brāhmaṇa surnames current during the period mention is made of two only, viz., Dīkṣita (38) and Miśra (566).

(vi) Bhaṭṭa was employed as an epithet of respect for the learned Brāhmaṇas; it could be used both before (529, 563, 565) or after (365) the proper name.[1] The words *Bhaṭṭa-putra* (37, 75, 79), *Bhaṭṭa-sūnu* (59), *Bhaṭṭa-suta* (60, 80), *Bhaṭṭa-tanaya* (88) and *Bhaṭṭa-dāyāda* (138) denoted the son of a learned Brāhmaṇa and, like Bhaṭṭa, were used as titles of honour.[2]

While it is difficult to classify all the personal names found in the poem in a systematic manner, the following observations will be of some interest.

Among courtesans names containing words indicating lasciviousness were very common. We come across, for example, names like Madanasenā (36, 350, 351), Kāmasenā (360), Manmathasenā (537), Anaṅgadevī (539), Suratadevī (356), Suratasenā (366), Smaralīlā (357), Keli (345), Dayitikā (346) and Madirākṣī (747)[3]. Similar names were borne by men also, e.g., Madanaka (344), Kandarpaka (347), Vilāsaka (348), Matta (357), Kallola (334), Vibhrama (351) and Līlodaya (352).

Some names referred to physical charms, e.g., Lalitā (362), Śaśiprabhā (285, 343) in the case of women and Abhirāma (363) in the case of men, and others to auspiciousness or human virtues, e.g., Śubhadeva (38) and Guṇapālita (210).

A few names, both male, e.g., Viśeṣaka (343) and Maṇi-kaṇṭha (560), and female, e.g., Hāralatā (277), Hārā (355) and Kuvalayamālā (352), are indicative of Indians' proverbial love of ornaments.

Names connected with the vegetal world were very popular among women, e.g., Mālatī (20) or Mālatikā (129), Mañjarī (37, 736) or Mañjarikā (810), Kesarasenā (38), Kesarā (349), Tilakamañjarī (353), Mukulā (361), Kusumadevī (363), Ketakī, (403), kusumalatā (525), Kundamālā (523), Kamala-

1. The title Bhaṭṭa is frequently applied to Brāhmaṇas in inscriptions. See *EI*, xxii, pp. 108, 137, 151, 156, 159, 189, 191, etc.; xxiii, pp. 32, 77, 80, 129, etc. The title appears for the first time in a Yūpa inscription from Barnala, dated Kṛta year 335-A.D. 279. Vide *ibid.*, xxvi, p. 173, text line 1.

2. For epigraphical references, see *ibid.*, xxii, pp. 156, 158; xxiii, pp. 16, 78, 266, 268, 269; xxvi, p. 167, etc.; Sircar, *Indian Epigraphical Glossary*, p. 52. Vide also *supra*, p. 18.

3. According to the *Nāṭya-śāstra* (xix-33), names of courtesans usually ended in *dattā*, *mitrā* and *senā*.

devī (522), Kadambakā (563), Citralatā (699), Kumudinī (750). Similar names were also adopted by men though not so commonly, e.g., Kiñjalkaka (346), Indīvaraka (353), Makarandaka (354), Kadambaka (565) and Kuśakarṇa (748).

Names derived from fauna were also borne both by males and females, e.g., Kalahaṁsaka (345), Mṛgadevī (525), Kuraṅgī (745) and Hariṇī (746).

We also come across the name of a river borne by a woman, viz., Narmadā (35, 540).

Names derived from those of deities were in vogue both among men and women. Thus, we have names like Vāsudevabhaṭṭa (365), Keśavasvāmin (530), Rāmasena (540), Nandisena (538), Ravideva (542), Bhāskaravarman (561) and Vasuṣeṇa (745) in the case of men and Indralekhā (359), Śivadevī (538), Mādhavasenā (526), Śaṅkarasenā (520) and Suradevī (744) for women. Sometimes names of divinities themselves were used as personal names, e.g., Purandara (193), Narasiṁha (37, 562), Vāsudeva (365), Madhusūdana (536), Viṣṇu (563), Vāmadeva (564) and Nīlakaṇṭha (566).

Other names are of a miscellaneous character and need not be discussed here.

It follows from the above that in naming a boy or girl some of the rules laid down by Dharmaśāstra writers were not only not followed but flagrantly violated. Thus we have some male names containing an uneven number of letters and female names comprising an even number of letters which is against the injunctions of the Dharmaśāstra works.[1] Likewise names borrowed from the vegetal world and rivers go counter to Manu who disapproves for marriage girls named after asterisms, trees and rivers.[2]

VII. FOOD AND DRINKS

The stories and the subject-matter of the poem gave Dāmodaragupta no opportunity to offer a systematic account of contemporary practices appertaining food and drinks. The

1. *Āśvalāyana-gṛhyasūtra*, i.15.4-10; *Baudhāyana-gṛhyasūtra*, ii.1.25; *Mānava-gṛhyasūtra*, i.18. Vide also *HDS*, ii (i), pp. 242-3, 250.

2. *Manu-smṛti*, iii. 9; *Āpastamba-gṛhyasūtra*, iii. 13.

following observations are, therefore, based on some stray allusions found in the *Kuṭṭanī-mata*.

Food

Rice was undoubtedly an important item of food, and our poet refers to three different varieties of paddy, viz., *śāli*[1] (871), *kalama*[2] and *aṇu* (229). We have an allusion to the unhusking of *śāli* with the help of a pestle (871).

Of the pulses popularly consumed during his period, our poet mentions three kinds—*caṇa* (horse gram) *kulattha*[3] (*Dolichos uniflorus*) and *masūra* (*Ervum hirsutum*). Beggars and ordinary travellers, who received these different sorts of rice and pulses as alms from different houses had to eat them mixed up together (229).

Of the various milk products which must have formed an important ingredient of diet, mention is made only of clarified butter which was specially noted for its unctuousness (997).

Honey claims an interesting reference. The bees, it is said, leave the honeycomb after extracting honey, leaving only wax (645).

Meat diet was quite common in those days as at present. The fact that the *Nīla-mata* found it necessary to proscribe meat-eating on the days dedicated to Viṣṇu's worship indicates the popularity of animal food in ancient Kashmir.[4] In the 13th century A.D. Marco Polo found that flesh with rice and other food grains formed the principal food of the Kashmiris.[5]

Consumption of meat-juice (*māṁsa-rasa*) is said to cure bodily pain. Prostitutes consumed meat soup for removing the body ache caused by wanton sexual intercourse with men (307). Kṣemendra in his *Deśopadeśa* (iii.32) also states that a prostitute regains youth by consuming fish-juice, ghee, milk and onions. Kalhaṇa also mentions fish-broth as an aphrodisiac.[6]

1. It corresponds to the transplanted variety now called *jaḍahan*.
2. According to Monier Williams (*Sanskrit-English Dictionary*, s.v. *kalama-śāli*), it is sown in May or June and harvested in December or January.
3. Now called *kulathī*.
4. Ved Kumari, *op. cit.*, p. 119.
5. Henry Yule, *Travels of Marco Polo*, i, p. 166.
6. *RT*, vii. 522.

Of the animals whose flesh was consumed particular reference is made to the fish. Our poet describes the manner of catching, cooking and eating the fish. A snare stained with flesh was thrown into the water ; when the fish was thus caught, it was cooked with spices; after eating the flesh, its skin and bones were thrown away (734-35).[1]

Wine

As in the rest of India, so in Kashmir wine was lavishly consumed by the people. The great popularity of wine in Kashmir is evident from the fact that on certain religious festivals like the New Snowfall Day, the second Mahimāna and the Irāmañjarī-pūjana the drinking of wine is recommended in the *Nīla-mata*,[2] whereas the Dharmaśāstra texts vehemently condemn this practice.

Wine was taken both by men (395) and women (392). Prostitutes were particularly addicted to drinking (359) which imparted fragrance (414) and a coppery complexion to the face (965). Men were very anxious to partake of the wine offered by their beloved after she had tasted it (351).

As stated above,[3] the Brāhmaṇas, as a class, abstained from taking wine as a religious duty.

Community Feast

Mention is made of a feast wherein the members of a particular community alone, including women, participated (852). Persons known to be guilty of some serious social breaches were excluded from such a feast. But sometimes they had to be tolerated as a matter of courtesy. It corresponds to the present community feasts (*jāti-bhojana*) which are arranged on occasions like marriage, atonement for an offence and re-entry into the community.

1. See *supra*, p. 117. Also cf. *RT*, v. 119 ; vii. 522.
2. Verses 465, 523, 676.
3. *Supra*, pp. 101-102

VIII. DRESS AND ORNAMENTS

Dress

The use of dress and adornments in accordance with the requirements of time and clime was regarded as a sign of refined taste.[1] Under the name *nepathya-prayoga* it is incorporated in the catalogue of sixty-four subsidiary arts (*aṅga-vidyās*) in Vātsyāyana's *Kāma-sūtra* (i.3.16).[2]

Textiles

Garments fashioned from cotton (*kārpāsa*, 366, 870), wool (*ūrṇā*, 366), China silk (*cīn-āmbara*, 344) and a fabric called *paṭikā* (742) were commonly used by the people. We get a reference to the cultivation of cotton (870) and the domestication of rams for wool (366). Chinese silk was a very costly textile. The gift of a pair of garments made from China silk was sufficient to lure a courtesan (344). China silk enjoyed great popularity in ancient India at least from the Maurya period, and from that time onward we have a continuous chain of references to it in Sanskrit and Prakrit literature indicating its wide-spread use over a long period of time.[3] *Paṭikā*, which was a costly fabric and used only by the aristocrats, is noted for its softness. So far as I know, it is not mentioned anywhere else ; but it may be the same as the *paṭṭa* silk (modern *pāṭ*) fre-

1. न त्यागः कालदेशवेषस्य, *K* 580.
कालप्रदेशव्यापारस्थिति, *ibid.*, 688.

2. Yaśodhara explains *nepathya-yojana* as follows:—
देशकालापेक्षया वस्त्रमाल्याभरणादिभिः शोभार्थं शरीरस्य मण्डनाकारः

3. For some references, cf. *Ācārāṅga-sūtra*, ii. 5.4.1 referred to in J.C. Jain's *Life in Ancient India as Depicted in the Jain Canon*, p. 129; *Mahābhārata*, ii. 47.22 where it is admired for its correct measurement, excellent colour and fine texture; *Arthaśāstra*, ii. 11. 114; *Divy-āvadāna*, p.316; *Abhijñāna-Śākuntala*, i.34; *Kumāra-sambhava*, vii. 3; *Amaru-śataka*, verse 75; *Samaya-mātṛkā*, vii. 48; *Upamiti-bhava-prapañca-kathā*, 220; *Viddha-śāla-bhañjikā*, iii.

The reference to Cīnabhūmi as the source of *cīna-paṭṭa* in the *Arthaśāstra* is sometimes cited as an evidence indicating a late date for the composition of this work. For according to some Sinologists, the name China came to be used to denote the whole country only after the First T'sin or Chin Dynasty (221-209 B.C.) had established its hegemony over the whole of China. To avoid this difficulty, K. P. Jayaswal suggested to identify the Cīnas mentioned in Indian literature with Shina, a Gilgit tribe. Vide his *The Hindu Polity* p. 212, note 1. Following this view, Dr. Motichandra identifies it with the Kafiristan, Kohistan and Darad region where Shina is spoken. See his *Prācīna Bhāratīya Veśa-bhūṣā*, p. 101. But it seems more reasonable to derive the name China from the state of Tsin in the north-west of China which is known to have existed in the Chun Chin period (722-481 B.C.) and in the period of the

quently met with in literature and inscriptions.[1] We find mention of *aṁśuka* also (126, 524, 841) which, on the authority of the *Anuyoga-dvāra-sūtra,* appears to have been a kind of silk.[2] It is equally possible, however, that in our work the word *aṁśuka* is employed to denote cloth in general, and not in the sense of a particular sort of cloth. Garments interwoven with the threads of gold dazzling the eyes (*uccaṇḍa-kanaka-garbhita,* 66) were also in use.

Male Dress

Men wore a variety of garments. The rich wore clothes fashioned from costly textiles like China silk (344) and *paṭikā* (742). Their clothes were sometimes interwoven with threads of gold (66). Coloured garments were very much in favour. We have reference to the son of an influential government officer attired in garments dyed with saffron and worked with golden threads. The poor dressed themselves in old tattered garments,[3] sometimes made by joining many a piece together. Their clothes were made from a rough variety of cotton textiles.[4] Clothes stuffed with cotton were also in vogue, evidently in winter.[5] Such clothes are still in use.

Warring States (481- 221 B.C.) and came into prominence as early as 636 B.C. It is through this state that the western world including India came into contact with China. This Sino-Indian trade through the state of Tsin had probably started in the 6th or 5th century B.C., and the name of the state through which this trade had to be carried on was probably employed for the whole of China sometime about that date. Vide *The Age of Imperial Unity,* p. 644; Manomohan Ghosh, Origin and Antiquity of the Sanskrit Name China as the Name of China, *ABORI,* xlii (1961), pp. 150-54; R.P. Kangle, *The Kauṭilīya Arthaśāstra : A Study,* pp. 74-75.

1. According to the commentator of the *Anuyoga-dvāra-sūtra, paṭṭa* was manufactured from the insects that gathered round the flesh stored for the purpose in the jungle. Vide J.C. Jain, *op. cit.,* p. 129, note 72. The wearing by ladies of a pair of *paṭṭa* clothes is referred to in the Mandasor inscription of a silk-weavers' guild. See *CII,* iii, p. 82, line 12. For some other references, see Motichandra, *Prāchīna Bhāratīya Veṣa-bhūṣā,* pp. 28, 148.

2. J.C. Jain, *op. cit.,* p. 129; Motichandra, *Prācīna Bhāratīya Veṣa-bhūṣā,* p. 148; V.S. Agrawala, *Harṣacarita : Eka Sāṁskṛitika Adhyayana,* p. 76.

3. पटच्चरावरणः, *K* 34; कर्पटकावृतमूर्तिः, *ibid.,* 219. Also cf. *ibid,* 407.

4. स्थूलघनतन्तुसन्ततितानितनानापटच्चरावरणम्, *Ibid.,* 407. This is a variant reading quoted by Tripathi. Kaul's reading नानाम्बरावरणम् also gives the same sense.

5. This is based on the reading adopted by Tripathi, viz., तोनिततूलाम्बरावरणम्.

Brahmacārins wore girdles (*mekhalikā*, 198) which, when broken, were replaced. *Kaṭitra* or waist-band was also an important item of dress (407).

Ascetics put on ochre-coloured garments (*kaṣāya*, 748) and carried a staff (*daṇḍa*, 492, 748).

Men, rich and poor alike, used shoes (*caraṇa-tra*, 64, 408, 742). Shoes were a necessary luxury; but the poor could ill-afford to change them every now and then, and, as such, they continued to use them until they became completely unserviceable (408). The rich, on the other hand, wore luxurious shoes fitted with steel-made soles imported from Central Asia (*Tauruṣkika-khumbhikā*) and with bees-wax placed inside for a soothing touch.[1] They were also fond of using shoes producing noise as the wearer moved.[2]

Dress of Women

The standard female attire consisted of a pair of clothes, upper and lower (*vasana-yugala*, 29; *ambara-yugalaka*, 344). Ordinarily both these garments appear to have been unstitched, the lower one being like the present-day *dhotī* and the upper one being used in the fashion of the *uttarīya* or scarf. This is indicated by references to the *aṁśuka* fluttering and slipping from the body and the partial visibility of the shoulders, bosoms and the navel because of the unstability of the *aṁśuka* (126, 841).

They wore the lower garment by putting a knot (*nivi*) to it (842).

Fashionable ladies loved to wear soft, clean and perfumed clothes (149). They were very fond of Chinese silk (344).

Like men, women were also fond of using coloured clothes. Garments dyed with saffron commanded special favour (346). *Abhisārikās* (ladies going to visit their lovers at night secretly)

1. अन्तर्निविष्टसिक्थकतौरुष्किककुम्भिकादिचरणत्रः,
K 64.

It may also mean that a perfume or incense prepared from *turuṣka* was applied to the shoes, as suggested by Tripathi. But it is more probable that here we have a reference to the use of imported iron soles.

2. शब्दोल्वणचुचुंराङ्कचरणत्रः *ibid.*, 742 (Tripathi);
शब्दोल्बणलुच्चुवाकचरणत्रः, (Kaul).

The popularity of such shoes in Kashmir in the eleventh century A.D. is vouched for by Kṣemendra. Vide *Samaya-mātṛkā*, vi. 34.

are described as attired in black garments (184), evidently in dark nights so that they could not be easily detected by others.

However, elderly women had a preference for clean white clothes (29).

Side by side with unstitched clothes, stitched garments were also in vogue. Our poet mentions two such items of dress, viz. *kañcuka* (523) and *vārabāṇa* (899-900). From our references both these clothes appear to have been very much similar to one another and served the same purpose. The *kañcuka* covered the shoulders, arm-pits, bosoms and the sides which became visible as it was put off.[1] The *vārabāṇa* is said to have been worn on the breasts and put off at the time of sexual intercourse. It intervened between the bosoms and the necklace.[2] It may be noted in this connection that many Sanskrit writers regard these words as synonymous.[3] From literary evidence it appears that both men[4] and women[5] wore the *kañcuka*. In the case of the former it was something like a sleeved long coat covering practically the whole body from the neck to the feet.[6] Among women two kinds of *kañcukas* were in vogue, viz., (i) a kind of long sleeved tunic covering the whole body from the neck to the feet (Pl. XII. 19),[7] and (ii) a

1. कञ्चुकमपकर्षन्त्याः प्रकटीभवदंसकक्षकुचपार्श्वम् ।
साभिनिवेशं दृष्टं भवता किं कुन्दमालायाः ॥
K 523.

2. करपीडनोपमर्दव्यतिकरसमये कदर्थ्यमानोऽपि ।
स्तनमण्डले स्थितोऽहं त्वं पुनराकृष्य कुत्रचित् क्षिप्तः ॥
अधुनाऽन्तरयसि मामिति कोपादिति वारबाणमभिरामम् ।
बहुचित्रपदन्यासैर्वल्गन्त्या हन्ति हार उच्छलितः ॥ *Ibid.*, 899-900.

3. *Amara-kośa*, ii.8.63; Mallinātha on *Raghu-vaṁśa*, iv.55; Śaṅkara on *Harṣa-carita*, iii, p. 148; Śrutadeva on *Yaśastilaka-campū*, ii, p. 51, quoted by Gokulachandra Jain in his *Yaśastilaka kā Sāṁskṛtika Adhyayana*, p. 131 & note 85.

4. *Amara-kośa*, ii. 8. 63; *Bṛhat-saṁhitā*, lvii. 46-48; V.S. Agrawala, *Harṣa-carita : Eka Sāṁskṛtika Adhyayana*, pp. 79-80, 150.

5. *Harṣa-carita*, i, p. 50, iii, p. 148; Gokulachandra Jain, *op. cit.*, p. 131.

6. *Bṛhat-saṁhitā*, lvii. 46-48.; Ajay Mitra Shastri, *India as seen in the Bṛhat-saṁhitā of Varāhamihira*, pp. 140-41, 226.

7. *Harṣa-carita*, i, p. 50, where Sarasvatī's attendant Mālatī is said to have been donned in a *kañcuka* reaching the feet (*āprapadīna kañcuka*). It is represented in paintings at Ajanta. Vide V.S. Agrawala, *Harṣa-carita : Eka Sāṁskṛtika Adhyayana*, Pl. 24, figs. 72-72a.

half-sleeved jacket resembling modern *colī* or *polakā* (Pl. XII. 18).[1] The latter fashion came into vogue in the post-Gupta period and is found represented in the terracotta figures from Ahicchattra datable from *c.* 550 to 750 A.D.[2] Kalhaṇa speaks of ladies dressing their breasts in jackets (*kañcukas*) which covered but half the length of their arms.[3]

So far as men are concerned, the *vārabāṇa* also denoted a full-sleeved coat, but its length was less than that of the *kañcuka.* It came to India probably with the Kuṣāṇas about the beginning of the Christian era and gradually became popular with the royalty. The Kuṣāṇa and the Gupta emperors are shown attired in the *vārabāṇa* on their coins.[4] How far it differed from *kañcuka* in the case of women is difficult to say in the present state of insufficient information. But the fact that Sanskrit commentators take the two words as synonyms and explain them by one another[5] indicates that they denoted the same garment, and that the difference, if any, between them must have been of a very minor character.

As stated above,[6] married women generally used veil (*avaguṇṭhana*) which, like humility, speaking in a low voice and slow gait, was regarded as a sign of chastity and modesty (848) and distinguished them from women of easy virtue (895). Sometimes a knitted piece of cloth was used for this purpose.

We have no means to ascertain if, like men, women also used shoes; probably they did not.

Ornaments

"Decoration precedes dress" is a well-known dictum. This is particularly true of the people of the Orient who are

1. *RT*, vii. 930.
2. *Ancient India*, iv, p. 172, Figs. 246, 307, 308; Agrawala, *Harṣa-carita: Eka Sāṁskṛtika Adhyayana*, Pl. 5, fig. 27.
3. *RT*, vii, 930.
4. It has been suggested that *vārabāṇa* is a sanskritised form of some Pahlavi word. Its various forms are : *barvan* (Pahlavi), *varapanak* (Aramaic), *gurmanaka* (Syriac). *ZDMG*, xci, p. 91; *Transactions of the Philological Society of London*, 1945, p. 154n.; Agrawala, *Harṣacarita* : *Eka Sāṁskṛtika Adhyayana*, p. 80, fn. 1, p. 151.
5. *Śaṅkara on Harṣa-carita*, iii, p. 148; Śrutadeva on *Yaśastilaka-campū*, ii, p. 51; Gokulachandra Jain, *op. cit.*, p. 131.
6. *Supra*, pp. 107-108.

known to have cherished excessive love of ornaments. In our period people of both sexes decked various parts of the body with appropriate ornaments. There is no part of body for which an appropriate ornament was not designed. The rich and poor were alike crazy for adornments and satiated their cravings in accordance with their respective means. Thus while the rich used costly ornaments, people of modest means had to remain contented with adornments fashioned from cheaper materials.

The wearing of proper ornaments on appropriate parts of the body was regarded as an art worth cultivating, particularly for ladies (556). At another place we get a reference to a courtesan putting on decent adornments (*agrāmya maṇḍana*, 149), indicating thereby that wearing indecent or vulgar ornaments was treated as a sign of bad taste. Vātsyāyana, too, mentions the art of wearing ornaments according to the refined taste (*bhūṣaṇa-yojana*) as one of the sixty-four *aṅga-vidyās* connected with erotics.[1]

Materials

A variety of materials was used for fabricating ornaments. Gold ornaments were certainly most popular, and in most of the cases, where the material is specifically mentioned, they are said te have been fashioned from gold. Several words are used for gold, e.g., *cāmīkara* (63), *heman* (295, 626), *jāta-rūpa* (64, 741), *kala-dhauta*[2] (53, 594), *kanaka* (55, 359), *svarṇa* (740). Whether they denote different varieties of gold or are synonyms meaning the species in general is difficult to ascertain. The word *kaladhauta*, however, undoubtedly refers, as indicated by the term itself, to purified gold wherefrom blackish tinge has been removed. Lead (*sīsa*) was also employed for fashioning ornaments. We have a reference to an ear-ornament made out of a sheet of lead (65). No other metal used for making ornaments is mentioned. A variety of necklaces was fashioned from pearls (*muktā*, 606). Ornaments of glass (*kāca*) and conch-shell (*śaṅkha*) were also in vogue,

1. *Kāma-sūtra*, i. 3. 16.

2. Another connotation of the word is silver. Cf. *Amara-kośa*, iii. 3. 76. But in the present context it is undoubtedly employed in the sense of gold.

particularly among people of ordinary means. Mention is made of a necklace formed out of glass beads (66) and bangles made of conch-shell (67). *Kāca-maṇis* or imitations of jewels in glass also appear to have been in use. It is stated that a glass-jewel breaks up when heated in fire (717). This method was probably adopted for testing the genuineness of a jewel and for checking the fraud of the traders who manufactured and circulated such fake jewels. Gold ornaments with precious stones set in them also appear to have been very much in favour,[1] evidently among the rich. Their great popularity is vouched for by the fact that it had become proverbial to speak of a combination of two excellences in terms of the setting of precious stones with gold.[2] Mention is also made of moonstone (*śaśa-dhara-kānta*, 102), but nothing is said about its use in ornaments. Various kinds of flowers and sprouts of trees were also used as ornaments by both men and women.

Ornaments of Men

References to the ornaments worn by men are found in connection with the descriptions of Cintāmaṇi, his betel-box-bearer and prince Samarabhaṭa. The ornaments mentioned in these contexts include a variety of ear-rings, necklaces, armlets, bracelets and finger-rings. It would be noted, however, that as compared to the ornaments of women named by our author, ornaments of the male were simpler and fewer in number.

Ear-Ornaments

Besides the common ear-ring (*kuṇḍala*, 740), mention is made of three other ornaments worn on the ears, viz., *dala-viṭaka*, *sīsa-patra* (65) and *danta-paṅkti* (62). These ornaments are not known to have been referred to in other texts. According to Tripathi, *dala-viṭaka* may denote betel wrapped in a leaf

1. रञ्जयति मनो नितरां कलधौतनिवेशितं रत्नम् ॥
K 594.

2. It is said that natural love by mutual consent and marked by mutual attachment is like the combination of a precious stone and gold :—

उभयेच्छया प्रवृत्तं निरुपाधि प्रेम भवति रमणीयम् ।
अन्योन्यसमासक्तौ संस्थानमिवाभिजातमणिहेम्नोः ॥
Ibid., 626.

and in the present context an adornment resembling it.[1] We are, however, inclined to take it as referring to an ear-ornament with a knob in the centre and leaf-like projections along its edge. It is found represented in sculptures at Khajuraho (Pl.XIII. 20),[2] Markandi (Pl.XIII. 21)[3] and other places. It has come down to our own times and is in popular use in Maharashtra under the name *biri* while in the Chhattisgarh region of Madhya Pradesh it is known as *viri* (Pl.XIII.22), both the names being undoubtedly derived from a word like *vīṭaka*. Dr. Moti Chandra's statement that it was a heart-shaped ornament[4] has nothing to commend itself.

Sīsa-patra, as indicated by the name, was probably fashioned from a sheet of lead. It may be pointed out here that coiled circlets of lead strips, which may have been used as ear-ornaments, have been reported from the excavations at the Sātavāhana site of Bhokardan (Pl.XIII.23) and other places. Although wrought from a cheap material, it appears to have been in favour even with the well-to-do men of fashion; it is said to have been worn by Cintāmaṇi.

Cintāmaṇi is described as wearing *dala-vīṭaka* in one ear and *sīsa-patraka* in the other (65). The popularity of the practice of wearing ornaments of different designs, and probably of different materials, in the two ears in ancient India is vouched for by profuse literary[5] and archaeological[6] evidence (Pl.XIII. 25).

Danta-paṅkti, which was evidently fashioned from ivory,

1. *Dala-vīṭakaṁ pallav-āntaḥ-sthita-tāmbūlam; tat-sadṛśa-bhūṣaṇa-viśeṣo-pi-dala-vīṭakam*, Tripathi's commentary on *K* 65.
Vidya Prakash, *Khajuraho : A Cultural Study*, Pl.IV.3.

2. Urmila Agrawala, *Khajuraho Sculptures and their significance*, Pl, IV.23, Both Vidya Prakash (p.31) and Agrawala (p. 151), however, call it *karṇaphūla*.

3. S.B. Deo, *Mārkaṇḍi Temples*, Pl. XLVI. 1.

4. *Costumes, Textiles, Cosmetics and Coiffure in Ancient and Mediaeval India*, p. 105.

5. The *Vāsudeva-hiṇḍī* mentions the practice of wearing a *kuṇḍala* in the left ear-lobe and *karṇikā* in the right ear. Vide Jamkhedkar, *op. cit.*, p. 320.

6. V. S. Agrawala, Terracotta Figurines of Ahichchhatra, *Ancient India*, No. 4, July 1947-January 1948, nos. 146 (*b*) (*danta-patra* in the left ear and *tāṭaṅka* in the right), 147 (*d*) (leafy ornament in the right ear and disc in the left), 148, p. 101, fig. 8 (*danta-patra* in left and *cakra-kuṇḍala* in right ear), no. 149 (leafy ornament in right and large round *kuṇḍala* in the left ear). For an image of Baladeva wearing ear-rings of different designs, see my *India as seen in the Bṛhat saṁhitā of Varāhamihira*, Fig. 8.

is described as resembling a saw. *Paṅkti* is mentioned as an ornament in the Buddhist work *Mahā-vyutpatti*.

Neck-Ornaments (*Gala-maṇḍana*)

The *kaṇṭha-sūtrikā* of gold was a golden chain worn round the neck (63). It is obviously the same as the *sūtraka* which is referred to in the *Nāṭya-śāstra* (xxi.17, 32) as a neck-ornament of both men and women.

Ṭiṭṭibhaka, which is also styled neck-ornament (*kandharābharaṇa*, 740), was probably a torque or nacklace shaped like the *ṭiṭṭibha* bird.

There is also a vague allusion to neck-ornaments of gold (64).

These ornaments were worn by the rich. The poor, on the other hand, wore adornments made from cheaper materials. The betel-box-bearer (*tāmbūla-karaṅka-vāhin*) of Cintāmaṇi is said to have put on a necklace of large-sized glass beads (*sthūlatara-kāca-vartaka-mālā*, 66).

Armlets

Keyūra was the generic name for the circular ornament worn round the upper arm which consequently came to be known as the "place of *keyūra*" (*keyūra-sthāna*, 741). Samarabhaṭa is said to have worn on the place of *keyūra* an amulet of lac sanctified with a charm (*mantra*) and covered with gold.[1]

Wristlets

The wrist was also called *kaṭaka* (241) after the ring (*kaṭaka*) worn round it.[2] Another word used to denote the same limb was *maṇi-bandhana* (741) which also brings in relief the popularity of jewelled wristlets. Samarabhaṭa is represented as wearing on his wrists a string of golden beads of dazzling brilliance.[3] Fashionable men of modest means wore conch-shell bangles (*śaṅkha-cakra*).[4]

1. केयूरस्थानगतस्वर्णावृतमन्त्रगर्भजतुगुडकः । *K* 741.
Kaul's reading is as follows :
केयूरस्थानगतसुवर्णभृतमंत्रगर्भजतुगुडकः ।
Moti Chandra's description of it as amulets filled with leaf' (*Costumes, Textiles*, etc., p. 105) is not supported by the text.
2. The Hindi word *kaṛā* is its modern descendant.
3. मणिबन्धनविन्यस्तप्रचलाङ्कुरजातरूपमणिमालः ।। *K.*, 741.
4. करमूलनिबद्धशङ्खचक्रेण । *Ibid.*, 67. It evidently means the circular (or wheel-like) ornament (*cakra*) of conchshell (*śaṅkha*) worn on the wrist

Finger-Ornaments

The only finger-ornament of men mentioned by our poet is *mudrikā*,[1] obviously identical with *aṅguli-mudrā*, which, according to the *Amara-kośa* (ii.6.108), was an inscribed finger-ring. Literature[2] and archaeology[3] furnish sufficient evidence to vouch for the popularity of inscribed finger-rings, particularly those bearing the name of the wearer.

Ornaments of Females

Women's ornaments naturally evinced a much greater variety than those used by men. The number of ornaments worn by them also was much larger. Although men had also a craze for ornaments, women were much more crazy. It was a *sine qua non* of their personal embellishment and they took particular care to put on ornaments while going out to meet their lovers in private (594).

Necklaces

The largest number of references that we come across appertain neck-ornaments (*kaṇṭha-bhūṣaṇa*, 469). Like other Sanskrit poets, Dāmodaragupta takes great delight in describing the necklace (*hāra*,[4] *hāralatā*[5] as enjoying the company of the heavy bosoms.[6] These necklaces usually consisted of one or more strands of pearls (*muktā-hāra*, 606). At one place a necklace is described as pierced from inside (*antarbhinna*, 297), which obviously refers to the boring of pearls for stringing them together. Another stanza mentions the combination of the *tarala* with a pearl-necklace.[7] Kauṭilya mentions *tarala-pratibaddha* as one

(*kara-mūla-nibaddha*)'. Tripathi, however, thinks that it refers to the wearing of conchshell, wheel, etc., for warding off evil eye:—

शङ्खचक्रादि च हीनदृष्ट्याद्यवरोधाय धार्यंते ।

1. करशाखार्पितमुद्रिक, *K* 63.

2. According to the *Rāmāyaṇa* (v. 36. 2), Hanumān showed to Sītā a finger-ring inscribed with Rāma's name in order to convince her of his reliability. Duṣyanta's finger-ring bearing his name plays an important role in Kālidāsa's *Abhijñāna-Śākuntala*. The *Vasudeva-hiṇḍī* also refers to such finger-rings. Vide Jamkhedkar, *op. cit.*, p. 323.

3. Marshall, *Taxila*, ii, pp. 448-449, specimen nos. 14, 15, 56.

4. *K* 102, 103, 610.

5. *Ibid.*, 190.

6. *Ibid.*, 136, 899-900, 983, 987. Cf. *Nāṭya-śāstra*, xxi.19, 34, which style necklaces *vakṣo-vibhūṣaṇa*, i.e., ornaments of breasts.

7. हारलतास्तरलसङ्गता, *K* 190.

of the varieties of pearl-strings.[1] According to the *Amara-kośa* (ii.6.102), the word *tarala* denotes the central gem of a necklace (*taralo hāra-madhyagaḥ*). It would thus follow that *tarala-hāra* was a kind of pearl-necklace the central gem of which was of a larger size, and perhaps of a different material, than other pearls which were probably of a uniform size.

There is also a reference to the wearing of a thread round the neck (*gala-sūtra*) to which were tied various medicinal herbs and precious stones.[2] It was particularly worn by elderly ladies and was obviously a sort of amulet the kind of which is still in vogue.

Ear-Ornaments

Of the various kinds of ear-ornaments that were in use in those days only one, viz., *kanaka-tāḍī*, is referred to.[3] This was evidently an adaptation in gold of an ornament consisting of a strip of rolled palm leaf which, there is evidence to show, was quite popular with women of modest means in the Deccan.[4] It is even now worn by lower class people in South India. Its golden counterpart is mentioned as *kāñcana-tāla-patra*,[5] *kanaka-patra*,[6] *hema-tālī-puṭa*[7] and *hema-tālī-paṭṭa*[8] in some other texts indicating the high degree of popularity enjoyed by this ornament over a long period of time. Probably this very ornament is referred to under the name *tāḍī-yuga* (a pair of *tāḍīs*) by the Kashmiri poet Kṣemendra,[9] showing thereby that it continued to enjoy popularity in Kashmir in the eleventh century A.D.

1. *Artha-śāstra*, ii.11.6. R.P. Kangle's explanation of *tarala-prati-baddha*, based on the Malayalam gloss known as Bhāsa-vyākhyānam or Bhāsa-Kauṭilīyam, viz., a string of uniform-sized pearls throughout, does not appear to be correct. Vide his *The Kauṭilīya Arthaśāstra*, ii, p. 112, fn. 6.

2. विविधौषधिमणिसनाथगलसूत्राम् । *K* 29.

3. The reading *kanaka-nāḍī*, found in some manuscripts and adopted by Pandit Madhusudan Kaul, is undoubtedly a mistake.

4. *Gāthā-sapta-śatī*, iv. 98; C. Sivaramamurti, *Amaravati Sculptures in the Madras Government Museum*, p. 109.

5. *Pāda-tāḍitaka* (*Caturbhāṇī*), p. 237, verse 113.

6. *Caura-pañcāśikā*, verse 79.

7. V. S. Agrawala, *Kādambarī : Eka Sāṁskṛtika Adhyayana*, 95/112.

8. *Ibid.*, 191/186.

9. *Samaya-mātṛkā*, ii.70.

In art we find it depicted in two different forms, one shaped on the model of a rolled palm leaf[1] and the other cylindrical.[2]

Armlets

Besides the common golden armlet (*kanak-āṅgada*, 50), mention is made of a special kind of ornament called *valaya-kalāpī* which was worn on the upper arm (343). It is undoubtedly the same as *kalāpī* or *śaṅkha-kalāpī* of Bharata's *Nāṭya-śāstra* (xxi.35) and *mayūra-keyūra* of Aśvaghoṣa's *Saundara-Nanda* (x.8) and, as suggested by the word, was modelled on the pattern of a peacock-head. We find some beautiful illustrations of this ornament in the Kuṣāṇa art. Thus a terracotta figurine of Viṣṇu from Ahichchhatrā assignable to the end of the Kuṣāṇa period (*c.* 300 A.D.) shows on the upper arms armlets shaped like a framed peacock-head (Pl. XIII. 27).[3] Similar armlets are to be noticed on a Bodhisattva figure of the Kuṣāṇa age from Mathurā.[4] If we accept the reading *śaṅkha-kalāpī* in the aforesaid passage of the *Nāṭya-śāstra*, it would follow that this ornament was fashioned from ivory.

Bracelets

The ornament worn on the wrist was commonly known as *valaya* (101, 127, 443) and *kaṭaka* (295, 987). It was fashioned from gold (*hema-kaṭaka*, 295). The number of bracelets to be worn on a wrist was not fixed. A number of *valayas* (*valay-āvali*) was sometimes put on on each wrist as would follow from reference to the noise (127, 443) produced by bracelets if the wearer happened to move suddenly. In art we often find women represented as wearing numerous bangles on each hand (Pl. XI. 17).[5]

1. C. Sivaramamurti, *Amaravati Sculptures in the Madras Government Museum*, p. 109, Pls VIII.1; XVIII.1.

2. *Ancient India*, No. 4, Pl.L.157, 158.
This ornament is still in use and is known as *taraunā* in Hindi.

3. V.S. Agrawala, Terracota Figurines of Ahichchhatra, *Ancient India*, No. 4, July 1947-January 1948, p.127, no. 90, p. 101, fig. 3, Pl.XXXVII. 90.

4. J. Ph. Vogel, *Catalogue of Archaeological Museum at Mathura*, p. 58, No. A.45, Pl. X.

5. Sivaramamurti, *Amaravati Sculptures in the Madras Government Museum*, Pl. VIII. 7, 14; R. C. Kak, *Handbook of the Archaeological and Numismatic Sections of the Sri Pratap Singh Museum, Srinagar*, p. 26, Nos. Bc 64.

At one place we read of the thinning down of the arm of Hāralatā because of separation from her lover so as to allow the *hema-kaṭaka* to slip out of the wrist and fall on the ground.[1] The motif of the thinning of the separated lover's arms and the falling of bracelets is very common in ancient Indian literature. The *Megha-dūta* (i.2) describes how the golden bracelet (*kanaka-valaya*) slipped from the wrist of the Yakṣa after he had spent some months in separation from his beloved. The same idea is repeated in the *Abhijñāna-Śākuntala* (iii.10) where Duṣyanta complains that because of the emaciation caused by the pangs of separation from his beloved his golden bracelet slips again and again from his wrist. Amaruka describes how at the very idea of separation from the lover bracelets of a woman slipped down from her wrist.[2]

Finger-Ornaments

A small ring (*bālikā*), fashioned from gold, is said to have been worn on the root of the finger (Pl. XIII. 28).[3]

Girdles

Elaborate girdles, referred to as *raśanā* (987) and *raśanā-guṇa* (296) were worn on the hips. According to the *Nāṭya-śāstra* (xxi. 38), *raśanā* means a girdle comprising sixteen strands. Whether in our text the word has this technical sense or is used to denote a girdle of any sort cannot be ascertained. The latter, however, appears more likely.

Anklets

There is a reference to the tinkling sound produced by anklets (*nūpuras*) as a lady wearing them moved playfully (902). We have some beautiful sculptural representations of ladies in the act of tying anklets with tinkling bells to their feet (Pls. (XIV. 29, XV. 30.)

Candra

Courtesans are described as adorned with *candra* (5). According to Sanskrit lexicographers, the word *candra* denotes,

1. प्रशिथिलभुजलतिकायास्तस्याः पतितस्य हेमकटकस्य ।
यत् प्रापणं पृथिव्यास्तस्मिन् खलु मुक्तहस्तता हेतुः ॥
K 295.

2. *Amaruka-śataka* (edited by C. R. Devadhar, *ABORI*, xxxix-xl), verse 35. For the same motif, also see *Padma-prābhṛtaka*, vv. 28, 40.

3. तन्वीमङ्गुलिमूले तपनीयमयीं च बालिकां दधतीम् । *K* 29.

among other things, gold.[1] It is possible that our author meant to say that prostitutes were decorated with gold i.e., golden ornaments. However, it is more likely that here we have a reference to some adornment shaped like the crescent moon, for we have numerous references to and artistic representations of such ornaments. Śūdraka in his *Padma-prābhṛtaka* (verse 36) refers to *śaśi* as adorning the edges of breasts.[2] Bāṇa mentions a forehead-ornament called *candra-lekhikā* which was fashioned from gold and set with pearls.[3] The *Vasudeva-hiṇḍī* speaks of the use of replicas of the sun and moon in necklaces (*caṁda-sūra-mālā*).[4] Syāmilaka in his *Pāda-tāḍitaka* describes crescentic ear-ring reflection whereof fell on the cheeks and shoulders of the wearer.[5] Such ear-ornaments are illustrated in art.[6] For want of necessary data it is difficult to ascertain as to which of these ornaments our author had in his mind.

IX. HAIR STYLES

Let us now turn our attention to various modes of hair-dressing prevalent among the fashionable people of those days. People of both sexes devoted considerable thought to arranging and decorating their hair in a variety of attractive ways.

Hair-Styles of the Male

The fashionable aristocrats kept rather long hair which were tied with multi-coloured shining ribbons.[7] Some kept a long thick tuft of hair measuring five digits.[8] Others arranged their hair with a long piece of cloth tied on three-fourths of the head, leaving one-fourth portion bare, and applied a thick layer of saffron paste to the hair close to the ears.[9] The fashion-

1. *Amara-kośa*, iii.3.182.
2. *Caturbhāṇī*, p. 51. According to Motichandra and V.S. Agrawala, it refers to a crescent-shaped bead in a necklace called *candra-lekhā*.
3. V.S. Agrawala, *Kādambarī : Eka Sāṁskṛtika Adhyayana*, p. 186.
4. Jamkhedkar, *op. cit.*, p. 327.
5. *Caturbhāṇī*, p. 239.
6. *Ibid.*, p. 239, fn. 114(6).
7. नानावर्णविवेष्टितबहलदशापाशबद्धततकेशः ।
   K 65.
8. स्थूलस्थापितचूडः पञ्चाङ्गुलमात्रकेशविन्यासः ।
   Ibid., 62.
9. मूर्धत्रिभागसंस्थितबृहदम्बरचीरकेशसंयमनः ।
   ·····घनकुङ्कुमलिप्तकर्णकेशाग्रः ॥
   Ibid, 739.

conscious men in rural areas, however, did not arrange their hair in a tasteful manner but just managed to decorate them with garlands of flowers (866).

Hair-Styles of the Female

Women bestowed much more thought to hair-dressing; for their beauty depends, in a large measure, on the manner in which they arrange their hair. Consequently a variety of hair-styles came into vogue. Ladies did not normally appear before their lovers with undressed hair (163). Flowers were used to decorate the hair, and it is said that the bee, even though feeling the heat of her sighs caused by the separation from her lover, does not leave the flower of her hair (293).

Of the numerous kinds of hair-styles prevalent during the period three are mentioned by Dāmodaragupta, viz., (1) *veṇī*, (2) *dhammilla*, and (3) *alaka* or *alak-āvali*. *Veṇī* was a twisted braid of hair. At one place it is described as long (964). It became unstable and dangled with the movement of the person (469). It was often decked with bunches (*niryūha*) of flowers (901).[1] This mode of dressing the hair has been in vogue from very early times (Pl. XVI. 32) and is popular even today.

Dhammilla was a form of coiffure in which the hair were tied into a big single knot over the head.[2] It was adorned with a garland of flowers (*śekhara*, 901). It figures in South Indian literature[3] and art[4] from the early centuries of the Christian era, but in North India it makes its appearance for the first time in the Gupta period, one of its earliest representations being found in cave no. 17 at Ajanta (Pl.XVI.33).[5] Its popularity in Kashmir in later times is evidenced by a reference in Bilhaṇa's *Caura-pañcā-śikā* (79).[6] In view of its rather late appearance in the North as

1. For some other references to *veṇī*, see V.S. Apte, *The Students' Sanskrit-English* Dictionary, s.v. *veṇi, -ṇī*. In literature, *veṇi* is often associated with women whose husbands have gone away. We notice no such association in our work.

2. Cf. *Amara-Kośa*, ii.6.97.

3. *Gāthā-sapta-śatī*, iii.91; vi.44.

4. C. Sivaramamurti, *Amaravati Sculptures in the Madras Government Museum*, p. 107, Pl. viii, fig. 23; *Sanskrit literature and Art—Art Mirrors of Indian Culture, MASI*, No. 73, pp. 31-32.

5. Panta Pratinidhi, *Ajiṇṭhā*, Pl. 69; V.S. Agrawala, *Harṣa-carita : Eka Sāṁskṛtika Adhyayana*, Pl. XIV, fig. 53. Vide also *Ancient India*, No. 4, Pl. XLV.

6. For some other references to *dhammilla*, see *Amaruka-śataka*, 96; *Śṛ ṅgāra-śataka* (of Bhartṛhari), 49; *Gīta-govinda*, 2.

compared to the South and on linguistic grounds V.S. Agrawala suggests to derive the word *dhammilla* from the ancient name of the Tamil country, viz., Sanskrit Dramiḍa or Draviḍa, Ceylonese Damila, Greek Damirica.[1] The problem deserves further investigation.

Alak-āvali, as suggested by the word, consisted of the arrangement of the hair in rows of spiral locks on the forehead. At one place we read of the dark black ringlets of curly hair falling on the forehead giving her appearance of the shadow of the face of Rāhu projected in the crescent moon.[2] This mode of hair-dressing is beautifully illustrated by some paintings at Ajanta (Pl. XVI. 34) and terracotta figurines from Ahichchhatrā.[3] Particularly noteworthy in this connection is the artistically superb head of Pārvatī found in the Śiva temple, dating between *c.* A.D. 450 and 650, wherein the *alak-āvali* and *dhammilla* styles are combined. (Pl. IV. 5)[4] This feature is also noticed in a beautiful sculpture of Gaṅgā dating from Vākāṭaka period at Paunar in the Wardha District of Maharashtra (Pl. XVI. 35).

X. TOILETTE

We get some interesting information about toilette too. Beauty aids appear to have been more commonly used in those days than at present. Both men and women made an extensive use of cosmetics and perfumes to enhance their bodily charm. A note of warning must, however, be struck at the very outset. It was only the fashionable people who were very much addicted to the use of beauty aids, while others contented themselves only with absolutely necessary articles of toilette, for we do not find any reference to toilette articles in connection with the description of the Brāhmaṇa youth Sundarasena and his father Purandara. Further, toilette varied according to one's resources and

1. V.S. Agrawala, *Harṣa-carita : Eka Sāṁskṛtika Adhyayana*, p. 96.
2. शशधरबिम्बार्धगतां छायामिव सैंहिकेयवदनस्य ।
अलिपटलनीलकुटिलामलकावलिमलिकसन्निधौ वहति ॥
K 110.

Vide also verse 293 which speaks of the decoration of the ringlets of hair with flowers.

3. V.S. Agrawala, Terracotta Figurines from Ahichchhatrā, *Ancient India*, No. 4, figurine nos. 170, 267, 274, 275. Males also adopted this hair-style, Vide *ibid.*, p. 138.
4. *Ibid.*, Pl. XLV.

taste. In fact, toilette was an indication of the degree of one's refinement and culture. Many of the beauty aids, it will be noticed, were common to both sexes.

Flowers

Large-scale use of leaves and flowers was a typical feature of ancient Indian toilette. As stated above,[1] flowers were profusely employed for decorating the hair. Flower-garlands[2] were worn by both men (64, 84) and women (968). Belles were very fond of wearing floral ear-ornaments called *avataṁsaka* and *śruti-pūraka*. We meet with references to the *avataṁsakas* of fresh *aśoka* leaves (671, 676), *kiṅkirāta* (676), lotus (991) and *sinduvāra* (677) flowers and shoots of mango tree (677). Lotus flowers were also worn on the ears, and the poet speaks of ear-lotuses (112) and flowers put on as *śruti-pūraka*[3] (294) as being haunted by bees. At another place we are told that the lotus-like eyes of a beautiful damsel can be distinguished from the blue lotus flower worn on the ears only because the latter has filament shining like gold (981). Mention is also made of bracelets fashioned from lotus stalk (*mṛṇāla-valaya*, 101). These floral ornaments were particularly worn on the occasion of garden-sports in spring and summer. Men took great delight in picking up fresh flowers, leaves and shoots and putting them on the appropriate limbs of their lady-loves (671, 676-77) which made women mad with joy and kindled love in their hearts.

Beds made out of leaves (100), particularly fresh sandal leaves (992), were used in summer and during the period of mental anxiety[4] with the object of alleviating heat.

As we have seen above, ladies sent flowers together with betel to their lovers by way of present. Similarly, like betel, flowers were offered to a respectable guest (757) and a flower-garland was presented to convey a feeling of high appreciation of a dancing performance (84).

Tāmbūla (Betel)

Betel (*tāmbūla*) was another item of make up common to both sexes (522, 740). As suggested by the word *vīṭikā*[5]

1. *Supra*, p. 147.
2. *Kusuma-dāma*, *K* 64; *sumano-mālā*, 84; *sraj*, 968.
3. The same as the present *karanphūl*.
4. In the present case. anxiety to meet the lover.
5. Hindi *bīḍā*, Marathi *vīḍā* are derived from *viṭaka*. Also cf. *tāmbūla-paṭalaka*, *K* 990.

(759), *tāmbūla* was prepared by rolling the leaf as at present. We have no information about the ingredients used in preparing it, but the reference to the colour produced by chewing it (999) alludes to the use of catechu.

Some people used such a large quantity of betels at a time that it led to an apparent swelling of their cheeks (70). Princes (759) and aristocrats (67) had their own betel-box-bearers (*tāmbūla-karaṅka-bhṛt, tāmbūla-karaṅka-vāhin*), and it was an art to receive betel from them. Prince Samarabhaṭa is said to have taken betel with his left hand in the *khaṭakā-mukha* pose from the betel-box-bearer's hand which was in the *sandaṁśa* attitude (759).[1] In this context it will be of interest to refer to an episode of king Jayāpīḍa's life reported by Kalhaṇa. The king, we are told, reached Puṇḍravardhana in the Gauḍa country and there went to the temple of Kārttikeya to view the dancing and singing performed in accordance with Bharata's precepts. The performance over, he quickly came out and seated himself on a stone at the gate of the temple. As the people overawed by his exceptional dignity withdrew from his side, a dancer named Kamalā noticed him. She was astonished to see that his hand reached, from time to time, quickly to the back of his shoulder. It then occurred to her that he must be a disguised king or *rāja-putra* born of a great family and that he must be accustomed to take thus rolled betel-leaves from attendants standing at his back, and therefore his hand moved at every moment to the back of his shoulder. After returning home she sent an intimate friend close up to him. When his hand moved again as before, she put betel-nuts into it. These the king put into his mouth, and then turning round he noticed the girl.[2] It would thus appear that in the time of Dāmodaragupta's patron, Jayāpīḍa, the betel-box-bearer probably stood behind his master. In view of this it is possible, though by no means certain, that our poet has deliberately employed the root *anu-gam-to follow, to come behind*, in the description of the betel-box-bearer of Cintāmaṇi (67). The lovers were thrilled at the idea of transmitting betel from mouth to mouth[3] (549). Betel-chewing was particularly favoured by the fashionable

1. For these attitudes, see *infra*, pp. 219-20.
2. *RT*, iv. 421-431.
3. Cf. *Kāma-sūtra*, v.2.7.

as it imparted a pleasing colour to the tongue (999). Offering betel-rolls was regarded as a mode of expressing love. And as such if a man offered betel to a woman it could be construed as a proposal for love in disguise (522). When a woman deputed a message-girl with an errand, particularly a proposal of love, to a prospective lover she never forgot to send to him a .betel and flowers (90, 990). Betel-rolls were also offered while receiving a distinguished guest (757). The presentation of betels together with flower-garlands was also indicative of an appreciative feeling. Thus when spectators were pleased with a dancing girl's performance, they gave vent to their approbation by offering betel and garlands (84).

Unguents

Both men and women anointed their person with various kinds of coloured and perfumed pastes (*paṅka*, 101, 102; *gātra-rāga*, 739; *vilepana*, 758) prepared from a variety of aromatic articles such as saffron (63, 739), sandal wood, camphor (102) and andropogon (866). Men of taste were modest in their use of unguents (63, 739), while rustic men of fashion literally covered their body with a thick mass of paste (866). Again, while cultured men of resources evinced a preference for saffron paste (63, 739), less cultured people painted their person with multi-coloured pastes (758) made from comparatively cheaper ingredients like andropogon (866).

Male Toilette

We may now pass on to such items of make up as are referred to particularly in connection with males. They pained their nails with *vṛścika*[1] (67), applied antimony to their eyes with a rod specially meant for the purpose (*śalāk-āñjana*, 426) with a view to improve eye-sight,[2] and perfumed their

1. According to Tripathi, *vṛścika* here denotes *kurabaka* or *raktapunarnavā* leaves and flowers whereof are red. Is it possible to take it in the sense of *mehadī* ?

2. Cf. अज्ञानतिमिरान्धस्य ज्ञानाञ्जनशलाकया ।
चक्षुरुन्मीलितं येन तस्मै श्रीगुरवे नमः ॥
Guru-gītā, verse 47.

Also cf. *Harṣa-carita*, iii :
एकशलाकाञ्जनजनितलोचनरुचिः ।

clothes with various kinds of fragrant powders called *paṭa-vāsa*. *Paṭa-vāsas* were presented to honourable guests while receiving them (757). They were very popular in ancient India, and a formula for preparing one such powder is given in Varāhamihira's *Bṛhat-saṁhitā*.[1] Some fashionable persons also applied a *tilaka* mark on their forehead which was rendered uneven by the use of white mustard seeds (740). Some people, particularly those in high position, also carried a cane-stick (*vetra-daṇḍa*) which was held at the top (742).

Female Toilette

Women used lac-die (*alaktaka*) for reddening their feet (7) and lips (113).[2] The poet while describing Vārāṇasī fancies that the earth there assumes the appearance of a park of *sthala-kamalas* as it is rendered reddish by the liquid of the lac-die applied to the soles of the feet of belles constantly moving to and fro (7). This reminds one of sculptural representations of ladies applying lac-die to the soles of their feet (Pl. XVII. 36). Even if a woman's lips were naturally red, *alaktaka* was applied just for completing the make up. The practice of applying bees'wax to lips (310) was also common. It helped brighten the effect of *alaktaka* and cured the splitting of lips in winter. Rājaśekhara informs us that bees' wax was applied to lips only in the cold weather, its use being given up at the approach of the spring.[3] Collyrium (*kajjala*), too, was an important item of a woman's make up. The poet imagines that the drops of sweat, naturally white because of residing on the body of a fair damsel but mixed with collyrium-tinted tears, when falling on the edges of her bosoms bear resemblance to the confluence of the waters of the Gaṅgā and Yamunā at Prayāga.[4] Fashionable ladies perfumed their garments by fumigation (149). They also scented their mouths by various

1. Ajay Mitra Shastri, *op.cit.*, pp. 243-44.
2. Cf. verse 308 which also refers to the reddishness of lips. The custom of applying *alaktaka* to lips is referred to in other works also, e.g., *Kirāt-Ārjunīya*, viii.40; *Naiṣadhīya-carita*, xv.43.
3. *Karpūra-mañjarī*, i. 13.
4. वाससितं स्वेदजलं कज्जलमलिनाश्रुवारिणा मिश्रम् ।
कुचतटपतितं तस्याः प्रयागसम्भेदसलिलमनुकुरुते ॥

K 298.

For a sculptural representation of a lady applying collyrium t her eyes, see Pl. XVII. 37.

devices (*vadana-vāsa*, 164) one of which was to smoke an incense-wick (*dhūpa-varti*, 149). Formulae for preparing a variety of mouth-perfumes (*mukha-vāsakas*) are found in the *Bṛhat-saṁhitā*,[1] the *Agni-purāṇa*[2] and other works.[3] Padmaśrījñāna gives prescriptions for some kinds of *dhūpa-vartis* also.[4] Women decorated their face with a variety of designs called *tilaka* (251, 597, 764), *viśeṣaka*[5] (343) and *tamāla-patra* (16).[6] The popularity of leaf designs, suggested by the last-mentioned word, over a long period of time is vouched for by numerous references scattered in literature.[7] It is worth while to note in this connection that *viśeṣaka-cchedya* or making designs by cutting leaves is included in the catalogue of the sixty-four erotic arts.[8] The *patra-ccheda* mentioned by our author (74, 124, 236) has the same import. Young ladies were very particular about the *tilaka* designs and usually they did not appear without them in the presence of their lovers (257, 597). The reference to the washing away of the *tilaka* decoration of the widowed women of the enemy (764) probably indicates that the *tilaka* mark on the forehead had by now come to be regarded as an essential item of the toilette of the ladies whose husbands were alive,[9] though *tilaka* was sometimes applied purely for decorative purposes (597) without any symbolic value being attached to it.

Belles pining for union with their lovers are said to have used a bed of leaves, floral ornaments, sandal paste, plantain staff, lotus flowers, fibres of the lotus-stalk, water, pearl-necklaces, camphor and moonstone in order to allay the heat generated by sexual appetite (100-103, 1020-1021). Such descrip-

1. Ajay Mitra Shastri, *op. cit.*, p. 241.
2. Ch. ccxxiv. vv. 34-38.
3. E.g., *Śārṅgadhara-paddhati*, verse 3250; *Nāgara-sarvasva*, iv. 7-9.
4. *Ibid.*, iv. 16-17.
5. Inferred from a personal name.
6. Cf. *Amara-kośa*, ii.6.123, which regards these words as synonyms.
7. *Saundara-Nanda*, iv. 20; *Pāda-tāḍitaka*, verse 105, etc.
8. *Kāma-sūtra*, i. 3. 16.
9. Although a red *tilaka* mark is to be seen on the forehead of some female figures in some wall paintings of Caves I and II at Ajanta, it is not very common even in the later group of frescoes. The available literary evidence points to the conclusion that the *tilaka* mark, which was originally only decorative in character, became an absolute necessity for married women by *circa* 8th century A.D. *Vide* P.V. Kane, 'The Tilaka', *JBBRAS*, NS, xxi (1945), pp. 33-37; G.S. Gai, 'A note on the Tilaka Mark and Kaṅkaṇī, *BDCRI*, xx, p. 301. It would, thus, appear that ours is one of the earliest references to this practice.

tions are to be met with so very frequently in classical Sanskrit and Prakrit literature that they appear to have become something like a *kavi-samaya* or poetic convention, and consequently a student of social history cannot take them seriously. These conventional descriptions seem to have been resorted to with the object of heightening the effect.

XI. SPORTS AND PASTIMES

The monotony of daily life was relieved by a variety of diversions which included a number of indoor and outdoor games and other recreations. We get information about many a pastime which is outlined below.

The Game of Ball

Ball-playing (*kanduka-krīḍā*) commanded great popularity, especially among girls who liked the game so much that they went on playing till they were completely exhausted and their palms became red and swollen (362). The high favour that the game enjoyed with girls is vouched for by innumerable references in other works. Thus, the *Pāda-tāḍitaka* of Śyāmilaka describes it as one of the four games particularly meant for girls (*duhitṛ-krīḍanaka*),[1] while the *Padma-prābhṛtaka* of Śūdraka affords a picturesque description of the game.[2] Daṇḍin refers to the festival of ball-play (*kanduk-otsava*) at Dāmalipta (=Tāmralipti, modern Tamluk in the Midnapur district of West Bengal) wherein the daughter of the king of the Suhma country performed ball-dance (*kanduka-nṛtya*) before the goddess Vindhya-vāsinī with the object of securing a suitable husband and played with a ball in public. He has poured all his poetic talent in the description of the play,[3] which is also represented in sculpture (Pl. XVIII. 38, 39).

The Game of Dice

Dice-playing has been widely prevalent in India from the

1. *Caturbhāṇī*, p. 210.
2. *Ibid.*, pp. 42-43, vv. 30, 31.
3. *Daśa-kumāra-carita*, Uttara-pīṭhikā, ucchvāsa vi, pp. 205-211. Elsewhere (ucchvāsa iv, p. 170), Daṇḍin refers to Kāntimatī, daughter of Caṇḍasiṁha, king of Kāśī, playing with ball with her companions for pleasing the god Śiva.

earliest known proto-historic times. The popularity of this game in ancient Kashmir is evidenced by Kalhaṇa's chronicle[1] and the *Nīla-mata-purāṇa*, the latter especially recommending it for the 15th of the dark half of the month of Kārttika[2] Our author mentions the game twice. At one place he states that in the game of dice the players try to intrude into the compartments assigned to others.[3] The game was evidently similar to the present-day *caupaṛa*. Another stanza informs us that the game was played with five dices.[4] Women also played the game, specially on the festival in honour of the god of love (895). There is also an allusion to the evil consequences of gambling (997). In this context one is reminded of a popular theme in early mediaeval Indian art wherein Śiva and Pārvatī are shown playing *causara* (Pl. III. 4)

Hunting

Hunting (*ākheṭaka*, 80, 950, 958; *ācchoṭana*, 949; *mṛgayā*, 951, 959) was an important outdoor game. Dāmodaragupta gives us a vivid description of the joys, pleasures and advantages derived from it. It was regarded as a hereditary art (*kula-vidyā*) of the princes (949). Due to the evil consequences of excessive attachment to it and the risk involved, elderly people did not like their wards indulging in hunting too much (80). Hunting, we are told, imparts skill in piercing an unstable target and sitting steady on a fast-galloping horse and the knowledge of the different divisions of the earth.[5] The animals chased included the deer, boar and hare (954-957).[6] The pleasure-hunter was assisted by professional hunters (954).[7] Music was played in order to attract and divert the attention of the deer so that it could be easily caught alive (955). A hunter hiding himself beneath a tree derived immense pleasure

1. *RT*, vii. 1003; viii. 1740.
2. Verse 403.
3. परगृहरोधस्तथाऽक्षेषु । *K* 11.
4. पञ्चाक्षद्यूतगति, *Ibid.*, 997.
5. चललक्ष्यवेधकौशलमश्वप्रजवे स्थिरासनाभ्यसनम् ।
भूमिविभागज्ञानं भवन्ति मृगयाभियोगेन ॥ *Ibid.*, 951.
6. It appears from *RT*, vi. 181, 183, 184; vii. 171; viii. 699, that jackal hunt was also very popular in Kashmir.
7. According to Kalhaṇa (*ibid.*, vi. 182), these were Ḍombas and junglefolks.

in felling a leaping deer brought close up to him by professional hunters by resorting to deceptive tricks (954). In the boar hunt the forest was put aflame in order to compel the animal to come out of its hiding in the dense forest (956).[1] Of the weapons employed in hunting mention is made of bow alone (953). Hunting dogs (*viśva-kadru,* 953) were also used to frighten animals.[1a] A caparisoned fast-moving horse with foot-rests (*pāda-kaṭaka*) was used as the most convenient mount (951, 952). Hunting the deer was a feat of hunting skill and archery and could be achieved only by those who had a good experience of shooting (710). Winning an unsteady target was the greatest thrill of chasing (80).

It may be mentioned in this connection that a number of hunting scenes are found represented on some tiles discovered in archaeological excavations at Harwan a little distance from Srinagar. Thus one tile shows an armoured horseman riding a fully accoutred horse at full gallop and drawing his bow (Pl. IV. 6).[2] Another panel bears a huntsman with bow and arrow riding at full gallop and chasing a stag (Pl. V. 7-8).[3] Yet another tile displays a mounted hunter aiming an arrow at a fleeing deer (Pl. VI. 11).[4]

Fishing also appears to have been a favourite pastime. Dāmodaragupta tells us how nets smeared with flesh were employed for this purpose (734). The popularity of fishing in ancient Kashmir is vouched for by Kalhaṇa.[5]

Ram-Fight

Animal fights were another popular means of diversion. Of these, mention is made only of ram-fight (361). There was keen rivalry among the participants who made advance preparations for the contest and gave a special diet to their respective rams. Hetairai took keen interest in these animal fights. It is interesting to note in this connection that Vātsyāyana mentions the use of quail-fight, cock-fight and ram-fight, the talk of parrots and mainas and dramatic performances as

1. For a sculptural representation at Koṇārka, see Pl. V.9.
1a. Cf. *RT*. vi. 182.
2. R.C. Kak, *Ancient Monuments of Kashmir,* pl. xxiii.3.
3. *Ibid.,* pl.xxix.19-20.
4. *Ibid.,* pl.xxviii.14.
5. *RT,* vii. 170.

pretexts to bring a client to the residence of a courtesan or *vice versa*.[6]

It would be of interest to note here that some scenes of animal fights are found sculptured on a few tiles from Harwan assignable to the early centuries of the Christian era. These include cock-fight[1] and ram-fight.[2]

Taming Animals and Birds

The taming of animals and birds was another source of recreation. Of the animals and birds tamed for this purpose we have references to the mongoose (360), parrot (356) and *śārikā* (913, 914). The mongoose was given milk and if the attendant in charge of it failed to perform this duty properly it was a source of unhappiness to the tamer. The young ones of parrots were trained in imitation language while the *sārikā* was regarded as an intelligent bird. In plastic art we often come across depictions of ladies playing with birds (Pl. XX. 41, 42).

Garden-Sports

Then there were garden-sports (*upavana-līlā*) which also amused the sophisticated people. In the spring season when cuckoos were warbling sweet, fresh leaves and sprouts had replaced the old ones and the *kiṅkirāta*, *sinduvāra*, mango and other trees were in full bloom and parks assumed beauty beyond description, young men and women felt an irresistible attraction towards them. Vātsyāyana furnishes a graphic account of garden-parties. In the morning on a day already fixed for the purpose men accompanied by courtesans and followed by attendants riding horses went to a garden. They spent the whole day there diverting themselves with various recreations like cock-fighting, dice-playing, spectacles and other favourite sports and taking with them some momento of the party returned home in the evening.[3] This description is beautifully illustrated by our poet. Men went to these gardens with their beloved prostitutes and enjoyed pleasures of love in secluded spots like creeper-bowers. They walked together with their hands placed

6. *Kāma-sūtra*, vi. 1. 25. For representation of a scene of ram-fight in an Ajanta painting, see XIX. 40.

1. R.C. Kak, *Ancient Monuments of Kashmir*, pls. xxx.21; xxxix. 41.
2. *Ibid.*, p. 109.
3. *Kāma-sūtra*, i.4.40.

on each other's shoulders. The beloved asked her man to pick up flowers or leaves of different trees and creepers and decorate her body with them and the lover felt obliged to carry out the request. They also enjoyed a swing from the branches of a tree, creepers serving as the swing (665-684). Although not explicitly stated, it may be reasonably assumed that married men and women also enjoyed garden-parties.

Water-Sport

Water-sports also provided great fun. According to Vātsyāyana, water-sport (*jala-krīḍā*) was resorted to by the *nāgaraka* in summer.[1] In this sport the lover and his beloved bathed in a pond and struck at each other with water coming out of a syringe (*karayantra*) or a vessel of the leaves of the lotus plant or *palāśa* tree and with lotus stalk. They dived deep into the water and unnoticed threw up each other jocularly, thereby providing much laughter to the people around. To see the charming physique of a woman covered with wet transparent garments was a matter of great joy to her lover who found himself lustily excited (685-691).

Gatherings

The various kinds of *goṣṭhīs* or social gatherings prevalent in ancient India were a good source of entertainment to the cultured people of refined taste and belonging to a higher social plane. Dāmodaragupta refers to the gatherings of the virtuous (*sajjana-goṣṭhī*, 209) and of the clever (*vidagdha-goṣṭhī*, 235). These appear to have been the first kind of *goṣṭhī* described by Vātsyāyana. In these *goṣṭhīs*, which met at the residence of a courtesan, a public hall meant for the purpose (*sabhā*) or at the house of a man about the town (*nāgaraka*), people equal in age, learning, intellectual pursuits, character and wealth accompanied by hetairai came together and amused themselves by intellectual diversions such as befitting conversation and discussions on matters relating to poetry and arts. In these gatherings the participants exchanged gifts as a mark of affection, and respect was shown to those who deserved it on account of their popularity and excellence in learning and arts.[2] Thus

1. *Kāma-sūtra*, i. 4. 41.
2. *Ibid.*, i.4. 34-36.

these gatherings afforded opportunities for men and women of sophisticated nature and refined manners to display and augment their proficiency in arts and letters. These *goṣṭhis* were in fact an important feature of ancient Indian life and, if the testimony of the *Kāma-sūtra* is to be relied upon, formed a regular item of the life of a *nāgaraka*. Such gatherings appear to have been fairly popular during the period under reference also, and Sundarasena is represented to have witnessed the gatherings of the clever (*vidagdha-goṣṭhīs*) in the course of his peregrinations (235).[1]

Mention is also made of *pānaka-goṣṭhīs* (795) and *surata-goṣṭhīs* (1013). The former were a sort of drinking bouts in which courtesans and their lovers participated. Vātsyāyana refers to such gatherings as *āpānaka* and informs us that they were held at the residences of the *nāgarakas* where courtesans offered various sorts of liquor to the *nāgarakas* and then drank themselves.[2]

The *surata-goṣṭhīs*, in which the clever participated, appear to have been gatherings meant for conversation on erotics.

Festivals

Reference must be made here to certain festivals[3] of a socio-religious nature which characterised ancient Indian life and wherein men and women from all walks of life freely participated and found some relief from worries of daily routine. One such festival, and probably the most popular one, was the Spring Festival observed with great pomp and show in the month of Caitra in honour of the Indian god of love, Kāma. People maddened at the approach of the spring season freely engaged themselves in *carcarī* performances wherein men and women danced in joy; there was no distinction between children, the young and the old, between ladies observing seclusion and those coming out in public freely; all of them exchanged obscene words without caring a farthing for propriety and indulged in various

1. Cf. *vidyā-goṣṭhīs* mentioned by Bāṇa as taking place in the assembly of Brahmā. Vide V.S. Agrawala, *Harṣa-carita : Eka Sāṁskṛtika Adhyayana*, p. 12.

2. *Kāma-sūtra*, i. 4. 37-38.

3. These were known as *parvan* (886, 894, 917), *maha* (925) and *kṣaṇa* (822).

sports ; they used fresh flowers to deck themselves and threw coloured powders (*piṣṭātaka*) on each other so much so that the whole atmosphere appeared to have grown yellowish ; not to speak of the young, even old men felt so very overjoyed that they danced at random to the accompaniment of clapping and instrumental music losing all sense of their advanced age; they sang various songs and sprinkled water from a syringe (*śṛṅgaka*) on one another ; the whole ground became wet with water and strewn with cloth-perfumes (*paṭavāsa*) and bunches of flowers (*kusuma-niryūha*) worn as ornaments and fallen because of the violent movements of the people; even women of respectable families gave up all sense of decency and indulged in obscene dialogues and dice-playing (886-904).[1]

Then there were *deva-yātrās* or processions of divine images which attracted large crowds and provided opportunities for young men and women to meet one another. These contacts sometimes developed into love affairs (969).

1. The meaning of *carcarī* (886) or *carcarikā* (904) is not quite certain. At one place Dāmodaragupta speaks of the seeing of *carcarī* on the festival of Kusumāyudha (886) and on another occasion of the singing of *carcarikā* (904). It would thus follow that the word denoted both a play which could be seen and a kind of song. The same uncertainty is to be noticed elsewhere. According to the Prabhā commentary on the *Ratnāvalī*, *carcarī* or *carcarikā* denotes a kind of song (*gīta-bheda*), (Act I, pp. 22, 30), and it is quite in keeping with the expression 'street resounding with the sound of *carcarī*' (*carcarī-śabda-mukhara-rathyā*) in that play (p. 21). At one place the play contrasts between *carcarī* and *dvipadī-khaṇḍa* (p. 30). Elsewhere (p. 17) the commentator takes the word in the sense of a kind of musical instrument, mixture of many sounds, joyous play, and clapping. The *Saṅgīta-ratnākara* (iv. 292-293) states that *carcarī* should be sung in Prakrit on the occasion of *vasant-otsava* and that it is a kind of metre. Raghunātha in his gloss on the *Vikram-orvaśīya* also takes it to be a kind of song (*gīti-viśeṣa*). In the *Bhāva-prakāśa* (Ch. 9) it is described as a kind of acting wherein a couple of women participated. In the 4th act of Rājaśekhara's *Karpūra-mañjarī* we find a beautiful description of *carcarī*. According to C.R. Lanman (*ibid.*. p. 279, fn. 6), it is a peculiar dance accompanied by various poses. But while dance was surely one of the connotations of *carcarī*, it was not the only meaning of the word. From the description in the *Karpūra-mañjarī* it appears that *carcarī* is employed there to denote merry-making in general including dances (e.g., staff-dance and *callī* dance), mask-making and playing with coloured water.

Dolls

The Indian game of wooden dolls has a long history and continues to enjoy great popularity even today. That it must have been a source of popular amusement, particularly to the young, in ancient Kashmir also is evidenced by an interesting stanza which informs us that these dolls were fashioned from wood, adorned with appropriate clothes and ornaments and fitted with mechanical devices for movement with the help of a string and performed a variety of acts to provide fun to the spectators at the instance of the doll-player.[1]

Samudgikā

Samudgikā, which is described as decorated outside, hollow inside, hard and making sound by the application of a mechanical device,[2] also appears to denote some kind of toy. It is strange that no lexicon gives this meaning.

Wrestling

Wrestling was a popular means of entertainment in ancient Kashmir. The *Nīla-mata* refers to wrestlers as being honoured by the people.[3] Verse 76 of our poem mentions the terms *vasu*, *nanda*, *citra* and *daṇḍaka* which probably denoted various tricks employed in wrestling.[4] Bhārgava Paraśurāma was traditionally regarded as the ideal wrestler as also the expert wielder of various weapons.

There is reason to believe that dance and musical and theatrical performances also provided diversion to the people, especially the elite. This is indicated by numerous references which will be dealt with in a subsequent chapter.

XII. FURNITURE

Of the items of household furniture we find mention of the seat (*āsana*, 163 ; *āsandī*, 30), couch (*paryaṅka*, 141, 356, 822; *palyaṅka*, 397; *talpa*, 395, 625) covered with a bed-sheet (*āstaraṇa*,

1. अन्यवशेन विसंज्ञा कृतभूषा यन्त्रसूत्रसञ्चारा ।
दारुमयीव प्रतिमा विदधामि विडम्बना बह्वीः ॥
K 728.

2. बहिरुपपादितशोभा अन्तस्तुच्छाः स्वभावतः कठिनाः ।
वेश्याः समुद्गिका इव क्वणन्ति यन्त्रप्रयोगेण ॥
Ibid., 323.

3. *Nīla-mata*, vv. 433, 863; Ved Kumari, *op.cit.*, p. 111.

4. For sculptural representation of a wrestling scene, see Pl. VI. 10.

822), pillow (*upadhāna*, 845; *upadhānaka*, 230), bedding (*śayana*, 232; *śayyā*, 164; *śayanīya*, 230), and foot-stool (*pāda-pīṭha*, 35). One sat on a seat while attending toilette (163). A canopy (*vitānaka*, 141) was spread to decorate the bed-chamber.

Of other household articles mention is made of the lamp (*dīpa*, 141, 430) burning as long as there is oil in it (314, 651), pitcher (*ghaṭa*, 863, 865, 868), small leathern bottle for keeping liquids (*kutupa*), gourd for keeping drinking water (*tumbikā*), fan (*dalavṛntaka*, 407) and other utensils (*bhājana*, 228), pestle (*musala*) for threshing the paddy (*śāli-kaṇḍana*, 871), and syringe (*kara-yantra*, 685; *śṛṅgaka*, 893) for throwing water on one another.

XIII. CORRESPONDENCE

The practice of communicating through letters had been in vogue in India from early times,[1] and the procedure of composing letters, both official and private, is adumbrated in many Sanskrit texts either partially or fully devoted to this topic.[2] Instances of epistles are actually found in several Sanskrit works.[3] In Purandara's letter to his son Sundarasena described in verses 411-424 we get some idea about letter-writing in ancient India.

An epistle was called *lekha* (410, 425), and the carrier of letters was known as *lekha-vāhaka* (408). Letters were sometimes sent to very distant places, and the letter in question is said to have been sent from Kusumapura to Mt. Abu. Letter-carriers must have taken a long time to cover such distances, and therefore carried with them such necessaries as a fan, leathern bottle for oil, gourd for water, and a waist-band, tied at one end of a stick kept on the shoulders (407). Because of long journey their shoes were torn, soles of their feet were cloven and body covered with dirt (408). They saluted the addressees with their heads touching the ground and placed the letters

1. For some textual references to letter-writing, vide Monier-Williams, *Sanskrit-English Dictionary*, s.v., *patra*, *lekha*, *likh*; Rhys Davids *Pali-English Dictionary*, s.v. *likhati*, *lekha*, *paṇṇa*.

2. For some Sanskrit works dealing with the subject, see K. V. Sarma (Ed.), *Praśastikāśikā* of Bālakṛṣṇa Tripāṭhin, Introduction, p. xii.

3. For some letters, vide *Mālavik-Āgnimitra*, act v; *Mudrā-Rākṣasa*, act iii; *Mahāvīra-carita*, acts ii, v; *Prabodha-candrodaya*, act ii.

on the earth wherefrom the addressees lifted them up and read (410).[1]

According to Kauṭilya's classification of the contents of a letter (*lekhaja artha*),[2] the present epistle belongs to the class of reproof (*upālambha*), for it reproves Sundarasena for his unworthy attachment to an ordinary strumpet in blatant violation of his high family traditions. The whole letter reverberates with the agony of a father who had high hopes from his son who had, however, gone astray.

The letter commenced with the benedictory word *svasti*; next came the name of the place of its despatch in ablative prefixed by the honorific *śrī*; it was followed by the name of the sender in nominative singular and that of the addressed in accusative singular; the preamble concluded with the word 'states' (*samabhidhatte*, 411).

This is strictly in agreement with the prescriptions in the manuals on the subject which appear to have been followed in practice. Thus, the *Lekha-paddhati* lays down that the word *svasti* should be written at the beginning of the letter for the fame or benediction or wellbeing of the addressee; then should be mentioned the name of the place of origin prefixed by *śrī* and ending in the fifth case; the sender should be mentioned in nominative singular and the addressee in objective singular.[3] It may also be noted that the composition of the initial portion of the missive said to have been sent by *Senāpati* Puṣyamitra to his son Agnimitra is very similar to that of the above-mentioned letter. It also begins with the word *svasti*, followed by the mention of the place of issue (the venue of sacrifice), name of

1. There is no reference to the mode of sealing and carrying a letter. For the description of the messenger carrying Prabhākaravardhana's letter to Harṣa, see *Harṣa-carita*, ucchvāsa v.

2. *Artha-śāstra*, ii.10.23, 31.

3. स्वस्तिशब्दं प्रसिद्ध्यर्थं मङ्गलार्थं च कारयेत् ।
क्षेमार्थं वाचकस्यापि तेनादौ लिखते बुधः ॥
श्रीकारमादितः कुर्यात् स्थाने प्राकारवेष्टिते ।
स्वस्थाने पञ्चमी देया परस्थानेषु सप्तमी ।
आत्मनः प्रथमा देया द्वितीया च परस्य च ॥

Lekha-paddhati (G.O.S., No.19), pp. 58-59.

the sender in nominative singular and that of the addressee in accusative singular.[1]

XIV. CUSTOMS AND MANNERS

The juniors saluted the elders with their heads touching the earth.[2] The seniors inquired of the juniors about their health and wellbeing and then the latter seated themselves with the permission of the former (31).

A lady saluted a respectable person by touching the feet of the latter with an end of her garment.[3]

For showing respect to an elder, one folded one's hands and left one's seat with all humility (32).

For consoling a disappointed person, the consoler caressed affectionately the back of the person to be consoled (43).

At the sight of an approaching guest, the host rose on one's feet, saluted him and offered him one's own seat (139).

Strangers addressed women as mother and sister, evidently depending on the age of the persons concerned (220, 222).

When bidding farewell to a friend, relation or guest, people accompanied him up to an oozing tree like banyan or a place of water.[4] Hāralatā is said to have accompanied her lover, Sundarasena, up to a banyan tree and was then asked by the latter to return home .

At the sight of a socially disapproved man people made faces and pointed their fingers at him (434).

Men of high socio-political rank such as princes had their own manners indicative of vanity typical of their class. They accepted betel-leaves from the betel-box-bearers by peculiar

1. *Mālavik-Āgnimitra*, act v, after verse 14.
2. विधाय क्षितिमण्डललीनमौलिना प्रणतिम् ।
K 31.
अवनितललीनशिरसा कृतनतिना ।
Ibid.,410.
3. प्रविधेयमञ्चलेन प्रस्फोटनमङ्घ्रियुगलस्य ।
Ibid., 139.
4. आ क्षीरवतो वृक्षादा सलिलाद् वा प्रिये प्रियं यान्तम् ।
अनुयायादिति वचनं तेन स्वमितो निवर्तस्व ॥
Ibid., 451.

In the *Abhijñāna-Śākuntala*, act iv, p. 145, also it is said that a beloved person must be accompanied up to a place of water.

hand poses called *sandaṁśa* and *khaṭakāmukha* which actually belonged to the domain of dance (759),[1] they touched with a stick one being described by another person to ascertain one's identity, obviously with the object of exhibiting their indifference (810). They indicated their approval not by words, but by raising their eye-brows (880).

While making a request one saluted the person so entreated with folded hands (519).

Priya-darśana = 'one of amiable appearance' is mentioned as a mode of address for one whose visit was eagerly awaited (371). The word has a long history, and it has been used for Aśoka Maurya in the Ceylonese chronicles.[2] The *Mudrā-Rākṣasa* (act ii) employs it for his grandfather Caṇdragupta. The epithet *priya-darśin* met with in Aśokan inscriptions has the same meaning.

XV. GENERAL LIFE

Before concluding our study of social life a few remarks about the general life of the people will not be amiss. The conditions described in the *Kuṭṭanī-mata* pertain mainly to the city life, for the principal centres of the episodes narrated therein are the cities of Vārāṇasī, Pāṭaliputra and Abu. We also get some glimpses of the village life in the description of the difficulties attending travel in those days (219-230) and in the conversation between prince Samarabhaṭa's minister and Mañjarī's mother (811-874). The rural people led a simple life. They had good neighbourly relations among themselves. Women in particular maintained friendly relations with one another and frequented neighbouring houses under the pretext of borrowing household utensils and other articles, and this provided occasions for friendly chat (227-228). Villagers were very much afraid of thieves and brigands and consequently hesitated to give shelter to the strangers. Probably there were no inns or public rest houses in villages,[3] and the travellers had to hide their

1. For these poses, see *infra*, pp. 219-20.

2. *Dīpa-vaṁsa* (edited and translated into English by H. Oldenberg, London, 1879), vi.2,3; xv. 88 *et seq*; xvi.5.

3. That there were rest-houses in towns appears certain. Cf. *Samaya-mātṛkā*, ii.3, where a *pānth-āvasatha* at Parihāsapura in Kashmir is mentioned.

heads under the roof of the village temple (219-228). Villagers were pre-occupied with agricultural operations and had little time to devote to comforts of life. This, however, does not mean that the village life was completely dull and dry. There were some fashionable people even in villages who imitated the fashions of urban life anointing their body with unguents and adorning their hair with flower garlands (866).

The attraction of town life and the spurt of fashion in rural areas was in no small measure due to the fashionable men about the town (*nāgaraka*) who had, perhaps owing to economic reasons, settled in villages situated not far from cities. Vātsyāyana has given us a detailed account of the life and pursuits of the *nāgaraka*.[1] The *nāgaraka* described by him was a cultured city-bred man of refined manners and artistic pursuits and his example was to be emulated even by the cultured section of the rural population.[2] A perusal of the *Kuṭṭani-mata* shows that Dāmodaragupta had a village-bred pseudo-*nāgaraka* in view while describing Cintāmaṇi, while the real *nāgaraka* is seen in prince Samarabhaṭa. The latter, belonging as he did to royalty, could afford the luxurious life of a *nāgaraka*; he is in the prime of his youth; his dress and manners reveal a refined taste; he has kept long hair which are arranged with ribbons covering three-fourths of his head; his body is anointed with a light unguent; the hair near the ears are coloured with saffron; on his forehead is the *tilaka* mark adorned with white mustard seeds; he has used betel; in his ears are to be seen earrings, while his neck is also adorned with the *ṭiṭṭibhaka*; to his arms are tied amulets, while in his wrists he is wearing an ornament comprising strings of shining gold beads; his hand is perched on the upper end of a cane-stick; his apparel is fashioned from soft silk; he wears noisy shoes; being a prince a dagger and a sword are suspended from his waist; every action of his has an artistic touch; he receives betel with a dramatic pose; he knows the intricacies of music, dance, dramatic performance and hunting and is able to describe them in minute details.

We may now turn to the pseudo-*nāgaraka*, Cintāmaṇi.

1. *Kāma-sūtra*, i.4.
2. H.C. Chakladar, *A Study in Vātsyāyana's Kāmasūtra*, pp. 103-120.

He has long hair with a thick tuft; his long hair are done up with multi-coloured tassels; he is very fond of ornaments; in the ears he wears three different types of ornaments at a time; he wears finger-rings and gold chains adorn the neck; his body is slightly yellowish on account of saffron rubbed on it; flower-garlands and other gold ornaments are suspended from his neck; he wears saffron-dyed clothes embroidered with gold and ornamental, noisy shoes fitted with iron soles and softened with bees'wax; he is accompanied by a betel-box-carrier who is equally showy; his neck is adorned with a necklace formed by thick glass beads and wrists with conchshell bangles; his nails are polished. He makes public appearance in theatre-halls accompanied by some sword-carrying attendants of a haughty mien; he sits on a thick-cushioned seat specially provided for him in the midst of *śreṣṭhins*, traders, jesters, etc., with the upper half of his body resting against a pillow and his hands touching the cheeks swollen on account of a heavy dose of betel inside the mouth. With his eye-brows raised up, he recites irrelevant verses in Prakrit which he has somehow managed to memorise; moving his head in surprise and pretending absorption in the sentiment he beats other spectators and with appreciative remarks like 'Oh well done', etc., disturbs other fellow spectators; he narrates episodes indicating the king's affection for and confidence in his father; whether he knows an art or not, he tries to publicise his proficiency in it; in his heart he enjoys the eulogy showered on him by his attendants attributing to him knowledge of dramaturgy, music, art of wielding weapons, wrestling, erotics, skill in hunting, and liberality; he poses to be well-versed in music and dance; without waiting for a proper occasion he, in a gesture of buoyant appreciation, offers a flower-garland taking it out of his own neck and betel to the dancing girl and praises her by using expressions which he has managed to cram but the real meaning of which he is unable to grasp.

CHAPTER V

EDUCATION, LEARNING AND LITERATURE

EDUCATION

The *Kuṭṭanī-mata* affords very meagre information about the system of education prevailing in contemporary Kashmir. We can, however, get some idea of the teacher-taught relations, curriculum of instructions, important centres of learning and allied matters from some casual allusions scattered throughout the poem.

Teacher-Taught Relations

The relationship between the teacher and the student appears to have been marked by harmony and cordiality. Students went to the residence of their teachers for study (433). It was deemed to be the duty of a student to render personal service to his teacher (421, 436).[1] Pupils were anxious to see their teachers happy (196). The teacher had a right to administer mild chastisement such as caning, evidently for correcting lapses on the part of the student.[2]

Method of Teaching

Education was mainly oral, and emphasis was laid on correct pronunciation (8). Boards, obviously of wood, were used for writing (1026)[3].

Curriculum of Instruction

As will be shown in the following section of this chapter, our work contains numerous references to ancient authors and texts and stray allusions to certain disciplines which give us some

1. It is interesting to note in this connection that Medhātithi speaks of the fetching of water in jars for the teacher's use (on *Manu-smṛti*, ii. 108) and massaging his body when he is tired (on *ibid.*, ii. 191) as examples of household work that a student was expected to do.

2. Medhātithi (on *Ibid.*, ii. 195) recommends the application of mild punishment by the teacher for the student's inattention only if persuasion fails to bear the desired effect.

3. For sculptural representation of a school scene at Khajuraho, see Pl. VII. 12.

idea about the courses of study besides bringing to a high relief the poet's great erudition. An analysis of this material indicates that the Vedas, Dharma-śāstra texts, Pāṇinian grammar, metrics, poetics, erotics, Purāṇas, the epics, political science, medicine, philosophy and creative literature as also fine arts were more or less vigorously studied.

Educational Centres

Vārāṇasī and Pāṭaliputra continued to enjoy high reputation as great centres of learning and education. As for the former, we find only vague allusions to its scholars (3, 17,) including grammarians engaged in grammatical discussions (12), poets devoted to dramatic and poetic compositions (15) and professors busy with their students (8).

As regards Pāṭaliputra, our author not only refers to its scholars (179) who were mostly Brāhmaṇas with their intellect sharpened by the study of various sciences (181) and to women who were capable of distinguishing between the good and the bad and were engrossed in studying the *śāstras* (181, 192) but styles the city as a permanent abode of Sarasvatī, the Indian goddess of learning (*Sarasvatī-kula-gṛha*, 176).[1] This great renown of Pāṭaliputra as a famous seat of learning in all India was in a large measure due to the enlightened patronage of the Pāla rulers. Unfortunately, however, we get no information about the nature of educational institutions at these places.

Educational Excursions

The importance of the role of journey for general education was fully realised in our period. We are told that those who are ignorant of the dress, customs and speech of the different countries and do not wait upon teachers are like oxen without horns.[2] Sundarasena, accompanied by his friend Guṇapālita,

1. Cf. *Uttarādhyayana-ṭīkā*, ii, p. 220, which states that when Rakkhita of Daśapura could not study further in his own town he proceeded to Pāṭaliputra for higher studies. Vide J.C. Jain, *Life in Ancient India as depicted in the Jain Canon*, p. 174.

2. देशान्तरेषु वेशस्वभावभणितानि ये न बुध्यन्ते ।
समुपासते न च गुरून् विषाणविकलास्त उक्षाणः ॥

K 212.

undertook an arduous educational excursion from Pāṭaliputra to Mount Arbuda with the object of learning the conduct of the virtuous people, the deeds of rogues, the aspirations of the various people, the jests of the sharp-witted, the sarcastic speech of women of easy virtue, the substance of the sciences which is otherwise to be known from the teacher, the character of the *viṭas*, and the tricks adopted by rakes for cheating others (214-15). It is further stated that in course of their sojourn they learned everything that might be expected. Thus, they witnessed the gatherings of the learned, practised the use of various weapons, got an insight into the essence of the *śāstras*, saw many a wonder, learned the art of making a variety of figures by cutting leaves, portrait-painting, modelling in clay, metal or bees'wax, dance accompanied by vocal music, musical instruments like stringed ones and tabor, understood the deceptive devices of cheats and humorous and ironical speech of the *viṭas* and unchaste women, and all the *śāstras* and manners of all the people (235-238).

The popularity of the practice of undertaking long journey for the avowed purpose of learning the manners and customs of different provinces is indicated by the fact that Bāṇa also had undertaken such a sojourn.[1] Medhātithi also advises students to go abroad for acquiring greater proficiency in the *śāstras*.[2] Rājaśekhara also avers that ancient poets used to visit foreign countries and islands and utilised the experience gained thereby in their works,[3] and that the employment in later times, when the conditions had undergone change, of descriptions based on such experience was to be treated as a poetic motif (*kavi-samaya*).[4]

Such foreign travel in those days must have been very difficult indeed. Dāmodaragupta furnishes a graphic description of the difficulties that attended it. When a traveller was tired after the day's journey and was in need of rest, it was a problem to get a shelter for the night. With all the energy at his command exhausted and his body covered with dust he

1. *Harṣa-carita*, i; Agrawala, *Harṣa-carita*: *Eka Sāṁskṛtika Adhyayana*, p. 27.
2. On *Manu*, ix.76.
3. *Kāvya-mīmāṁsā*, ch. iv, p. 12.
4. *Ibid.*, ch. xiv, p. 78.

moved from house to house requesting people to allow him to spend the night at theirs'. Housewives were extremely reluctant to accommodate him. And even if the master of the house allowed him to while away the night in a corner of the house, the neighbourers were alarmed and the housewife quarrelled with him suspecting the traveller to be a cheat. The village temple was perhaps the only place where the traveller might hope to find a shelter. Beds were not available; the bare earth served the bed and bricks the pillow. Then, there was difficulty of food. Food shops appear to have been rather rare in villages. The traveller had, therefore, not unoften to beg from door to door and ate all that he received mixed up together.[1]

II
LITERATURE

Dāmodaragupta was not only an accomplished poet but also an erudite and well-read scholar who had an extensive knowledge of a wide variety of the literary lore popularly cultivated during his age as vouched for by innumerable specific, as well as casual, allusions to earlier and near contemporary authors and texts found embedded throughout the poem. We may now proceed to study these references with a view to highlight the enormous learning and literature jealously cherished in contemporary Kashmir in particular and India in general.

(i) *Vedic Studies*—The study of the Vedic texts was specially cultivated in the Brāhmaṇa families. Discussions on the divergent interpretations of the Vedic passages often took place (199), and at least some Brāhmaṇas were skilled reciters of the Vedic hymns (414, 422).

(ii) *Dharma-śāstra*. Smṛtis and other Dharma-śāstra texts appear to have been popularly studied, particularly by the Brāhmaṇas, and there is an allusion to the observance of the *vratas* prescribed by them (419). At one place Manu is spoken of as a sage who had knowledge of the past, present and future (719). Another stanza tells us that illicit relations with the teacher's spouse are sure to cause one's downfall (296). It

1. *K* 229.

may be observed here that sexual intercourse with the teacher's wife was regarded as one of the five most heinous sins.[1]

(iii) *Grammar*. Kalhaṇa informs us that our poet's patron, Jayāpīḍa, encouraged the study of Pāṇinian grammar in his dominions. He brought competent grammarians from abroad and restored the study of the *Mahābhāṣya*. He learned grammar himself from a distinguished grammarian named Kṣīra.[2] The impression thus obtained about the popularity of grammatical studies in Kashmir during the period under study is confirmed by several references of grammatical import found in our work.

An allusion is made to the discussions among grammarians about the verb-roots.[3] The non-applicability of the *sandhi* rules in cases coming under the *pragṛhya* rules is also referred to.[4] That *upasargas* have got to be employed only in association with verbs is also stated. The sight of an *upasarga* without a verb is spoken of as a matter of surprise.[5] In another stanza an allusion is made to a number of technical terms in common use among grammarians, viz., *vṛddhi*, *puruṣa*, *guṇa*, *gaṇa* and *paribhāṣā*. A prince united with prosperity (*vṛddhi*) renowned for a multitude of masculine qualities (*puruṣa-guṇa-gaṇa-khyātiḥ*) and issuing royal decrees (*paribhāṣā*) is figuratively compared to the science of grammar which is characterised by *vṛddhi*[6] *puruṣas*, *guṇa*,[7] *gaṇas* and *paribhāṣās*.[8]

1. *Nirukta*, vi.27; *Chāndogya Upaniṣad*, v.10.9; *Gautama-dharma-sūtra*, xxi.1-3.; *Āpastamba-dharma-sūtra*, i.7.21.8-11; *Vasiṣṭha-dharma-sūtra*, i.19-21; *Yājñavalkya-smṛti*, iii. 227; *Manu-smṛti*, xi. 103-104, etc. Also vide Kane, *HDS*, iii, pp. 613-14.
2. *RT*, iv. 488-489.
3. पदवेदिषु यत्र धातुवादित्वम्,
   K 12.
4. सन्धिच्छेदः प्रगृह्येषु,
   Ibid., 13. Cf. *Aṣṭādhyāyī*, i.1.11-19; vi.1.125
5. उदयति न पण्डितानां कथमात्मनि कौतुकं गजेन्द्रगतिः ।
   यन्नवयसां पुंसां विना क्रियायोगमुपसर्गाः ॥
   K 980. Cf. *Aṣṭādhyāyī*, i.4.58-59.
6. *Ibid.*, i.1. 1-3.
7. *Ibid.*, i.1. 2-3.
8. तत्रापि वृद्धियोगस्तस्मिन्नपि पुरुषगुणगणख्यातिः ।
   परिभाषा तत्रापि व्याकरणान्नातिरिच्यते तेन ॥
   K. 782.

(iv) *Prosody*. Metrics claims a larger number of references. Piṅgala, the promulgator of the science of prosody, is mentioned by name (780). The science of metrics, it is said, is characterised by *yatis* (pauses), *gaṇas* (letter-groups) and the proper placement of the latter.[1] In a metre, a short syllable coming at the end of a quarter is regarded as long.[2] Mention is also made of the scanning of metres (*chandaḥ-prastāra*) by putting the *guru* (long) and *laghu* (short) marks. It is stated that the marks indicating length are not straight.[3]

As we have seen above, the whole of our poem is couched in the Āryā metre. It is mentioned by name several times.[4] Some varieties of Āryā are also referred to. The variety named more frequently than others is Gīti[5] or Gītikā.[6] Our author has many a time employed Gītis in order to introduce changes in the story.[7] Verses 255, 326-328, 427, 959 and 1042 are in the Gīti metre. For the same purpose Pathyā, another kind of Āryā, has been used once (465-466). Jaghanacapalā, yet another division of Āryā, is named twice (313, 780). Mention is also made of the Gāthās of the *mātṛkā* variety sung in accordance with the *dvi-padī* tune (339). Six other metres are also referred to in a stanza with *double entendre*, viz., Sragdharā, Suvadanā, Praharṣiṇī, Tanumadhyā, Rucirā and Mañjubhāṣiṇī.[8]

(v) *Erotics*. In a poem revolving round prostitutes references to the art and science of love, i.e., Kāma-śāstra are naturally to be expected. Dāmodaragupta evinces penetrating knowledge of the minutest detail of Kāma-śāstra (382) which is also mentioned under various other names such as Kandarpa-śāstra (639), Kusum-āyudha-śāstra (403), Manmatha-śāstra

1. यतिगणगुणसमुपेता या नित्यं छन्दसामिव प्रचितिः । *K* 10.
2. प्रकृतिलघोर्येन कृता अवन्यवर्णस्य गौरवापत्तिः । *Ibid.*, 708.
3. छन्दःप्रस्तारविधौ गुरवो यस्यामनार्जवस्थितयः । *Ibid.*, 14.
4. *Ibid.*, 22, 211, 425, 491, 948.
5. *Ibid.*, 254, 325, 1042.
6. *Ibid.*, 958, 960, 1044.
7. Sometimes Āryās also serve the same purpose.
8. सा स्रग्धरा सुवदना प्रहर्षिणी सैव सैव तनुमध्या ।
न करोति कस्य विस्मयमिति रुचिरा मञ्जुभाषिणी सैव ॥ *Ibid.*, 968.

(678), Manmatha-tantra (77), Mīna-ketu-śāstra (864) and Smaraśāstra (535). He refers to writers on erotics as *kandarpa-śāstrakāra* (639). Mention is also made of authors of works on prostitution (*vaiśika-śāstra-praṇetṛ*, 504).

The text most commonly perused by the literati in ancient India for acquiring an insight into erotics was, of course, the *Kāma-sūtra* of Vātsyāyana. Dāmodaragupta had adroitly studied this work and its impress is to be discerned throughout the poem. He has referred to Vātsyāyana by name twice at the head of the list of authorities on erotics (77, 123). Several descriptions in the poem can be shown to be based on or derived from the work of Vātsyāyana. Verse 385 states that when two lovers are united in a coitus-posture it is impossible to count their various acts inspired by sexual desire kindled by natural love,[1] an idea obviously based on the *Kāma-sūtra*.[2] The conception of sexual congress as a war[3] also follows the *Kāma-sūtra*.[4] The term *rati-cakra* (385), i.e., a cycle of coition, is also taken over from Vātsyāyana.[5] The classification of men into three divisions, viz., *śaśa* (hare), *vṛṣa* (bull) and *aśva* (horse), depending on the size of the sex organ (535, 999), has also its basis in the *Kāma-sūtra* (ii.1.1). The *sama-rata* or equal sexual congress

1. सद्भावरागदीपितमदनाचार्योपदिष्टचेष्टानाम् ।
क: परिगणनं कर्तुं रतिचक्राविष्टरमणयो: शक्त: ।। *K* 385. Also cf. 382.

2. शास्त्राणां विषयस्तावद् यावन्मन्दरसा नरा: ।
रतिचक्रे प्रवृत्ते तु नैव शास्त्रं न च क्रम: ।। *Kāma-sūtra*, ii.2.32.
Also cf. नास्त्यत्र गणना काचिन्न च शास्त्रपरिग्रह: ।
प्रवृत्ते रतिसंयोगें राग एवात्र कारणम् ।।
स्वप्नेष्वपि न दृश्यन्ते ते भावास्ते च विभ्रमा: ।
सुरतव्यवहारेषु ये स्युस्तत्क्षणकल्पिता: ।। *Ibid.* ii. 7. 30-31.

3. *Rati-saṅgara*, 152; *rata-saṅgara*, 415; *rati-samara*, 1052; *rati-yuddha*, 335; *surata-saṅgara*, 572; *rati-kalaha*, 1055; *surata-parimarda*, 383.

4. *Surata-sammarda*, ii.7.33. Also cf. *K* 1055 where coitus is said to resemble quarrel. The *Rati-rahasya* (x.52) also calls it *madana-yuddha*. In fact the description of coitus as war had become a literary motif which is met with in many works., e.g., *Padma-prābhṛtaka*, verse 39; *Dhūrta-viṭa-saṁvāda*, verse 53; *Pāda-tāḍitaka*, verse 138; Jāyasī's *Padmāvata*, 318. 1-9.

5. II.2.32. See note 2 above.

mentioned by our poet (652), which also involves the aforesaid three-fold classification of men and that of women into *mṛgī* (haress), *vaḍavā* (mare) and *hastinī* (she-elephant),[1] denotes, according to Vātsyāyana (ii.1.3), the union of the *śaśa*, *vṛṣa* and *aśva* types of men with the *mṛgī*, *vaḍavā* and *hastinī* females respectively. Dāmodaragupta states that two kinds of kiss-marks, *bindu* on the lower lip and *maṇi-mālā* on the neck, and the nail-mark called *śaśa-plutaka* on the breasts suggest a lover well-versed in erotics.[2] All these are detailed in the *Kāma-sūtra*.[3] The *udghṛṣṭaka* kind of embrace, which is defined by Vātsyāyana as the mutual rubbing of the bodies of lovers for a long time while walking in dark, a crowd of people or a lonely place,[4] is also mentioned in our poem.[5] The *Kāma-sūtra* counsels a woman to utter, at the time of coitus, words meaning 'mother' and expressing her desire to be relieved and her inability to bear it and make sounds (*sītkṛta*) resembling those, of a pigeon, cuckoo, *hārīta*, parrot, bee, *dātyūha*, swan, *kāraṇḍava* and quail.[6] Our author also administers a similar advice.[7]

Dāmodaragupta's description of the conduct of a courtesan, skilfully put into the mouth of Vikarālā, is also derived from Vātsyāyana. Thus the various ways adopted by a prostitute

1. *Kāma-sūtra*, ii.1.2.
2. अधरे बिन्दुः कण्ठे मणिमाला स्तनयुगे शशप्लुतकम् ।
   तव सूचयन्ति केतकि कुसुमायुधपण्डितं रमणम् ॥
   K 403.
3. *Kāma-sūtra*, ii.5.7 (*bindu*); 11, 40 (*maṇi-mālā*); ii.4.4,20 (*śaśa-plutaka*).
4. तमसि जनसम्बाधे विजने वाऽथ शनकैर्गच्छतोर्नातिह्रस्वकालमुद्घर्षणं परस्परस्य गात्राणामुद्घृष्टकम् । *Ibid.*, ii.2.12.
5. सहसा संकटवर्त्मन्यवितर्कितसंमुखागतेनापि ।
   अभिलषितेनोद्घृष्टकमनल्पशुभकर्मणा लभ्यम् ॥
   K 823.
6. अम्बार्थाः शब्दा वारणार्था मोक्षणार्थाश्चालमर्थास्ते ते चार्थयोगात् । पारावतपरभृतहारीतशुकमधुकरदात्यूहहंसकारण्डवलावकविरुतानि सीत्कृतभूयिष्ठानि विकल्पशः प्रयुञ्जीत । *Kāma-sūtra*, ii.6.7-8.
7. मा मा मामतिपीडय मुञ्च क्षणमदय नो समर्थाऽस्मि ।
   इति गद्गदस्फुटाक्षरमभिधातव्यस्त्वया कामी ॥

for extracting money and ousting an impoverished lover and then wooing another man who had been discarded earlier but had in the interval regained his prosperity, which are adumbrated in our poem, actually furnish illustrations of similar devices enunciated in the Vaiśika section of the *Kāma-sūtra.*[1]

At one place courtesans are described as well-versed in sixty-four acts which are capable of captivating the heart of a lover.[2] What these sixty-four acts or arts were is difficult to ascertain. This topic is dealt with at two different places in the *Kāma-sūtra*. First are enumerated sixty-four subsidiary arts (*aṅga-vidyās*) which are said to form part of the *Kāma-sūtra*. These include (1-2) music, vocal and instrumental, (3) dance, (4) painting, (5) cutting leaf-designs for adorning the face, (6) making various designs with rice and flowers, (7) arrangement of flowers, (8) dyeing teeth, clothes and body, (9) decorating the floor, (10) arranging the bed, (11) producing musical sounds from water, (12) splashing and squirting with water, (13) various secret formulas, (14) making a variety of garlands, (15) preparing floral head-ornaments known as *śekharaka* and *āpīḍa*, (16) wearing proper dress and adornments, (17) making leaf-shaped ear-ornaments, (18) perfumery, (19) making ornaments, (20) magic, (21) secret potions prescribed by Kucumāra, (22) smartness, (23) preparing a variety of vegetables, juices, food articles, (24) and various drinks, (25) needlework, (26) creating patterns from threads, (27) playing on the lyre and the drum called *ḍamaruka*, (28) posing and solving riddles, (29) competition of verse-recital wherein one has to recite verses beginning with the concluding letter of the verses recited by others, (30) recital of verses difficult to repeat, tongue-twisters, etc., (31) book-reading, (32) knowledge of

परभृतलावकहंसकपारावततुरगहृदयनिःस्वनितम् ।
अनुकार्यमुचितकाले कलकण्ठि रुतैस्त्वया रसतः ॥

K 158, 157. Also cf .155, 417, 501.

1. VI.2 (keeping a lover attached); vi.3 (squeezing wealth); vi.3 (ways of getting rid of an impoverished man); vi.4 (wooing a formerly rejected lover). Also vide *supra*, pp.115-16.

2. रमणहृदयानुवर्तनचतुरचतुःषष्टिकर्मकुशलानाम् ।
न स्पृशति तत्त्वचर्चा पण्यवधूनां विदग्धचेतांसि ॥

K 499.

dramas and anecdotes, (33) completing unfinished stanzas, (34) variety of cane-weaving, (35) making mechanical aids, particularly those used in sexual congress, (36) wood-work, (37) architecture, (38) examination of coins and precious stones, (39) metallurgy, (40) knowledge of the colours and sources of gems, (41)arbori-horticulture, (42) art of ram-fight, cock-fight and quail-fight, (43) training parrots and mynas to speak and sing, (44) skill in pressing the body with feet and hands and shampooing the hair, (45) the art of deciphering writing in cipher, (46) conversing with deliberate transposition of words and letters, (47) knowledge of various regional languages, (48) making flower-carriages, (49) knowledge of omens, (50) making mechanical devices, (51) the sharpening of memory, (52) chorus reading, (53) mental composition of verses, (54) knowledge of lexica, (55) metrics and (56) figures of speech, (57) impersonation, (58) covering private parts with clothes, (59) various kinds of dice games, (60) dice game known as *ākarṣa*, (61) making children's toys, (62-64) knowledge of proper etiquette, victorious rites, and physical culture.[1] Elsewhere Vātsyāyana informs us that according to some scholars there are sixty-four subdivisions of the sexual union and that the union itself is called 'Sixty-four'. The genesis of this nomenclature is given variously. According to one view, a sage named Pāñcāla stated the 'Sixty-four' in the *Ṛgveda*, and as the chapter on the sexual union was also composed by Bābhravya Pāñcāla, the name 'Sixty-four' came to be applied to it also. The followers of Bābhravya held that as each of the eight stages of the sexual union, viz., embrace, kiss, marking with nails and with teeth, coitus proper, shrieking and crying, the woman assuming the role of a man, and oral congress, has eight subdivisions, the science is named 'Sixty-four' (8x8=64). But as pointed out by Vātsyāyana, the subdivisions of some of the eight stages of the sexual union are less or more than eight and additional topics like strikings (*prahaṇana*), shrieking and crying (*viruta*), etc., are also dealt with, and, therefore, the name 'Sixty-four' is applied only loosely as are the expressions like the 'seven-leafed' tree (*sapta-parṇa vṛkṣa*) and 'five-coloured' oblation

1. *Kāma-sūtra*, i.3.16

(*pañca-varṇa bali*).[1] Vātsyāyana himself seems to hold, and it is certainly much more reasonable, that as the aforesaid arts number sixty-four and are connected with the sexual union, they are collectively called 'Sixty-four'.[2] It follows from the above that our author intended to describe courtesans as skilled in the sixty-four *aṅga-vidyās* listed above.[3]

Among other authorities on Kāma-śāstra mention is made of Dattakācārya, Rājaputra (77, 123), Madanodaya (123) and Viṭaputra or Viṭavṛtta (123).[4] Of these, Dattaka was traditionally regarded as an authority on the prostitute's profession. Vātsyāyana informs us that at the instance of the hetairai of Pāṭaliputra Dattaka composed a treatise on Vaiśika which constituted the sixth section of the *Kāma-sūtra*[5] which was originally composed by Nandin, the attendant of Mahādeva, and then successively abridged by Śvetaketu, son of Uddālaka, and Bābhravya Pāñcāla.[6] Some passages from

1. *Kāma-sūtra*, ii.2.1-2, 4-6.
2. *Ibid.*, ii.2.3.
3. Tripathi, however, thinks that as the word *karman* is used in connection with *catuḥṣaṣṭi*, we have to understand here sexual union, etc., together with their subdivisions elaborated by Bābhravya Pāñcāla and in the second section of the *Kāma-sūtra*. But many of the sixty-four *aṅga-vidyās* can also be styled 'acts' and with some of them the words *karman* and *kriyā* are actually used.
4. वात्स्यायनमयमबुधं बाह्यान् दूरेण दत्तकाचार्यान् ।
गणयति मन्मथतन्त्रे पशुतुल्यं राजपुत्रं च ॥
वात्स्यायनमदनोदयदत्तकविटपुत्रराजपुत्राद्यैः ।
उल्लपितं यत् किञ्चित् तत् तस्या हृदयदेशमध्यास्ते ॥

K 77, 123.

Kaul prefers the reading *Viṭavṛtta*. Vide verse 122 of his edition.

5. *Kāma-sūtra*, i.1.11. Yaśodhara in his commentary gives two legends about Dattaka that were evidently prevalent in his time. According to one of these legends, Dattaka, son of a Brāhmaṇa of Mathurā settled at Pāṭaliputra, lost his parents shortly after his birth and was brought up by a Brāhmaṇa lady who gave him the meaningful name Dattaka, i.e., adopted; in course of time Dattaka successfully laboured with various sciences and betook himself to courtesans with a view to become familiar with worldly matters. He mastered worldly matters so well that the courtesans of Pāṭaliputra headed by Vīrasenā requested him to write a manual on their craft in deference to which he composed an independent treatise on the subject. Another tradition would have us believe that because of the interruption of divine agency he had experience of both sexes and consequently composed a treatise on courtesanship. There is nothing to support the view of S.N. Sinha and N.K. Basu (*History of Prostitution in India*, Vol. I, p. 197) that Dattaka lived in the middle of the fifth century B.C.
6. *Kāma-sūtra*, i.1.8-10.

Dattaka's work called Dattaka-sūtra are cited by Yaśodhara in his gloss on the *Kāma-sūtra.*[1]

Nothing whatsoever is known about Rājaputra. A certain Rājaputra is referred to in the *Hasty-āyurveda* of Pālakāpya (iii.8.99). In the present state of insufficient information it is not possible to determine if the two Rājaputras are identical.

The work of Madanodaya has not come down to us nor is he elsewhere cited as an authority on erotics. But Rāghava-bhaṭṭa in his Artha-dyotanikā commentary on the *Abhijñāna-Śākuntala* (i.27) quotes a stanza in the Anuṣṭubh metre on the signs of attachment from a text known as *Madanodaya.*[2] Is it possible that Madanodaya was actually the title of a text on erotics which came to be regarded, in later times, as a secondary name of its author himself?

Viṭaputra or Viṭavṛtta still remains a shadowy figure as he is not mentioned anywhere else.

Writings of all these authors appear to have enjoyed great popularity and been assiduously studied during our period. Cintāmaṇi is said to have regarded Vātsyāyana, Dattaka and Rājaputra as insignificant before him (77), and a message-girl is asked to describe her mistress as skilled in the works of these authorities as also of Madanodaya and Viṭaputra or Viṭavṛtta (123).

(vi) *Poetics and Dramaturgy.* That poetics and dramaturgy were also popularly studied in our period is vouchsafed by the *Kuṭṭanī-mata* which mentions by name some authorities on these subjects.

Indian tradition traces the beginnings of most of the sciences to god Brahmā, and dramatics is no exception. Verse 75 of our work refers to the *Nāṭya-śāstra* promulgated by Brahmā (*Brahm-okta-nāṭya-śāstra*). This does in no way prove the existence of a work on dramaturgy attributed to Brahmā but only alludes to the popular tradition about the origin of this discipline which is narrated at length in the *Nāṭya-śāstra.* Its opening

1. On vi. 3.19.
2. विकारो नेत्रवक्त्रस्य तद्वाक्यश्रवणादरः ।
अन्यव्याजेन तद्वीक्षा अनुरागेङ्गितं भवेत् ॥

verse states that Bharata restated the *Nāṭya-śāstra* which was originally propounded by Brahmā.[1] Another stanza avers that Brahmā created Nāṭya-veda out of the four Vedas, borrowing *pāṭhya* from the *Ṛgveda*, *gīta* (music) from the *Sāmaveda*, *abhinaya* (acting) from the *Yajurveda* and *rasas* (sentiments) from the *Atharvaveda*.[2] The *Skānda Purāṇa* also tells us that it was the four-faced god (Brahmā) who transmitted the various divisions of acting to Bharata.[3]

The first standard work on the subject was Bharata's *Nāṭya-śāstra* which eclipsed earlier works and has been holding the field ever since its composition, and Dāmodaragupta gives enough evidence of his painstaking study of this text. In verse 82 we read of a dancing girl performing in accordance with the directions of Kohala and Bharata. Verse 124 refers to the study of Bharata's work by courtesans. At another place we read of a dramatic performance in the world of gods wherein Bharata played the hero, sages Kohala and others acted *kuśīlavas* (actors or instrumentalists), divine courtesans played female roles, Brahmā's son Nārada gave musical performance and the sage Mataṅga played hollow musical instruments.[4] This is obviously an allusion to Ch. I, vv. 25 ff. of the *Nāṭya-śāstra* wherein Bharata is said to have taught acting to his sons including Kohala, heavenly hetairai are represented to have played female roles and Nārada, etc., are stated to have given music. There is also an allusion to the lapses committed in acting in accordance with Bharata and the trainer's anger over it (1009). Yet another stanza states that the sons of Bharata taught the art of acting to the women of the harem of king Nahuṣa.[5] This

1. *Nāṭya-śāstra*, i.1.
2. *Ibid.*, i.17.
3. नाटयवेदं ददौ पूर्वं भरताय चतुर्मुखः ।Cited by Tripathi on *ibid.*, 75.
4. नायकभूमौ भरतः कुशीलवाः कोहलादयो मुनयः ।
अप्सरसः स्त्रीनाट्ये गान्धर्वे कमलजन्मनस्तनयः ॥
सुषिरस्वरप्रयोगप्रतिपादनपण्डितो मतङ्गमुनिः ।
यदि रञ्जयन्ति हृदयं भवतो भूमिस्पृशां कुतः शक्तिः ॥
Ibid., 876-877.
5. भरतसुतैरुपदिष्टं क्षितिपतिनहुषावरोधनारीणाम् ।
Ibid., 946.

evidently refers to the concluding chapter of the *Nāṭya-śāstra*, which describes the legend of the transmission, at Nahuṣa's request, of the art of acting to the earth wherein Bharata's sons are said to have played an important part.

These direct references apart, the *Kuṭṭanī-mata* contains much other material which appears to have been borrowed from Bharata's work. Thus, we come across references to the *sot-kaṇṭhā*[1] (distressed by separation), *vāsaka-sajjā* (dressed up for union, 251), *khaṇḍana-kupitā*[2] (enraged with her lover due to the latter's attachment to another woman), *kalah-āntaritā*, (separated from her lover due to a quarrel, 791-92) and *abhi-sārikā* (one who visits her lover, 596) types of *nāyikā* (heroine) definitions whereof are to be found in the *Nāṭya-śāstra* (xxii.211-220). Mention is also made of a number of technical terms like *hāva* (emotion), *līlā* (sportive mimicry), *vilāsa* (amorous gesture), *vicchitti* (dishabille), *vibhrama* (confusion due to intoxication, passion and joy), *kilakiñcita* (hysterical mood), *moṭṭāyita* (manifestation of affection), *kuṭṭamita* (pretended anger), *bibboka* (affected coldness), *lalita* (lolling), and *vihṛta* (want of response due to bashfulness, pretence and nature) for the explanation whereof we have to refer to Bharata.[3] The various stages of love described by Bharata[4] are alluded to in the account of the longing of Mālatī (97-106), Hāralatā (288-300) and Mañjarī (991-1028) for Cintāmaṇi, Sundarasena and Samarabhaṭa respectviely, while verses 51 and 300 make pointed reference to the tenth stage, i.e., death. Verse 805 refers to the *sāttvika bhāvas* (temperamental states)[5] which, according to Bharata, are as follows : paralysis (*stambha*), perspiration (*sveda*), horripilation (*romāñca*), change of voice (*svara-bheda*), trembling (*vepathu*), change of colour (*vaivarṇya*), weeping (*aśru*) and fainting (*pralaya*).[6] Verses 881 and 928 speak of the singing of the *prāveśikī dhruvā* when the *sūtra-dhāra* is about to appear on the stage and of the *naiṣkrāmikī dhruvā* to mark the

1. The *Nāṭya-śāstra* (xxii.214) calls her *virah-otkaṇṭhitā*.
2. The same as the *khaṇḍitā* of the *Nāṭya-śāstra*, xxii.217.
3. *Ibid.*, xxii. 10-24.
4. *Ibid.*, xxii.169-191.
5. Also cf. 272, 289-298, 506 where first five temperamental states are described.
6. *Nāṭya-Śāstra*, vii.94, 95-107.

exit of all characters at the end of the first act of the *Ratnāvali*. Both these are named and described by Bharata.[1] It is stated in verse 809 that the consequents (*anubhāvas*) of the *karuṇa* (pathetic) and *vipralambha śṛṅgāra* (erotic sentiment in separa tion) sentiments are the same, which is also based on Bharata.[2] Our author names two hand poses, viz., *saṁdaṁśa* and *khaṭakā-mukha* (759), which are also defined in the *Nāṭya-śāstra*.[3] A kind of bodily acting called *sūcī* and the pain caused by it are referred to in verse 191. It follows the *Nāṭya-śāstra* (x. 34).[4]

As we have seen above, Kohala, Mataṅga and Nārada were also regarded as authorities on dramaturgy. It would follow from our references that Kohala was thought to be an authority on dance, acting and instrumental music. And from references made to him in other works he appears to have written on all topics of Nāṭya-śāstra, particularly acting, music and dancing. In the *Nāṭya-śāstra* (i.26) he is mentioned as one of the hundred sons of Bharata whom he taught the theory and practice of Nāṭya-veda. Elsewhere the same work (xxxvii, 18) prophetically states that Kohala will treat of all matters left out (by Bharata) in a later or additional treatise (*uttara-tantra*). He is also said to have practised *Nāṭya-śāstra* (xxxvii. 24) on the earth. Abhinavagupta mentions him as coeval with Bharata and styles him actor (*naṭa*).[5] Śiṅgabhūpāla's *Ras-ārṇava-sudhākara* (i.50-52) mentions him as an author on Nāṭya.[6] A text called *Kohala-rahasya* treating of musical modes is attributed to Bharata's son Kohala who revealed the subject at the request of Mataṅga.[7] Three other works called *Saṅgīta-*

1. *Nāṭya-śāstra*, xxxii.27, 38, 311-312.

2. *Ibid.*, vi, pp. 306-309, 317. Although Dāmodaragupta speaks of the sameness of the *anubhāvas* of the *karuṇa* and *vipralambha śṛṅgāra* sentiments, it is actually the *anubhāvas* of the latter and the *vyabhicāri-bhāvas* of the former which agree with each other.

3. *Nāṭya-śāstra*, ix.110, 60.

4. P.V. Kane (*History of Sanskrit Poetics*, pp. 43-44) invites attention to some of these points to show that the important chapters of the *Nāṭya-śāstra* from the 1st to the 36th existed before 800 A.D.

5. On *Nāṭya-śāstra*, ii.1.

6. P.V. Kane, *History of Sanskrit Poetics*, p. 25.

7. *Triennial Catalogue of Sanskrit Manuscripts in Government Oriental Manuscripts Library*, Madras, Vol. IC, p. 787.

Meru,[1] *Tāla-lakṣaṇa*[2] and *Kohalīya Abhinaya-śāstra*[3] are also ascribed to him.[4]

Dāmodaragupta's description of Mataṅga as an expounder of hollow musical instruments is vouched for by the *Abhinava-Bhāratī* which quotes Mataṅga's view on *suṣira ātodya* i.e., wind instruments.[5] "The *Kohala-rahasya* introduces him as a disciple of Kohala. Jagadekamalla's *Saṅgīta-cūḍāmaṇi*[6] and Niḥśaṅka Śārṅgadeva's *Sangīta-ratnākara*[7] mention him as a great writer on music, while in Śiṅgabhūpāla's *Rasārṇava-sudhākara*, which regards him as one of Bharata's sons, he is spoken of as a writer on Nāṭya-śāstra.[8] M.R. Kavi ascribes him a work called *Bṛhad-deśī*.[9]

Nārada was traditionally regarded as the propounder of music,[10] and he is repeatedly mentioned by Bharata in connection with the music part of the drama.[11] He refers to him as an authority on *dhruvās* and on instrumental music.[12] The *Bhāva-prakāśana* speaks of him as one of the expounders of dramatics.[13]

Viśākhila and Dantila (*v.l.* Dattila), who were also treated as authorities on music and dramatics, are also named by our author (124). In Vāmana's *Kāvy-ālaṅkāra-sūtra-vṛtti* (i.3.7) Viśākhila is spoken of as a writer on *kalās*. Abhinava-gupta in his commentary on the *Nāṭya-śāstra* mentions Viśākhila in connection with music. He is also mentioned in the *Rasa-ratna-dīpikā* and *Saṅgīta-ratnākara*.[14]

1. *JAHRS*, iii, p. 24.
2. Eggling, *Catalogue of Sanskrit Manuscripts in India Office Library*, iii (1891), nos. 3025, 3089; *A Descriptive Catalogue of Sanskrit Manuscripts in Government Oriental Manuscripts Library*, Madras, xxii, no. 12992.
3. *Ibid.*, no. 12989.
4. For more information about Kohala, vide P.V. Kane, *History of Sanskrit Poetics*, pp. 24-25, 56-57; *Proceedings of All-India Oriental Conference*, 6th Session, pp. 577-80; S.K. De, *History of Sanskrit Poetics*, i, pp. 21, 24, 138; M.R. Kavi's Introduction to Vol. II of *Nāṭya-śāstra*, pp. vi-viii; *JAHRS*, iii, p. 24.
5. On *Nāṭya-śāstra*, xxx.1.
6. *IHQ*, xx, p. 87.
7. Kane, *History of Sanskrit Poetics*, p. 58.
8. *Ibid.*, p. 57.
9. *JAHRS*, iii, p. 24.
10. *Mahābhārata*, Śāntiparvan, 210.21. Also cf. Allahabad Pillar inscription of Samudragupta (*CII*, iii, p. 8, line 27) where the Gupta emperor is said to have surpassed Nārada in musical skill.
11. *Nāṭya-śāstra*, i.51,52; xxxiii.23 (*Iha Nāradena* is a variant for *Prapitāmahena*).
12. *Ibid.*, xxxii.1; xxxiv.2.
13. I, p. 2.
14. P. V. Kane, *History of Sanskrit Poetics*, p. 59.

The *Nāṭya-śāstra* (i.26) mentions Dattila as one of the sons or pupils whom Bharata taught Nāṭya-veda. Elsewhere (xxxvii. 24) it states that *Nāṭya-śāstra* was practised, among others, by Dhūrtita which, according to P. V. Kane, is possibly an error for Dantila.[1] The *Rasārṇava-sudhākara* (52-54) of Siṅgabhūpāla mentions him as one of Bharata's sons who wrote on dramatics, and the author of the *Rasa-ratna-dīpikā* claims to have consulted the work of Dattila.[2] Abhinavagupta quotes a stanza from Dattila on *dhruvās*.[3] A work named *Gāndharva-veda-sāra*, which is extant, is attributed to him.[4]

Mention may now be made of a few more points which have a bearing on the topic under study. Verse 15 refers to the occurrence of suitable characters in the dramas composed by good poets and sweetness in poetic compositions.[5] Another stanza mentions the *śṛṅgāra* sentiment originating from a youthful couple and accompanied by the *sāttvika bhāvas* like horripilation and by the *vibhāvas*.[6] The three kinds of heroine (*nāyikā*) called *svīyā* (one's own wife), *parakīyā* (another man's wife) and *sāmānyā* (prostitute) are alluded to in verse 511. Mention is also made of the famous poetic motif of *dohada-dāna* (578). As we have seen above,[7] our poet has skilfully employed a very large number of figures of speech of both word and meaning. Four of them, viz., *vyāja-stuti*, *ākṣepa*, *upamā* and *rūpaka*, are mentioned by name (783).

(vii) *Purāṇas.* The popularity of the study of the Purāṇas during our period is vouched for by the numerous Paurāṇic references discussed in connection with religious conditions.[8]

1. It is supported by the fact that in *Nāṭya-śāstra*, i.26, *Dhūrtila* is a variant for Dattila.
2. Kane, *History of Sanskrit Poetics*, p. 57, fn. 4.
3. On *Nāṭya-śāstra*, iv.326.
4. *JAHRS*, iii, p. 24.
5. ग्रनुरूपवृत्तघटना सत्कविकृतरूपकेषु लोके च ।
   रमणीवचने यस्यां माधुर्यं काव्यबन्धे च ॥
6. उत्तमतरुणप्रकृतिः पुलकादिकसूचितान्यतरशक्तिः ।
   स्फुटसन्निहितविभावो निवार्यते केन शृङ्गारः ॥

   K 506.
7. *Supra*, pp.32 f.
8. See *supra*, Ch. III.

(viii) *Epics.* The *Rāmāyaṇa* and the *Mahābhārata* had, long prior to our time, received their final form and assumed the role of the fountain head of much of Indian classical literature. Dāmodaragupta affords enough evidence to indicate his familiarity with these twin epics of India.

Rāmāyaṇa. It is stated that although courtesans of the three worlds were available to the lord of demons, i.e., Rāvaṇa, he kidnapped the spouse of Rāma, son of Daśaratha (861), that his attachment to Sītā was one-sided (627) and that he did not use force against her (786). The episode of Jayanta assuming the form of a crow and striking at Sītā's breasts with his beak which is described in the *Rāmāyaṇa* (v. 38) is also alluded to (1014).[1]

Mahābhārata. Verse 640 avers that according to Vyāsa mean men are two : a pauper running after a woman and one without authority resorting to anger.[2] This is only a restatement of *Mahābhārata*, Udyogaparvan, 33.61, which describes these two kinds of men as unhappy.[3] Nala's fame for beauty (551)and of Dharmātmaja, i.e., Yudhiṣṭhira, for truthfulness (194) is alluded to. The episode of Karṇa, son of Rādhā, giving away his mail to Indra is also referred to (78). Hostility between the Pārthas (Pāṇḍavas) and the sons of Dhṛtarāṣṭra (Kauravas) is hinted at in verse 984 which treats close contacts between them as the greatest wonder, while verse 252 represents the army of the Kuru king as covered by the multitude of the arrows of Arjuna.

(ix) *Daṇḍa-nīti.* References to the constituents of the state (*prakṛtis*), expedients (*upāyas*), measures of foreign policy (*guṇas*) and secret tests employed to ascertain the character of high state dignitaries (*upadhās*), discussed above,[4] suggest the prevalence of the study of texts on polity.

1. For references to some other legends found in the *Rāmāyaṇa*, see *supra*, Ch. III.

2. व्यासमुनिनाऽपि गीतौ द्वावेव नराधमौ लोके ।
योऽनाढ्यः कामयते कुप्यति यश्चाप्रभुत्वयुक्तोऽपि ॥

3. द्वाविमौ पुरुषौ लोके सुखिनौ न कदाचन ।
यश्चाधनः कामयते यश्च कुप्यत्यनीश्वरः ॥

4. *Supra*, Ch. II.

(x) *Medicine*. Some allusions of medical import found in our poem indicate not only the popularity of medical studies but also that Dāmodaragupta had a thorough going general knowledge of Āyurveda. Thus, at one place it is said that physicians make efforts to cure even an incurable disease (1029). Another stanza speaks of the use of bitter medicine causing temporary fear (427). We are further told that the use of a thing that is the cause of a malady also cures it (1033). This is a definite principle of Āyurveda and reminds one of the famous maxims 'poison is curative of poison'[1] and 'heat is cured by heat'.[2]

(xi) *Philosophy*. That Dāmodaragupta was familiar with the general principles of the Sāṅkhya system is indicated by verse 318 which refers to the well-known Sāṅkhya doctrines of Puruṣa (the soul), Prakṛti (the matter) and the apparent (not real) changes in the former caused by the latter's actions.[3]

The *svarga-cintakas* or thinkers about heaven mentioned in verse 824 were probably the Mīmāṁsakas.

(xii) *Creative Literature*. Jayāpīḍa's reign constitutes a period of unparallelled literary activity not only in the ancient history of Kashmir but of India as a whole, and our poet must have perused a vast mass of creative literature. However, curious though it might look, the *Kuṭṭanī-mata* affords very little direct evidence on this aspect. The only explicit reference we get appertains the *Ratnāvalī* the enactment of the first act whereof is narrated at length (801-809, 881-928).[4]

Mention is also made of the famous Kalacuri dramatist Anaṅgaharṣa Mātrarāja (800), the author of the *Udātta-Rāghava* and *Tāpasa-Vatsarāja*. Although our author does not refer to his plays, he must have undoubtedly been familiar with them.[5]

1. विषस्य विषमौषधम् ।
2. उष्णमुष्णेन शाम्यति ।
3. प्रतिपुरुषं सन्निहिताः कृत्यपरा विविधविकरणोपचिताः ।
बहुलार्थग्राहिण्यः प्रकृतय इव दुर्ग्रहा गणिकाः ॥
4. For full discussion, see *supra*, pp. 6-8.
5. For a detailed discussion on the identification of Anaṅgaharṣa, see *supra*, pp. 10-15.

That our poet was acquainted with the *Gāthā-satta-saī*, an anthology of some seven hundred Prakrit lyrics compiled by Hāla, is evidenced by verse 399 which is based on *Gāthā-satta-saī*, iv.60.[1]

1. *Supra*, p. 36.

CHAPTER VI

ECONOMIC CONDITIONS

The information afforded by our author about the economic conditions of contemporary Kashmir is much scantier than what we know about the religious and social life of the people. However, we do get a few incidental allusions of interest to a student of the economic history of ancient India which shed some welcome light on agricultural practices, flora, fauna, occupations, industries, trade and coinage. These references are discussed in the following pages.

I. AGRICULTURE

The bulk of the population of ancient Kashmir, as of other parts of the country, lived in villages and had agriculture as its principal occupation. As we have seen above,[1] government officers and other favourites of the king were often granted large pieces of arable lands and sometimes a whole village. Consequently much of the cultivable land was concentrated in a few hands. These officers led a luxurious life and had often to remain away from the villages assigned to them which must have, therefore, been cultivated by landless cultivators for a share in the produce or for wages. In this connection mention is made of the interesting title, *ṭhakkura*. This title occurs in a number of early mediaeval inscriptions and literary works. In some epigraphic records this title is applied to Brāhmaṇa donees and government officials.[2] The Pāṇḍukeśvara grants of Lalitaśūra (9th century A.D.)[3] and Padmaṭadeva (early 10th century A.D.)[4] and the Ramganj plate of *mahāmāṇḍalika* Īśvaraghoṣa of Ḍhekkeṛi in North Bengal[5] are addressed to a large number of government officials and dignitaries including

1. *Supra*, p. 52.

2. Ghumli plates of Bāṣkaladeva, V.S. 1045, *EI*, xxxi, p. 16, line 25; Kālañjar inscription of V.S. 1147, *ibid.*, p. 166, line 17; Kadambapadraka grant of Naravarman, V.S. 1167, *ibid.*, p. 107, line 28; Kamauli plates of Gāhaḍa vālas, *ibid.*, iv, p. 104, lines 26-27; p. 107, line 24; p. 109, line 27; p. 111, line 22; p. 120, line 31; p. 121, line 24; p. 123, line 35; p. 124, line 37; p. 126, lines 31-32; p. 128, line 31; p. 129, line 37, etc.

3. *Ibid.*, xxxi, p. 280, line 11.

4. *Ibid.*, p. 287, line 14.

5. N. G. Majumdar, *Inscriptions of Bengal*, iii, p. 153.

ṭhakkura. The Lucknow Museum plate of Kīrtipāla[1] refers to a chief priest who bore the title of *ṭhakkura*.[2] Kalhaṇa applies the title to small nobility, perhaps Rajputs.[3] Kṣemendra refers to the *ṭhakkuras* and the son of a *ṭhakkura* (*ṭhakkura-putra*) in such a manner as to indicate that they were rich and influential.[4] Scholars have experienced difficulty in interpreting this title, and no satisfactory explanation has been suggested so far. Dr. D. C. Sircar, for example, observes, "*ṭhakkura* is difficult to explain, but may mean nobleman".[5] Elsewhere he states that it is believed to have been derived from the Turkish title *te-gin* and seems to denote a nobleman or zamindar.[6] A stanza in the *Kuṭṭanī-mata* sheds welcome light on this question. Prince Samarabhaṭa tells the dance master that he is given a village comprising good and extensive area, that he should establish his residence there and that in due course he would become a *ṭhakkura*[7]. It leaves no room for doubt that *ṭhakkuras* were big land-lords and as such commanded much influence in village affairs.

Land was measured in terms of *hala* (937)[8]. *Hala* as a measure of land was well-established in early mediaeval times as would appear from epigraphic evidence. The word *hala* appears in some early Prakrit inscriptions also, but there it does not seem to denote a land measure.[9] The Modasa copper-plate inscrip-

1. *EI*, vii, p. 97.
2. D.C. Sircar translates the compound *mahā-purohita-ṭhakkura* as 'head of chief priests', evidently taking *ṭhakkura* to mean the 'head' and regarding the compound as *ṣaṣṭhī-tatpuruṣa*. Vide his *Indian Epigraphy*, p. 329. It would, however, be better to take the compound as *karmadhāraya* and regard both *mahāpurohita* and *ṭhakkura* as two independent titles enjoyed by the same person in this case.
3. *RT*, vii.290, 706, 738. Also see Stein's translation, i, p. 292, fn. 290.
4. *Samaya-mātṛkā*, ii.103: viii.107.
5. *Indian Epigraphy*, p.368.
6. *EI*, xxxi, p. 282, fn. 2; *Indian Epigraphical Glossary*, p. 340.
7. श्रास्ते लिखितो ग्रामो गृहाण तं सत्प्रदेशबहुभूमिम् ।
वासय तत्रावासं भवसि ततष्ठक्कुरो दिवसैः ॥ *K* 931.
8. Tripathi adopts the reading *analpa-phala-jīvanam*; but the reading *analpa-hala-jīvanam* followed by Kaul (in verse 936 of his edition) appears preferable.
9. The *Amara-kośa* also does not mention it as a measure.

tion of Paramāra Bhoja , dated V.S. 1067, refers to a charter granting two *halas* of land.[1] The Santa Bommali plate of Indravarman of the Gaṅga Year 87 aims at recording the gift of three *halas* of land towards meeting the expenses of offering regular worship and repairs to the temple.[2] According to Hārīta cited by Sarvajñanārāyaṇa and Kullūka on *Manu-smṛti*, vii.119, eight, six, four or two bullocks were yoked to a plough.[3] Kullūka says that the land that can be tilled by six bulls forms a medium *hala* (*ṣaḍ-gavaṁ madhyamaṁ halam*). It only indicates that there were different kinds of *hala* measure prevalent in different regions, and sometimes perhaps in the same area also.[4] However, as indicated by the name, originally *hala* must have denoted a piece of land cultivable by a single plough in the course of a year. The measure is still current, but its connotation is not the same everywhere. We have no means to determine the area of a *hala* in Kashmir during the time of our poet.

Coming now to agricultural produce, paddy appears to have been cultivated extensively as rice was the staple food of the people.[5] As stated above,[6] Dāmodaragupta mentions three varieties of rice, viz., *śāli*, *kalama* and *aṇu*. Pulses, three varieties of which, namely, *kulattha*, *caṇa* and *masūra*, are named by our author (229), also must have been widely grown throughout the happy valley. A considerable part of cultivable land was devoted to the cultivation of cotton. We have a clear reference to village women going to pick up cotton from fields (870). Mention is also made of feeding the sheep with cotton

1. *EI*, xxxiii, p. 197, lines 8-9 : *pradatta-hala-dvaya-bhūmi-śāsanam.*
2. *Ibid.*, xxv, pp. 194ff.
3. *HDS*, iii, p. 150, fn. 188. It appears more reasonable to take it to refer to the land that can be tilled by eight, six, four or two bullocks respectively. However, the Nirnay Sagar Press edition (10th, 1946) of the *Manu-smṛti* with Kullūkabhaṭṭa's commentary gives the reading *tri-gavam* instead of *dvi-gavam* followed by Kane. In that case the reference will be to the land tillable by three bullocks.
4. See D.C. Sircar, *Indian Epigraphy*, pp. 134, 411, 417; *Indian Epigraphical Glossary*, p. 125.
5. Cf. *Nīla-mata*, 14, which refers to an abundance of paddy and fruits in Kashmir. Kalhaṇa (*RT*, ii.18;v.270) speaks of fields covered with autumnal rice crop ripening in Bhādrapada.
6. *Supra*.p 131.

seeds (366). Saffron, which was used for a variety of purposes, was also widely cultivated (698). It is stated that Kashmiris, who possess an abundance of saffron, are not aware of its real value and regard indigo as more valuable unless they move out.[1] In fact Kashmir was well-known for its saffron throughout India. Amara (ii.6.123-124) gives *kaśmīra-janman* (grown in Kashmir) as one of the words meaning saffron,[2] while Bilhaṇa states that he was not aware of the growth of saffron in any country other than that of Śāradā (i.e. Kashmir).[3] Our author repeatedly refers to the use of saffron for toilette. It is curious to note that we get no reference to grapes and other fruits for which the valley was very famous in the past as it is even now.

II. FLORA

Our work contains some interesting allusions to ancient Indian flora. The information elicited from these references is outlined hereunder. Except for verses 250-253 which appear to describe the flora of the Abu region, no regional association is indicated, though it is not impossible that the floral wealth of Kashmir is intended.

The moon is said to be the lord of vegetation (245). Trees were planted not only in forests and parks but also on roadsides (*mārga-taru*, 208).

Dāmodaragupta makes no mention of any system of classifying the vegetal world; but a few words indicating some sort of classification have found their way in the poem. Thus, mention is made of milky (*kṣīravat*, 451) and thorny (*kaṇṭakin*, 722) trees. *Oṣadhi* (245) technically means plants withering away after fructification. According to Cakrapāṇidatta, commentator of the *Caraka-saṁhitā*, *oṣadhis* are of two kinds, viz., (1) annuals or perennials bearing fruits, and (2) plants withering away after maturing but without fructification.[4] But whether

1. अविदितगुणान्तराणां को दोषः प्राप्तदेशवासानाम् ।
स्वाधीनकुङ्कुमा अपि यद् विदधति बहुमतिं नीले ॥ *K* 698.

2. Also vide my book *India as seen in the Bṛhatsaṁhitā of Varāhamihira*, p. 320.

3. *Vikramāṅkadeva-carita*, i.21.

4. *Upavana-vinoda*, pp. 11-12.

our author has used this term in its technical sense or for herbaceous plants in general does not admit of verification. *Gulma* (472) denotes a tree without trunk or a group of tendrils with a single root. *Latikā* (135) and *vratati* (670) refer to creeping or twining plants.[1]

An alphabetical list of the flora named in the *Kuṭṭanīmata* is appended below.

1. *Abja* (510,[2] 655) or lotus so called as it grows in water. Other words used for ordinary lotus are *aravinda* (729), *kamala* (103, 264, 965), *padma* (927), *paṅkeruha* (102); *sarasija* (111), *saroja* (561, 996) and *saroruha* (991). Mention is also made of its fibrous root or stalk (*mṛṇāla*, 50, 101, 103, 1020 *mṛṇālikā*, 133, 685, 787), leaves (671, 690) and pollen (*makaranda*, 729). The root of lotus is noted for its softness (50),cooling touch (101, 103, 1020) and sap (133). We have repeated references to assemblages of lotuses (*abjinī*, 690; *saroruhiṇī*, 317; *sarojavatī*, or *-nī*, 996 ; *kamalavatī*, or *-nī*, 131). That the lotus buds open at the touch of the rays of the sun is stated in verses 131 and 317. The association of the bees and the lotus flowers is frequently alluded to. Verse 729 states that the female bee does not get satisfaction unless it drinks the louts pollen. Verse 655 speaks of a female bee entering the lotus flower attracted by the desire of drinking pollen being closed up inside in the evening after sunset.[3] Verse 996 refers to lotus as naturally red (*sahaja-rāga-raktā*), while another stanza (965) describes it as associated with bees, blossoming at a time other than night, i.e., day, possessing pollen and copper-red in colour.

The blue variety called *kuvalaya* is also mentioned. Eyes are often compared to it (169, 771) and its pollen is said to be as shining as gold (981).

2. *Āmra* (733), also called *cūta* (281, 677) and *sahakāra*[4]

1. Cf. *Amara-kośa*, ii. 4. 9, 11. For some of the classifications followed in ancient India, vide Ajay Mitra Shastri, *l.c.*, pp. 275-276.

2. It is a variant.

3. Also cf. verse 927.

4. According to a stanza quoted by Tripathi, *sahakāra* is a variety of mango tree which bears both flowers and fruits :

अपुष्पफलवानाम्रः पुष्पितश्चूत उच्यते ।
पुष्पैः फलैश्च संयुक्तः सहकारः स उच्यते ॥

Sahakāra was used as an ingredient in perfumes. Vide my *India as seen*, etc., Ch. IV, Section VI; V.S. Agrawala, *Harṣa-carita : Eka Sāṁskṛtika Adhyayana*, p. 169.

(672), *Mangifera indica*, is the well-known mango tree. Mention is made of the sprouts (*mañjarī*) surrounded by bees (281) and used as ear-ornaments (677). There is also a reference to the ripe mango fruits being thrown away after chewing (733).

3. *Arjuna, Terminalia arjuna*, is said to grow on the Arbuda mountain (252).

4. *Aśoka* (671, 676), *Jonesia Asoka*. Its fresh leaves were used as ear-ornaments.

5. *Atimuktaka* (668), *Aganosma caryophyllum*. During garden-parties people rested in the bowers formed by *atimuktaka* creepers.

5a. *Badara, Ziziphus jujube*, is said to be of bitter taste. It is a vąriant in verse 772.

6. *Bakula* (591), *Mimusops elengi*, is said to blossom in the rainy season.

7. *Bāṇa*[1] (252) is said to have grown in abundance at Abu.

8. *Bandhujīva*, *Pentapetes phoenicea*. Its flowers which blossomed in the noon (763), were noted for their dark red colour and female lips are compared to it (113).[2]

9. *Campaka*[3] (102), *Michelia champaca*.

10. *Candana*, *Santalum album*. The sandal creeper is said to be surrounded by serpents and wet with sap (998). In summer a bed made from fresh sandal leaves was highly craved for but difficult to procure (992). Sandal paste was noted for its cooling toûch (102) .

10a. *Citralatā* (699), *Rubia Cordifolia*.

11. *Dāḍima*, *Punica granatum*, is the well-known pomegranate tree. Its fruit is noted for its red complexion (56).

12. *Darbha* (603), *Poa cynosuroides*, a grass regarded as sacred and employed in religious ceremonies. Also called *kuśa* (415). Its blade is noted for its sharpness and one who uprooted it or walked through it was sure to get one's hands or feet cut (415, 603).

13. *Kadali* (102, 588, 1021), also called *rambhā* (54, 116, 699), *Musa sapientum*, is the famous plantain tree. Its

1. According to Tripathi, it is a plant called *nilajhiṇṭī* and *kālikoraṇṭī*.
2. In Hindi it is called *dopahariyā*.
3. It is a variant reading.

staff was noted for its soothing touch (102, 1021), and its inside for softness (588). Because of its smoothness female thighs are compared to it (54, 116).

14. *Kalpa-taru* (55) or *-vṛkṣa* (209) is the mythical wish-giving tree.

15. *Karīra* (722), *Capparis aphylla*, is known as *karel* in Hindi. It is a thorny tree with bitter sap.

16. *Khadira* (132, 722[1]), *Acecia catechu*, is described as non-straight, i.e., crooked, sapless, hard, rough and thorny.

17. *Kiṅkirāta*. Its flowers were used as ornaments (676).

18. *Kumuda* (208), water lily, which blossoms at the appearance of moon and fades at its disappearance (516). Assemblages of water lilies (*kumuda-ṣaṇḍa*,[2] 208; *kumudinī*, 516) were a common scene.

19. *Madana* (251), *Randia dumetorum*, growing in Abu region. It is popularly called *dhatūrā*.

20. *Mālatī* (714, 715) or *-tikā* (132), a jasminum species. Surprise is expressed that the *mālatī* creeper entwines round the crooked, hard and rough *khadira* tree (132). Verses 714-715 allude to the close association of the *mālatī* flower and bees.

21. *Mallikā* (866), a jasminum species. Garlands of *mallikā* flowers were used to adorn the hair.

22. *Mṛṣṭaka* (253), said to grow at Abu.[3]

23. *Palāśa* (250), growing in the Abu region.

24. *Pārijāta* (993), one of the mythical divine trees. A task difficult of achievement was figuratively compared to the desire of wearing a bunch of *pārijāta* flowers.

25. *Pīlu* (251), *Salvadora indica*, described as growing on the Arbuda mountain. This name is still current.

26. *Rohiṇī* (253), a creeper or plant represented as growing in the Abu region.

27. *Śāla* (10), *Shorea robusta*, is described as growing in forest.

1. This is the reading adopted by Kaul (verse 721 of his edition) in place of *badara* preferred by Tripathi.

2. This is Kaul's reading (verse 207 of his edition), while Tripathi follows *-khaṇḍa*.

3. *Mṛṣṭaka* is Kaul's reading (verse 252 of his edition), while *miṣṭaka* is given by Tripathi who thinks it may refer to the mango which is sweet (*miṣṭa*). *Mastaka*, which is another reading, means *devadāru*.

28. *Saptapatra* (250), *Alstonia scholaris*, adorned the Arbuda mountain.

29. *Siddhārtha* (740), white mustard.

30. *Sinduvāra* (806, 915), flowers whereof were used as ear-ornaments (677).

31. *Śrīphala* (766), *Aegle marmelos*, is the well-known *bel* (*bilva*) tree fruits whereof were, as at present, eaten.

32. *Sthala-kamala* (7) or-*linī* (56), *Hibiscus mutabilis*, is a variety of lotus grown on land. Dāmodaragupta speaks of forests of *sthala-kamalas* (*sthala-kamala-vanī*,[1] 7) which were noted for their dark red colour and consequently the earth reddened by the lac-dye of the soles of the feet of the constantly moving ladies (7) and crimson-red lips of beautiful damsels (56) were often compared to them.

33. *Tāla-taru* (190), *Borossus flabelliformis*, is the well-known palmyra tree which even now grows abundantly. It is correctly described as straight and tall (*stabdha*).

34. *Tamāla* (16), *Cinnamomum tamala*, is said to have been grown in rows in gardens. Young ladies adorned their cheeks with designs of *tamāla* leaves.

35. *Tilaka* (251) trees are represented to have grown on the Arbuda mountain.

36. *Uśīra* (866), *Andropogon laniger*, paste prepared wherefrom was applied to the hair.

37. *Vaṭa* (175, 450, 468, 474), *Ficus bengalensis*.

III. FAUNA

All the allusions to fauna are of a very general character and but for those met with in verses 951-957 describing the pleasures of hunting are in the form of similes. On the whole, there is no regional association except in verse 9 and verses 241-253 which refer to the fauna of the Vindhya and Abu regions respectively. There is no indication of any classification either.

Wild Animals

The lion (*siṁha*, 79) is noted for its bravery and is said

1. *Sthala-kamalinī* in verse 56 may also be taken to refer to an assemblage of *sthala-kamalas*.

not to spare even the deer which is given to fleeing.

The elephant, variously called *karin* (12), *vāraṇa* (9, 57) and *gaja* (980), is noted for its majestic gait, and the gait of a young beautiful damsel is often compared to it (57, 980). The ceasing of the ichor of the elephant after rutting is also referred to (12). Mad elephants (*matta-vāraṇas*) are said to have inhabited the Vindhya region (9). She-elephant (*kareṇu*) was used as a riding animal. She-elephants, we are told, are always mounted upon by men, look attractive on account of the application of artificial decoration and colours and are beaten on thighs, evidently for increasing the speed.[1]

The deer, called *hariṇa* (79, 189, 250, 419, 568, 955, 981) and *mṛga* (267, 964, 967), is particularly noted for its long unsteady eyes and eyes of ladies are very frequently compared to them (189, 267, 568, 964, 967, 981). There is a reference to the black antelope (*eṇa*, 200) also. Deer skin was worn while performing religious vows (200, 419). The great addiction of the deer to music is alluded to in verse 955 which informs us that hunters specially arranged music and when the deer was sitting motionless with its ears raised up in the act of hearing a song they easily caught it.[2]

Rhinoceros (*khaḍga*) was specially caught for use in ancestral rites (198).

The Monkeys (*plavaga*, 248) and the bear (*ṛkṣa*, 252) are said to have inhabited the Abu region.

To catch a boar (*sūkara*, 956) and a hare (*śaśa*, 999; *śaśaka*, 957) was regarded as a difficult test of hunting skill.

Domestic Animals

Of the domesticated animals, horse, variously known as *aśva* (951, 999), *gandharva* (10), *hari* (251), *turaga* (157, 244, 500) and *turaṅga* (952), is most frequently mentioned. Turkish horses were highly valued and Turkish army is said to have abounded in them (10). The presence of a large number of

1. पुरुषाक्रान्ताः सततं कृत्रिमश्रृङ्गाररागरमणीयाः ।
आहन्यमानजघनाः करेणवो वारयोषाश्च ॥ *K* 321.

2. गीतश्रवणोत्कर्णं निश्चलतृणकवलगर्भमुखहरिणम् ।
उपवेशितमस्पन्दं स्पृहणीया एव गृह्णन्ति ॥ *Ibid* 955.

horses at the gate of a royal palace is also alluded to (251). Horse, which was used as a riding animal, is noted for its speed and ability to move in an uneven area and to take a steady seat on it during hunting operations is highly spoken of. The rider kept his feet firmly on the *rakāb* called *pāda-kaṭaka* (951-952). A horse, it is stated, enters the mind of a rider even without an attractive complexion by its skill in taking turns, leaping, variety of gait, positions, speed and following instructions.[1]

The she-camel (*karabhī*, 722) is described as eating thorny trees with bitter taste like *karīra* and *badara* (or *khadira* according to another reading).

The she-buffalo (*mahiṣī*) is said to take delight in lying in mud (101).

Rams (*ūrṇāyu*, *meṣa*, 361; *uraṇa*, 366) were of great economic value as they supplied wool (366) for which Kashmir has been famous from time immemorial.

Mention is also made of hunting dogs (*viśvakadru*, 953), oxen (*ukṣan*, 212; *vṛṣa*, 999) and ass (*khara*, 650).

Aquatic Animals

There is an allusion to creatures living in a pond 197).

The fish, both male (*matsya*, 735) and female (*matsī*, 998; *jhaṣī*, 1035), is the only aquatic animal mentioned by our author. The female fish is represented as deriving unique satisfaction by looking steadily without twinkling (1035).

Birds

Of birds (*śakuna*, 1040), we have references to the pigeon (*pārāvata*, 157,[2] 581[3]) including the domesticated sort (*gṛha-kapota*, 501[4]) the peacock, male (*kalāpa-bhṛt*, 591) and female

1. वलितप्लुतचित्रगतिस्थितिवेगैश्चोदनानुवृत्त्या च ।
राागस्पर्शेन विना विशति मनः सादिनां तुरगः ॥ *K* 500.

This is Kaul's reading. Tripathi prefers *-bodhai-* to *-vegai-*, but gives *-vegai-* in a note. He gives *valita-* in the text, but seems to adopt *valgita-* in his gloss.

2. It recommends the imitation of the sound of a pigeon by a woman during sexual intercourse.

3. It refers to a kind of embrace called *pārāvat-āvagūhana*.

4. It states that the imitation of the sound of *gṛha-kapota* increases sexual appetite of the youth.

(*mayūrī*, 101, 1035), noted for its hostility towards serpents (101), sweet voice (591) and becoming delighted at the thundering sound of clouds (1035); the cuckoo (*pika*, 105, 299; *para-bhṛta*, 48, 157[1], 501[2], 682; *-tī*, 313; *kala-kaṇṭha*, 668) noted for its sweet melodious voice and natural reddishness of its eyes (313); ruddy goose (*cakrāhva*, 516, 581[3]), the female (*-vadhū*) meeting its male counterpart in the morning (516); *hārīta* (a kind of pigeon, 501) found in the Abu area (247); the swan, both male (*haṁsa*, 57, 292)[3a], 581, 695; *-ka*[4], 157) and female (*haṁsī*, 101), characterised by its attachment to lotus-stalks (101), beautiful gait (57, 292), melodious voice (157[4a]) and ability to separate milk from water (695); *kala-haṁsī* (a sort of white female ruddy goose with red beak and legs, 260) noted for its taking abode in the proximity of rivers; the parrot (*śuka*), said to live in the Abu region (247) and noted for its skill in imitating human speech (356); the sky-lark (*bharadvāja*) which inhabited the Abu region (247); the crow (*kāka*, 133); the owl (*kauśika*) with its liking for the night (*priya-doṣa*, 11); the quail (*lāvaka*, 157[5]); and the *sārikā* (talking maina, *Garcula religiosa*), called *medhāvinī* (913) evidently so called in allusion to its intelligent imitation of human speech.[6]

There is also an allusion to strong sexual appetite of birds (1040).

Reptiles

Among the reptiles mention is made of serpents (*bhujaṅga*, 48, 101, 314, 998; *bhogin* 19; *vilāsin*, 18; *bhujaga*, 191; *pavana-bhojana*, 241; *gandhavaha-bhojana*, 248) with their traditional

1. It speaks of the imitation by a woman of the sound of a cuckoo during sexual intercourse.

2. It avers that the imitation by a woman of the sound of a cuckoo augments sexual longing of young men.

3-3a. It mentions embraces called *cakrāhva-pariṣvajana* and *haṁsa-samāśleṣa*.

4-4a. The stanza refers to a woman's imitation of the sound of swan during cohabitation.

5. It speaks of a woman's imitation of the voice of *lāvaka* at the time of sexual intercourse.

6. The relevant portion of the *Ratnāvalī* (p. 39) mentions only the *sārikā* bird, while *K* uses the word *medhāvinī*.

fear of the *garuḍa* (18), proneness to find out others' holes (191), crooked gait, two tongues and natural inclination to destroy others (413) and their taking abode near the sandal creeper (998); the mongoose (*nakula*, 581[1]) with its natural enmity with snakes (314) and fondness of milk (360[2]); and the lizard (*kṛkalāsa*, 854) known for frequently changing its colour.

Insects

There is an interesting reference to the honey-making bees (*kṣudrā*) which, it is said, leave a honeycomb wherefrom honey has been extracted and where only wax remains (645).

The insect most favourite with classical Sanskrit writers is the large black bee variously called *ali* (110, 112, 927), *indindira* (668), *dvirepha* (682), *bhṛṅga*[3] (105, 299), *bhramara* (667), *madhukara*[4] (293, 715), *madhupa* (715), *madhuliha* (281) and *madhuleha* (294). It is represented as moving in a group (105, 667, 668), drinking the pollen of the lotus flower (729) and sometimes being closed in it in the evening (655) and as being specially fond of the *mālatī* flower (714, 715) and fresh mango sprouts (281). The noise of a multitude of *bhramaras* (105, 668, 682) is a great favourite of the poet who also represents young ladies as frightened by them (667).

IV. INDUSTRIES AND OCCUPATIONS

The different industries and crafts which supplied the various needs of the people must have absorbed a considerable section of the population of Kashmir. Of these, the textile industry was one of the oldest and most flourishing. As we have seen above, Dāmodaragupta refers to the great popularity of fine silk textiles. As at present, Kashmir was very famous for its woollen textiles. A large number of people must have earned their livelihood by taking to woollen industry. The extent to which it had become a part and parcel of Kashmiri life is evident from an interesting simile: a man who enjoyed the company of a courtesan without any payment in return is compared to the

1. The reference is to an embrace known as *nakula-pariramhha*.
2. The verse speaks of giving milk to a domesticated mongoose.
3. The female is called *bhṛṅgī* (517, 729).
4. The female is mentioned as *madhukarī* (552) and *-rikā* (655).

sheep eating cotton seeds without yielding even a thread of wool.[1] Mention is also made of *kutapa*, a kind of woollen blanket made from goats' wool. A variety of woollen textiles like *lohita-kambala*, *sthūla-kambala*, *kutha* and *prāvāra* are mentioned in the writings of Kṣemendra and Kalhaṇa. Kashmir also appears to have grown enough cotton to meet the requirements of her flourishing textile industry. The Chinese traveller, Yuan Chwang, who visited Kashmir about one century and a half earlier, noticed that the people used a rich variety of clothing materials such as the *kauśeya* (*kiao-she-ye*) silk derived from a wild silk-worm, muslin (*tieh*), calico (*pu*), linen (*ch'ü*-(or *ch'u*)-*mo*=*kṣauma*) and wool (*han* (or *kan*)-*po-lo*=*kambala*) and *ho-la-li* (*ral*?), a texture made from the wool of a wild animal.[2] All these textiles appear to have been produced locally.

No society wedded to a settled agricultural life and accustomed to the use of weapons can go without a flourishing metal industry. The different kinds of agricultural implements and steel-made weapons, of which *asidhenu*, *khaḍga*, *kṛpāṇa* and *bhallī* are mentioned by our author, must have been manufactured by skilled blacksmiths. Dāmodaragupta particularly refers to iron particles (*loha-kaṇikā*, 448) noted for their hardness and mentions loadstone (*cumbaka*) that attracts iron objects coming within the sphere of its gravity.[3] Another metal of common utility that attracted the attention of our poet was copper (*tāmra*, 965), and if we were to rely on Kalhaṇa, there existed copper mines in early Kashmir.[4]

As noted above, people of both sexes were crazy for ornaments, and the goldsmith must have had a busy time satiating the demand of golden ornaments (53, 322, 981). We have references to the touchstone (*nikaṣa-bhūmi*, 181; *nikaṣ-opala*, 208; *kanaka-nikaṣa-pāṣāṇa*, 209) which was used for testing the purity of gold, and the description of an individual capable

1. न ददात्येकामूर्णामुरणः परमत्ति कार्पासम् ।। *K* 366.
2. Watters, *op. cit.*, i, p. 148.
3. परमार्थकठोरा अपि विषयगतं लोहकं मनुष्यं च ।
चुम्बकपाषाणशिला रूपाजीवाश्च कर्षन्ति ।।
K 320.
4. *RT*, iv. 616-617.

of correctly evaluating virtues and defects as a touchstone of qualities had become an estasblished convention.

Gold ornaments set with precious stones were also in great demand (947) and jewellers, too, must have had a flourishing trade. Of the precious stones, diamond was specially noted for its hardness (312, 448).[1] The art and science of testing jewels (*ratna-parīkṣā*) had reached a high pitch of development in ancient India, and our author speaks of a gem being tested by a skilled examiner (947).

Leather-working was another important industry. Footwears, ornamented and ordinary, and other leathern articles[2] were in daily use. The Chinese sources inform us that the 7th century Kashmiris wore leather doublets.[3]

Glass industry also appears to have occupied an important place in the economic life of ancient Kashmir. Ornaments fashioned from glass beads were commonly used by people of ordinary means (66). That glass imitations of precious stones (*kāca-maṇi*) were also in circulation and that such copies break to pieces when heated in fire is clearly mentioned (717).

There were also a number of other vocations in which a sizeable section of population found its livelihood. The huntsmen (*lubdha*, 196, *vyādha*,957; *mṛgayu*, 954) fulfilled an important economic function inasmuch as they supplied flesh which formed an important item of food. The watchmen (*yāmika*, 624) kept watch during the night. The actors (*naṭa*, 502) and dancers (*nartaka*, 757, 760; *nartakī*, 82), the latter regarded as craftsmen (*śilpa-jīvin*, 878), entertained people by their performances. Senior dancers (*nartan-ācārya*, 355; *nartak-ācārya*, 875; *nṛty-ācārya*, 793; *nṛty-opadeśaka*, 83) provided training to their followers. The minstrels (*vandin*, 788; *vaitālika*, 761; *nagn-ācārya*, 920) earned their subsistence by satisfying the ego of the princes and noblemen. Theirs was a specialised occupation demanding literary skill, an imaginative mind and an exaggerating speech. We have a beautiful example of the kind of praises they showered

1. Ocean as a source of various jewels is mentioned in *K* 179.

2. According to a variant reading, verse 407 mentions *kutupa* or a small leathern bottle for storing liquids.

3. S. Beal, *Si-yu-ki* or *Buddhist Records of the Western World*, i, p. 148.

on their patrons (762-787, 790-792). Then there were menial servants like water-carrying maids (*ghaṭa-yuvati*, 863) who helped people in their household work. Many a people earned their bread by entering government employment (*rāj-ānujīvin*, 938). We have an interesting description of government servants who were dissatisfied with their lot and often made representations before their employers.[1]

Money-lending was a very flourishing occupation. Money-lenders (*vārdhuṣika*, 616) were known for their notoriety and dishonest practices. More often than not the borrower could not repay the debt and thereby lost his/her pledged deposits (606, 610). There is an express mention of a mischievous usurer who cheated people by entering more money than actually lent and was proud of his tactics.[2]

V. TRADE AND COMMERCE

Occupying a most strategic geographical position, Kashmir had developed commercial relations with other parts of the Indian subcontinent and the outside world quite early. Kashmir's flourishing trade resulted in the emergence of a rich trader class, and in our work we read of bankers (*śreṣṭhin*, 68, 757) and traders (*vaṇik*, 68, 605, 757, 759, 794) leading a luxurious life and playing an important role in the society.[3] Kalhaṇa furnishes an instance of a businessman whose palatial residence was provided with greater amenities, comforts and luxurious decoration than even the royal palace.[4]

Big cities, it may be presumed, were provided with well-arranged markets which were superintended by a government officer called *haṭṭa-pati* (540).[5]

Sometimes dealers accepted deposits which served as the basic capital (*bhāṇḍa-sthāna*) and sold their commodities on

1. See *supra*, p. 53.
2. वञ्चयति जनं योऽसौ हरिणि ह्रो धूर्तताभिमानेन ।
   लिखति शतं दशवृद्ध्या स निमग्नस्तरलिकावर्ते ॥ *K* 746.
3. They are represented as witnessing dance in a richly furnished theatre hall (68) and as receiving a prince (757) who inquires about their welfare (759). The *vaṇiks* are said to have patronised dramatic art (794).
4. *RT*, iv. 13ff. The story relates to the business magnate Noṇa and the Karkoṭa king Durlabhaka Pratāpāditya.
5. For information about the *haṭṭa-pati*, see *supra*, p. 51-2.

credit also; they recorded credit sale account in a register (*sampuṭaka*) which was afterwards totalled, the total being called *piṇḍalikā*; they had a hard time collecting their dues[1]. Sometimes help of a third party was sought in ascertaining the value of the deposits (*madhyastha-sthāpita-mūlya*, 610).

There is an interesting allusion to the weighing balance (*tulā*) which, we are told, even though tied with a strong rope, when raised, allows its pan to go down if only an article is placed on it.[2]

Dāmodaragupta does not supply us with any definite information about Kashmir's trade relations with the outside world. Jayāpīḍa and his predecessors had by their extensive conquests not only improved the political image of Kashmir but must have substantially expanded the scope of her trade with other parts of Northern India also. Jayāpīḍa, in particular, went as far as Bengal in course of his tour of adventure. The manner in which our author describes the cities of Vārāṇasī, Pāṭaliputra, the confluence of the Gaṅgā and Yamunā, i.e., Prayāga, Mt. Abu and Devarāṣṭra seems to indicate that the Kashmiris during his time had acquired an intimate knowledge about the different regions of India where these places were situated. There can be no doubt that Kashmir must have had flourishing commercial relations with these areas. In a later period, Bilhaṇa, in course of his sojourn to the South, went to Vārāṇasi; from Kashmir he made his way to the banks of the river Yamunā along which lay the high road linking north-west with Central India; he first reached Mathurā; then crossing the Gaṅgā northwards he reached Kannauj; then following the course of the Gaṅgā he arrived at Prayāga and finally Vārāṇasi[3]. The same route must have been followed for commercial pur-

1. यत्तु घनसारकुङ्कुमधूपादि मुक्तकं दत्तम् ।
तत् सम्पुटके लिखितं शृणु पिण्डलिकां करोमि ते पुरतः ॥
एतावन्तं कालं नावसरेऽभ्यर्थिता मया त्वमसि ।
रिक्तं भाण्डस्थानं सांप्रतमिति याचनं क्रियते ॥ *K* 607-608.

2. उचितगुणोत्क्षिप्ता अपि पुरतोऽपि निवेशिते सुवर्णलवे ।
झगिति पतन्ति मुखेन प्रकटप्रमदा यथा च तुलाः । *Ibid.*, 322.

3. Bühler (ed.), *Vikramāṅkadeva-carita*, xviii. 84-103. Vide also Intro-

poses also. The *Kathā-sarit-sāgara* also describes a mendicant going from Kashmir to Pāṭaliputra and a student from Pāṭaliputra to Kashmir.[1] The customs officers (*śaulkika*) and their chief (*śaulkik-ādhyakṣa*, 531) who levied customs taxes on all commodities exported from and imported to Kashmir must have played an important part in Kashmir's foreign trade. Dāmodaragupta does not mention items of either export or import. Her exports, however, must have included wool and manufactured woollen goods and saffron. Her imports included Indigo among other things. Our poet clearly tells us that his countrymen did not attach so much value to saffron as to Indigo (699). It was probably imported from Gujarat. Chinese silk must have been another important item of import. The steel-made soles of shoes were also probably imported from Central Asia. We have an interesting reference to the predominance of a strong cavalry in the Turuṣka forces (10). It is not impossible that Turkoman horses were also imported.

VI. SLAVERY

The institution of slavery was an economic necessity in all ancient civilizations, and, as in the rest of the country, it was prevalent in Kashmir also. Mention is made of the writing of *dāsa-patra* (834) which, according to Dharma-śāstra writers, was a variety of the *jānapada* (private) documents and denoted a deed of bondage to serve executed by an individual suffering from want of clothing and food.[2]

VII. COINS AND MEDIA OF EXCHANGE

The numismatic material contained in the *Kuṭṭani-mata*, though very scanty, is not devoid of interest as will appear from the following discussion.

duction, pp. 18-19.

1. Tawney, *The Ocean of Story*, vol. v, pp. 178-179.
2. वस्त्रान्नहीन: कान्तारे लिखितं कुरुते तु य: ।
   कर्माणि ते करिष्यामि दासपत्रं तदुच्यते ॥

Bṛhaspati cited by Tripaṭhi on *K* 834 and in the *Vācaspatya*, vol. vi, p. 4831, under *lekhya*.

Vide also *HDS*, iii, p. 311.

Cowrie Shells

The lowest denomination of prevailing currency which had an exchange value in contemporary market was the cowrie-shell (*varāṭikā*). While elaborating the tricks a strumpet should adopt in order to get rid of an impoverished paramour, Dāmodaragupta states that at her behest a maid, not being seen by but within the hearing distance of the man, should pointedly tell that the value of such a deplorable man as is deridedly laughed at by the servants at the instance of their mistress is not even as much as five cowrie-shells.[1]

Cowrie-shells served as a medium of exchange from a remote antiquity, and even after the invention of metallic currency they continued to be used in day-to-day transactions side by side with coined money. Thus, notwithstanding the abundant monetary issues in gold, silver and copper struck by the Imperial Guptas, the Chinese pilgrim Fa-hian found the market places in the Gupta empire flooded with cowrie-shells.[2] Similar was the case in ancient Kashmir. Abundant copper currency called *Toramāṇa* circulated widely in Kashmir in the sixth century A.D. and for a long period thereafter.[3] From the seventh century A.D. onwards the Karkoṭa kings issued an extensive currency in electrum,[4] silver and copper.[5] Coined money continued to be minted by the rulers belonging to the

1. अवगम्याभिप्रायं स्वामिन्याः परिजनोऽपि यं पुरुषम् ।
अवहसति तिरस्कार्यं तस्य न मूल्यं वराटिकाः पञ्च ॥ *K* 634.

2. H.A. Giles, *The Travels of Fa-hsien* (399-414 A.D.), *or Record of the Buddhist Kingdoms* (Cambridge, 1923), p. 21.

3. In the excavation of the Avantisvāmin temple at Avantipura *Toramāṇa* coins were found in association with the coins of the Muslim rulers. Vide *ASI, AR*, 1913-14, pp. 50-51. Their prevalence as late as the 15th century A.D. is shown by *Śrivara's Chronicle*, iii. 213.

4. The electrum coins having a mixture of gold, silver and copper in different proportions may have actually been intended to circulate as genuine gold coins.

5. Cunningham (*Coins of Mediaeval India*, p. 29) thought that the Karkoṭas did not issue copper coins at all. He regarded the abundant copper coins bearing the names of the Karkoṭa kings who issued them as forgeries which were guilt for passing as genuine gold coins. (Smith *Catalogue of Coins in the Indian Museum*, Calcutta, vol. i, pp. 268- 69), on the other hand, describes the copper coins of Pratāpāditya II Durlabha and Vinayāditya Jayāpīḍa. S. C. Ray (*JNSI*, xiv, pp. 122-24) has given

Utpala and Lohara dynasties.[1] But this metallic currency could not drive cowrie-shells out of market, and the extant evidence, literary and archaeological, indicates that they continued to be in circulation up to a comparatively late period. Dāmodaragupta is not the only literateur to refer to the use of cowrie-shells. Kṣemendra (11th century A.D.) mentions the use of cowrie-shells for ordinary daily transactions such as the purchase of vegetables.[2] The poet-historian Kalhaṇa also refers to cowrie-shells in connection with the same period[3].

Rūpaka

Dāmodaragupta makes mention of the silver coin called *rūpaka* also. Dilating upon the greediness of courtesans, he represents Guṇapālita as telling his friend Sundarasena that for prostitutes a wealthy man is verily the god of love, a man with a variety of *rūpakas* is the most handsome, a man possessed of riches is the real lover, while one without wealth is dull.[4] The word *rūpaka* is employed in literature and inscriptions in the sense of silver coins. The silver coins of the Guptas[5] and the Kalacuri king Kṛṣṇarāja[6] were called *rūpakas*. There is no reason to doubt that Dāmodaragupta has also used *rūpaka* in this sense. But silver coins of ancient Kashmir are rare in the extreme. Of the early rulers of Kashmir, only Pravarasena II (*cir.* 580 A.D.) is known to have issued silver coins weighing

cogent reasons to show that the Karkoṭaka kings issued copper coins alongside the electrum coins. The point is clinched by Kalhaṇa who states that from a mountain situated in Karmarājya Jayāpīḍa obtained copper sufficient to coin hundred crores less one *dinnaras* which bore his name. Vide *RT*, iv. 617.

1. Smith, *Catalogue of Coins in the Indian Museum*, Calcutta, vol. i, pp. 269-273.

2. *Samaya-mātṛkā*, viii. 80; *Kalā-vilāsa*, ii. 5,7 (*kapardikā*).

3. *RT*, vii. 112.

4. प्रद्युम्नः प्रद्युम्नो विरूपकः खलु विरूपकः सततम् ।
सुस्निग्धः सुस्निग्धो रूक्षो रूक्षस्तु गणिकानाम् ॥ *K* 305.

5. D.C. Sircar, *Select Inscriptions* (2nd ed., Calcutta 1965), p. 357, text line 6, note 1.

6. V.V. Mirashi, *Inscriptions dated in the Kalachuri-Chedi Era*, *CII*, iv, p. 151, lines 38-9.

about 120 grains.[1] But Dāmodaragupta's reference to *rūpakas*, first noticed in these pages, seems to indicate the prevalence of silver coins in a large number, and it is quite possible that one day we may come across more examples of silver coins. That silver coins continued to be in circulation in Kashmir as late as the eleventh century A.D. is evidenced by their mention by Kṣemendra.[2]

Kedara

However, the most interesting piece of numismatic evidence offered by our poet is the mention of the coin denomination called *Kedara*. As a means of inciting a paramour to give his wealth to the prostitute he loved a money-lender tells the prostitute that on the pearl-necklace she had pledged with him her maid has already borrowed thirty *Kedaras* and wants to borrow more for her (prostitute's) paramour.[3] *Kedara* as a coin denomination is also mentioned in the *Kāśikā* (on *Aṣṭādhyāyī*, v.2.120).[4] As indicated by the name itself, it evidently denoted the coins of ancient Kashmir issued in imitation of the gold and base gold coins of the Little Kuṣāṇas who were also known as Kidāra Kuṣāṇas as the dynasty was probably founded by a chief named Kidāra. The gold coins of the Kidāra Kuṣāṇas bore the effigy of the king standing to left with the legend *Kidāra* in Brāhmī characters under his left arm on the obverse and the goddess (Ardoksho) seated on throne with cornucopiae in her left hand on the reverse.[5] The Toramāṇa copper coins, the

1. Cunningham, *Coins of Mediaeval India*, p. 43; Stein, *RT*, Engl. tr., ii, p. 319.
2. *Samaya-matṛkā*, viii 71.
3. पूर्वं दत्तस्योपरि मुक्ताहारस्य केदरास्त्रिंशत् ।
परिचारिकया नीता अन्यानपि मृगयते वयस्यकृते ॥ *K* 606
व्ययस्य कृते is a variant.
4. Kṣemakīrti, while commenting on a passage of the *Bṛahatkalpabhāṣya*, mentions *ketara* as a coin-name. *Ketara* is probably the same as our *Kedara*. See *JNSI*, xii, pp. 198-99; xiv, p. 109 ; *JAIH*, iii, pp. 163-64.
5. Cunningham, *Later Indo-Scythians*, pp. 66ff. The Little Kuṣāṇas issued silver and copper coins also. The silver coins carried the bust of the king facing front with the Brāhmī legend *Kidāra Kuṣāṇa Sāhi* on the obverse and the fire-altar guarded by two sword-bearing attendants on the reverse. The copper coins bore male bust to left within a beaded circle on the obverse and legend in Brāhmī on the reverse.

gold and silver coins of Pravarasena II and the gold coins of Narendrāditya, issued in imitation of the Kidāra Kuṣāṇa coins, bear the word *Kidāra* on the reverse.[1] But the first regular series of Kashmir coins started with Durlabhaka, the founder of the Karkoṭa dynasty. The copper and electrum coins of all the Karkoṭa kings from Durlabhaka to Jayāpīḍa-Vinayāditya, which are close copies of the gold coins of the Kidāra Kuṣāṇas, show, as a rule, the name *Kidāra* or its abbreviations (*Kida*, *Ki* or *Ke*) under the left arm of the standing king.[2] The presence of this name reminds one of the originator of this type of coins, the first Little Kuṣāṇa king Kidāra. This is analogous to the occurrence of the name of the Ohind king Sāmantadeva on the coins of the Cāhamāna rulers of Delhi and Ajmer, Someśvara and Pṛthvīrāja III, although he had ceased to rule long ago.[3] The word *kedara*, therefore, appears to denote the coins of the Karkoṭaka rulers of Kashmir bearing the name Kidāra or its abbreviations. It is interesting to note in this connection that on the copper coins of Jayāpīḍa, the patron of our poet, we find *ke* as an abbreviation for Kidāra[4] instead of *ki* found on the coins of other kings.

To borrow thirty copper coins against a pearl necklace would amount to attaching too high a value to copper coins. In all probability, therefore, the word *kedara* as used by Dāmodaragupta denoted the electrum coins which were originally intended to pass as gold coins.

1. Cunningham, *Coins of Mediaeval India*, pp. 43ff.
2. *Ibid.*, pp. 43-45; Smith, *op. cit.*, pp. 268-69.
3. *Ibid.*, pp. 261-62.
4. *Ibid.*, p. 269.

CHAPTER VII

FINE ARTS

Our work affords a good deal of material to throw light on the state of fine arts in early medieval Kashmir. Most of the allusions pertain to the trio of music, dance and drama, information about other arts being extremely scanty.

I. MUSIC

Music is referred to as *saṅgīta*[1] (793) and *gāndharva* (876) and musicians as *gandharva*[2] (10, 180). Nārada, son of Brahmā, as stated above, was traditionally regarded as the expounder of music (76, 875), while Mataṅgamuni is said to have been an expert in the employment of hollow instruments (877). Dhenuka is described as the composer of a particular *tālaka* or beating time (83).[3] Vārāṇasī (10) and Pāṭaliputra (180) are said to have abounded in musicians.

We have references to both vocal and instrumental music. Verses 75 and 929 draw a distinction between singing (*gīta*) and playing on instruments as well as the sound created by the latter. A singer is called *gātṛ* (757, 944) and an instrumentalist *vādaka* (942).

Musical instruments, called *vādya* (16, 236, 576) and *ātodya* (125, 880, 929), were traditionally divided into four classes, to wit, (i) *tata* or stringed, (ii) *avanaddha* or percussion, (iii) *ghana* or cymbal, and (iv) *suṣira* or wind instruments, fashioned respectively from strings, skins, brass and bamboo[4]

1. The word *saṅgīta* was probably employedin a wider sense so as to include acting (*nāṭya*) also within its connotation. For in reply to Samarabhaṭa's query about the state of *saṅgīta* the dance-master described the condition of drama (793-794).

2. Even today there is a class of musicians called *gandharva* at Vārāṇasī. They give their daughters training in music and dancing and are consequently looked down upon. But their daughters-in-law are treated as respectable ladies. Cf. Dāmodara's *Ukti-vyakti-prakaraṇa*, 56/6, pp. 82-83.

3. *Tāla* also denotes a musical instrument fashioned from bell-metal. Cf. *Nāṭya-śāstra*, xxviii. 2. *Dhavaluka* and *tānaka* and *bhāṇaka* are variants for *Dhenuka* and *tālaka* respectively.

4. ततं चैवावनद्धं च घनं सुषिरमेव च ।
चतुर्विधं तु विज्ञेयमातोद्यं लक्षणान्वितम् ॥

and illustrated by lyre, tabor, cymbal or bell and lute. Of these, only the first and the last (877) are explicitly referred to in the *Kuṭṭanī-mata*, the former under the name *tantrī-vādya* (16, 236, 576). The stringed instruments are said to produce sound at the stroke of nails.[1] Elsewhere (236), *tantrī* or lyre and *muraja* or tabor are described as varieties of instruments (*vādya-bheda*). All the varieties of musical instruments are collectively called *sakal-ātodya* (880).

The fact that *vīṇā* claims the largest number of references[2] indicates that it was the most popular among the instruments in vogue. The sound of *vīṇā* is referred to as *parivāda* (14). Verse 576 speaks of the production by stringed instruments of the particular sounds called *kuharita*, *recita* and *kampita*, which according to Bharata refer to the trembling notes enshrined in throat, head and heart.[3] Among other instruments mention is made of *muraja* (75, 236), *vaṁśa* or lute[4] and *tūrya*[5] (891). The lute-player was called *vāṁśika* (757, 881).

We get some interesting information about vocal music also. The best tone is that which is flawless at the three sources, viz., the heart, throat and head (*tri-sthāna-viśuddha-nāda*, 790). Seven musical notes (*svaras*), viz., *ṣaḍja*, *ṛṣabha*, *gāndhāra*, *madhyama*, *pañcama*,[6] *dhaivata* and *niṣāda*,[7] six qualities of song, namely pleasing sound, sentiment, attachment, sweetness of component

ततं तन्त्रीकृतं ज्ञेयमवनद्धं तु पौष्करम् ।
घनं तालस्तु विज्ञेयः सुषिरो वंश उच्यते ॥

Nāṭya-śāstra, xxviii.1-2.

Also cf. *Viṣṇu-dharmottara*, iii.19; Yaśodhara on *Kāma-sūtra*, i.3.16, p. 30:

घनं च विततं वाद्यं ततं सुषिरमेव च ।
कांस्यपुष्करतन्त्रीभिर्वेणुना च यथाक्रमम् ॥

1. नखप्रहाररणितं तन्त्रीवाद्येषु, *K* 16.

2. *Ibid.*, 14, 264, 265, 357. Also called *tantrī*, 236.

3. *Nāṭya-śāstra*, xxix. 21-22, 43.

4. Implied in *vāṁśika*=lute-player, 757, 881. It was so called because it was made of bamboo (*vaṁśa*).

5. At present called *turahī* in Hindi. It is a kind of hollow (*suṣira*) instruments.

6. Also mentioned in 881.

7. Cf. *Saṅgīta-ratnākara*, i.24. As pointed out by Tripathi, seven *mārgas* may also be intended.

letters and adornment, and the modes of the three *layas*, to wit, *sama*, *sroto-vaha* and *go-puccha*, are alluded to (940).[1] The good qualities of a song are referred to. They are conformity with the prescribed measure, flawlessness at the three sources, appropriate rise and fall of tone, proper use of the *druta*, *madhya* and *vilambita layas* (time) of the *tālas* (beating times), expression of the sentiment, employment of tunes appropriate to particular *rāgas* or sentiments, and bringing about harmony when there is a conflict between the definition and the defined in particular *rāgas*.[2] Mention is also made of *dvipadī laya* (881) and the song called *carcarikā* (904) and *dhruvās* (928)[3], the last one said to have been sung for eight *kalās*[4] and endowed with proper *tālas* and *layas* (883).

Vocal and instrumental music was often combined, and perfect harmony between the two was highly appreciated. Verse 881 refers to the harmony between the sound of the lute and the tone of the singer. A good instrumentalist was one who showed skill in producing deep melodious sound to the accompaniment of a variety of songs and did not, at the same time, violate the beating time.[5]

Music played an important part in drama as indicated by the account of the performance of the first act of the *Ratnāvalī*. Prior to the commencement of the play the stage-manager had to get all instruments ready (880). The play began with a lute-player and a singer performing music. The stage-manager made his appearance on the stage at the end of the*p rāveśikī dhruvā* and sang a *dhruvā* endowed with proper *tāla* and *laya* (881, 883). The play ended with the *naiṣkrāmikī dhruvā* marking the exit of the hero and other characters and sound of songs and instruments coming to a close (928-929).

1. सप्ताश्रयः षडात्मा शारीरस्त्रिप्रमाणपरिमाणः ।
सत्त्वाधिक्याज्ज्येष्ठो व्यस्तसमस्तैस्त्रिभिर्विनिष्पाद्यः ।। *K* 940.

For a detailed discussion of this verse, see Tripathi's gloss.

2. नियमितदीपनगमनं द्रुतमध्यविलम्बितालयुतम् ।
रसवत् स्वरोपपन्नं कृतसाम्यं साधु गातृभिर्गीतम् ।। *Ibid.*, 944.

3. For *dhruvās*, see *Nāṭya-śāstra*, Ch. xxxii.

4. A *kalā*=5 *nimeṣas* or time necessary for pronouncing five short syllables. Vide *ibid.*, xxxi. 4.

5. गम्भीरमधुरशब्दं परिबृंहितगीतविविधभङ्गयुतम् ।
दर्शयतो वैचित्र्यं न भ्रष्टो वादकस्य लयकालः ।। *K* 942

Besides the professional singers and instrumentalists referred to above, mention is also made of minstrels (*vaitālika*, 761; *vandin*, 788; *nagnācārya*, 920) who adopted versified eulogy of the members of the royalty for their occupation.

The idea that we get from the *Kuṭṭanī-mata* about the popularity of music in ancient Kashmir is corroborated by independent archaeological and literary evidence. The Buddhistic site of Harwan dating from not later than the fourth century A.D. has yielded some tiles bearing depictions of music scenes. On one of these tiles are represented three musicians playing a flute, a cymbal and a pair of drums from left to right respectively (Pl.IX.15).[1] On another tile we see standing a female musician playing on a drum.[2] which is slung over her left shoulder. Kalhaṇa also makes some interesting references to music, which had become popular even with the Buddhist monks.[3] We learn from the *Nīla-mata* that on every feṣtival, whether purely religious, semi-religious, seasonal or agricultural, the chief item of the celebrations was music—vocal as well as instrumental.[4]

II. DANCE

As we have seen above,[5] dancing girls were hereditarily attached to temples, and dance must have formed a regular feature of the temple ritual. The wide popularity enjoyed by classical dances is vouched for by the reference to the dance performed in conformity with the precepts of Kohala and Bharata (83). It may be mentioned in this connection that our author's patron, King Jayāpīḍa, is said to have gone to the temple of Skanda at Puṇḍravardhana in order to witness a dance performed in accordance with Bharata's instructions.[6] Dances often took place on the spot where four roads met

1. R.C. Kak, *Ancient Monuments of Kashmir*, pl. xxviii.14 : upperb and.
2. *Ib.*, pl. xxvii.11.
3. *RT*, i.140. Also cf. v. 364 which refers to thes inging of two Domba girls.
4. Ved Kumari, *l.c.*, p. 100.
5. *Supra*, pp. 86-87
6. *RT* iv.; *supra*, p. 28.

(*śṛṅgāṭaka*) or in an assemblage of the *viṭas* (*viṭa-khaṭaka*),[1] who were evidently regarded as the most competent connoisseurs. One expressed one's appreciation of dance by offering a flower-garland taking it out of one's own neck and betel and by thanking the dancing girl (84). There were also male dancers (*nartaka*) who took to dancing as a means of subsistence (878). There were regular dance teachers called *nṛty-opadeśaka* (83), *nṛty-ācārya* (793), *nartan-ācārya* (355) and *nartak-ācārya* (875) who trained their pupils in the art of dancing and acting.[2] Dance was regarded as a craft (*śilpa*, 878). The celestial nymph Rambhā was traditionally treated as an ideal dancer (86).

Reference may now be made to some interesting technical terms connected with dance and employed by Dāmodaragupta. One such word is *preṅkhaṇaka* which is found used in verse 83. Although normally employed in the sense of one of the eighteen kinds of *uparūpaka*, a drama of an inferior class,[2a] from the context[3] it also appears to have denoted dance in general or a kind thereof.[4] The movements of feet in dance are referred to as *parikrama* (86, 804, 928).[5] *Vasu*, *nanda* and *citra*, mentioned in verse 76, may, according to one view, refer to some varieties of *parikrama*.[6] Another stanza speaks of people practising dance experiencing pain because of *sūcī*.[7] According to Sanskrit, lexica, *sūcī* is a kind of dance or physical acting (*āṅgik-ābhinaya*)[8] while the *Saṅgīta-ratnākara* takes it to mean the movement of

1. *Sṛṅgāṭaka* and *viṭa-khaṭaka* are variant readings in verse 82. Tripathi splits the latter into *viṭa* and *khaṭaka* and takes it to mean the dance-type desired to be seen (*khaṭaka*) by the *viṭas* or a subject difficult to be understood even by the *viṭas*. Cf. *Haima* :—*khaṭas=tṛṇe kaphe ṭaṅke-andha-kūpe prahāre* (quoted by Tripathi); *Medinī*:—*khaṭo=ndha-kūpa-khapayoḥ prahār-āntara-ṭaṅkayoḥ* (quoted in the Rāmāśramī gloss on the *Amara-kośa*).

2. For the representation of a dance teacher, see Pl. IX. 14, and of a dance school, Pl. VIII 13.

2a *Sāhitya-darpaṇa*, 547.

3. Cintāmaṇi is represented as inquiring of a dance master about his proficiency in *preṅkhaṇaka*.

4. Tripathi derives the word from the root *pra-ikkhi*=to move violently.

5. It is technically called *cārī*. Vide *Nāṭya-śāstra*, Ch. 10.

6. See Tripathi's commentary on verse 76.

7. सूचीव्यथानुभूतिर्नृत्याभ्यासप्रवृत्तानाम् । *K* 191.

8. सूची तु सीवनद्रव्येऽप्याङ्गिकाभिनयान्तरे ।

arms in dance indicating future event[1]. Mention is also made of two attitudes of hands at the time of dance, viz., *sandaṁśa* and *Khaṭakāmukha* (759). The former denotes a kind of hand pose resembling a pair of tongs wherein the foreparts of the fore-finger and the thumb touch each other without in any way affecting the bottom and middle of these fingers.[2] According to a stanza quoted by Arjunavarmadeva in his Śṛṅgāradīpikā commentary on the *Amaruka-śataka* (verse 1), that attitude wherein something is pressed by the thumb in the middle of the forefinger and middle finger and where the ring finger also comes into contact is known as *katakāmukha*.[3] Verse 804 mentions performing a variety of *sthānakas* while another stanza (85) speaks of flawlessness in respect of *sthānaka* (*sthā-naka-śuddhi*). *Sthānaka* is a variety of the movements of feet in dance and is said to be of six kinds.[4] In verses 85-86 which contain Cintāmaṇi's appreciative remarks about the performance of a danseuse we get an idea about the then notions of the chief contents of dancing. They are: various movements of arms,[5] keeping the limbs straight and steady, elegance, the lifting of the limbs above, turning sideways, flawlessness of the *sthānakas*, allround skill,[6] ability to distinctly express various feelings and sentiments by means of novel undulations and a

Medinī.

स्त्री सूचिनृत्यभेदे च व्यधनीशिखयोरपि *Ratna-kośa.*

1. वर्तना सा भवेत् सूची भाविवाक्योपजीवनात् ॥

Saṅgīta-ratnākara, vii.27. Quoted by Tripathi.

For another definition see *Nāṭya-śāstra*, iv. 137, pl. xiii. 76.

2. तर्जन्यङ्गुष्ठसन्दंशस्त्वरालस्य यदा भवेत् ।
आभुग्नतलमध्यस्थः स सन्दंश इति स्मृतः ॥ *Nāṭya-śāstra*, ix. 110.

3. तर्जनीमध्यमामध्ये पुङ्खोऽङ्गुष्ठेन पीयते ।
यस्मिन्ननामिकायोगः स हस्तः कटकामुखः ॥

Cited by Tripathi. For another definition see *Nāṭya-śāstra*, ix. 60.

4. *Nāṭya-śāstra*, x.51.

5. In case the variant reading *bhuja-patana* is accepted, it would refer to the falling of the arms from the waist which takes place prior to the commencement of the dance and to the movement of arms for expressing feelings.

6. This is based on Tripathi. It may alternatively refer to the graceful pose of the body at the beginning of all kinds of dance.

variety of movements of feet.[1] Keeping time with feet (*pada-mātrā*) was one of the most essential principles of dance and formed the main basis of its appreciation by the lay people and sometimes even by pseudo-*nāgarakas* (87). An item that marked the conclusion of a dance performance is referred to as *apasāraka* (87). It is not mentioned in texts on dramaturgy but, as suggested by Tripathi, may denote music indicating the exit of the dancing girl at the end of the performance. There is also a reference to an excellent dancer (*nartakī bhadrā*, 82). According to Bharata, a good danseuse is one who is maddened by youth and other accomplishments, is well-versed in dancing and singing, is ever eloquent and bold, free from laziness and fatigue and unparallelled in an assemblage of beautiful young ladies as regards merits.[2] Various systems or methods of dancing are mentioned as *prasthāna* (82).

Dancing was one of the chief means through which people expressed their exuberant joy on festive occasions like Madanamaha (888, 896, 904). Like music, dance was also an important ingredient of dramatic performances.

The popularity of dance in ancient Kashmir is vouched for by independent evidence. A tile from the ancient site of Harwan bears the representation of a dancer wearing large ear-rings and dressed in loose robe and trousers, with a long scarf held in both hands, which she waves over her head.[3] The *Nīla-mata* prescribes dances on religious occasions like the awakening of the god Viṣṇu,[4] Śiva-caturdaśī,[5] the birth-day of

1. भुजवलनगात्रसंस्थितिलालित्योद्वहनपार्श्ववलितानि ।
अनयैव निर्मितानि स्थानकशुद्धिश्च चातुरस्र्यं च ॥
प्रविभक्तैर्भावरसैरभिनवभङ्गया परिक्रमैश्चित्रैः ।
रम्भामप्यतिशेते किमुतेतरमर्त्यनर्तकीलोकम् ॥

2. यौवनादिगुणोन्मत्ता नृत्तगीतविचक्षणा ।
सदा प्रगल्भा च तथा त्यक्तालस्या जितश्रमा ॥
समागतासु नारीषु रूपयौवनकान्तिषु ।
न दृश्यते गुणैस्तुल्या नर्तकी सा प्रकीर्तिता ॥ *Nāṭya-śāstra.*

3. R.C. Kak, *Ancient Monuments of Kashmir*, pl. xxvii.12.
4. *Nīla-mata*, vv.408, 412.
5. *Ibid.*, 559.

the Buddha,[1] worship of Aśokikā and Umā,[2] Bhadrakālī[3] and Śyāmā,[4] the installation of divine images[5] and the New Snowfall day,[6] in social gathering held in honour of seasons,[7] on agricultural festivals,[8] and on such horticultural occurrences as the ripening of grapes.[9] Kalhaṇa not only refers to the association of dancing girls with temples but also speaks of personal interest shown by some kings in this art. King Kalaśa took to the collecting of dancing girls as a hobby.[10] King Harṣa personally instructed dancing girls in the art of acting keeping awake at night.[11]

III. DRAMA

In connection with the enactment of the first act of the *Ratnāvalī* which is described in detail in vv. 801-809, 880-928, and its appreciation by prince Samarabhaṭa in vv. 940-947, Dāmodaragupta makes numerous interesting references to various aspects of the theory and practice of the art of theatrical performance. As we have already seen,[12] Bharata, Kohala, divine damsels, Nārada, Mataṅgamuni, sons of Bharata, and the ladies of the harem of king Nahuṣa were traditionally associated with the origin and descent on earth of drama.

The words *prekṣaṇaka* (929, 1010), *prekṣā* (949), *nāṭya-prayoga* (930) and *prayoga* (940, 1009) are employed to denote a dramatic performance. The spectators were technically called *sāmājika* (798, 882, 938), while those fond of drama are referred to as *nāṭyaprajā* (879). Acting, like dancing, was regarded as a craft (*śilpa*, 1008). Dance and drama were closely connected with each other, and training in acting was often imparted by dance masters (793, 875).

Knowledge of dramatics is said to have been a family-learning (*kula-vidyā*) of the princes (949), while another stanza

1. *Ibid.*, 758.
2. *Ibid.*, 801.
3. *Ibid.*, 788.
4. *Ibid.*, 464, 468.
5. *Ibid.*, 862.
6. *Ibid.*, 674.
7. *Ibid.*, 519, 527-28, 547, 750.
8. *Ibid.*, 801.
9. *RT*, vii. 606.
10. *Supra*, pp. 183-84.
11. *Ibid.*, vii. 1140.
12. *Ibid.*, 688.

(939) refers to kings' proficiency in drama. These statements are corroborated by the appreciative remarks skilfully put in the mouth of prince Samarabhaṭa (940-947). Plays were often enacted for the entertainment of princes, as was the first act of the *Ratnāvalī* for the recreation of Samarabhaṭa. Dance masters, who were in charge of dramatic performances, seem to have eagerly awaited royal visits to get an opportunity to exhibit their skill with the hope of being suitably rewarded, and we actually find prince Samarabhaṭa granting a village to the *nartak-ācārya* (931). Big business magnets (*śreṣṭhin*) and traders (*vaṇij*) were also noted for their patronage of theatrical art (68, 794).

There is an interesting reference to large theatre-halls provided with thick cushioned seats and back-rests which appear to have been managed by *śūlā-pālas*.[1] It is likely that these halls were attached to courtesans' houses. Although the reference is in connection with Vārāṇasī, it is probable that such halls existed in ancient Kashmir also. The precincts of temples also served as venues of theatrical performances, and the first act of the *Ratnāvalī* appears to have been staged in the courtyard of the temple of Vṛṣabhadhvaja at Vārāṇasī. The prevalence of this latter practice in ancient Kashmir is vouched for by Kalhaṇa who compares the fleeing forces of a king to people caught by a down-pour while watching a theatrical performance.[2] The *Nīla-mata* also describes a number of functions as celebrated around bonfire outside the houses or in open fields.[3]

As regards the pre-requisits of success in dramatic performance, we are told that skill is unthinkable without mental

1. श्रेष्ठिवणिग्विटकितवप्रधानरङ्गस्य सुमहतो मध्ये ।
शूलापालस्थापितकतिपयबद्धोरुपीठिकासीनः ॥

K 68. For back-supports, see verse 70.

In case the other reading °*Vadhr-oru*° is accepted, the seats would appear to have been fashioned from leather.

2. ततश्चिचलिषावेष राज्ञि तत्कटको दिशः ।
स वृष्ट्यम्बुहतो रङ्गप्रेक्षिलोक इवाभवत् ॥ *RT*, vii. 1666.

3. Ved Kumari, *op. cit.*, p. 109.

concentration, while the beauty of acting depends on skill.[1]

Dramatic performance is said to be of two kinds, viz., (i) *amiśra* or pure consisting of recitation (*pathyā*) alone, and (ii) *miśra* or mixed which combines recitation, music both vocal and instrumental, and dance with one of them preponderating over the rest (805).[3] Theatrical art is styled bodily (*śārīra*) as its constituents like music and dance depend on the body; it is said to have three sources (*tri-pramāṇa*), to wit, *loka* or world, *veda* and *adhyātma* or metaphysics (940).[4] Mention is also made of the various *vṛttis* or styles of dramatic composition which are known to be four, viz., *bhāratī*, *kaiśikī*, *sātvatī* and *ārabhaṭī*.[5] A drama was to be staged with tender and entertaining actions and expression of various transitory feelings.[6] *Paṭhita* or text was an important constituent of drama: it was in a variety of languages, generally speaking in Sanskrit and Prakrit.[7] A text recited without leaving appropriate places, viz., heart, throat and head, and in conformity with the sentiment, with expressive changes of voice (*kāku*),[8] clear in meanings and words, beautifully, flawlessiy and without unnecessary pause was highly lauded.[9] Faithful imitation of dress and make up suitable to

1. चेतोऽन्तरा न सत्त्वं सत्त्वे सति चारुता प्रयोगस्य । *K* 799

चेतोवशिता is a variant.

2. उद्यमसाहित्यवशाच्छोभातिशयेन मदनुबन्धेन ॥ *Ibid.*, 903.

3. *Vādye* and *nādye* are variants in place of *nāṭye*, Vide Kaul's edition.

4. Cf. लोको वेदस्तथाऽध्यात्मं प्रमाणं त्रिविधं स्मृतम् ॥

लोकाध्यात्मपदार्थेषु प्रायो नाट्यं व्यवस्थितम् ॥ *Nāṭya-śāstra*, xx.7

5. भारती सात्वती चैव कैशिक्यारभटी तथा ।

चतस्रो वृत्तयो ह्येता यासु नाट्यं प्रतिष्ठितम् ॥

Ibid., vi.24b-25a. Also of. *ibid*,, i.41.

6. सुकुमाराविद्धक्रिय उपरञ्जकरञ्जितो विविधवृत्तिः ।

आदेयहेयमध्यैर्भावैः संपादितः प्रयोगोऽयम् ॥ *K* 941.

विविधनृत्तः and विविधनृत्यः are variant readings.

7. For a detailed treatment of *pāṭhya* and languages, see *Nāṭya-śāstra*, ch. xvii.

8. For various kinds of *kāku*, see *ibid.*, xvii. 106ff.

9. अपरित्यक्तस्थानकरसकाकुव्यञ्जितस्फुटपदार्थम् ।

अभिरामाविश्रान्तं पठितं निरवद्यभाषासु ॥ *K* 943.

०मखिलभावयुतम् is a variant.

various dispositions (e.g., king and jester) and states of mind is said to be the very basis of the twin success in acting and recitation.[1] Good characters and a composition couched in pleasing words are also fundamental to the success of a theatrical performance. So is also its criticism by well-versed connoisseurs An appropriate employment of *sandhis* or joints also contributed to it.[2] As pointed out above,[3] music with seven *svaras* or *mārgas*, six qualities, three *layas* and *tālas* and a variety of dances also constituted essentials of a drama.

In the praise said to have been bestowed by spectators on Mañjarī for her excellent acting we get an idea of what was regarded as the best measure of the success of an actor or actress. The laudable features of her acting were as follows: performing a variety of *sthānakas* and movements of feet, elegance in the movements of body, meanings and words distinguished by changes in voice corresponding to changing feelings, the perfection of the sentiment, the stability of the feeling of complete identity with the role performed, development of the *sāttvika bhāvas*, perfect imitation, application of coloured pastes and adornments befitting the role, and non-violation of the *layas* in mixed and unmixed drama.[4] The greatest criterion of the success of a dramatic performance was indeed the disappearance of the distinction between the imitation and the role imitated (*anukāry-*

1. प्रकृतिविशेषावस्थाप्रतिपादकवेषरचनसामग्र्या ।
अनुकरणमभ्यतीतं सिद्धिद्वयसम्पदाधारम् ॥ *K* 945.

We prefer Kaul's reading (verse 944 of his edition). Tripathi adopts the reading संपदा धाराम् which does not give good sense. Also cf. verse 805.

2. सुश्लिष्टसन्धिबन्धं सत्पात्रसुवर्णयोजितं सुतराम् ॥
निपुणपरीक्षकदृष्टं राजति रत्नावलीरत्नम् ॥ *K* 947.

Kaul prefers to read the first line as सुश्लिष्टसन्धिबन्धं सर्वत्र सुवर्णयोजितं सुभगम्.

3. *Supra*, pp. 216-17, 221.

4. विविधस्थानकरचनापरिक्रमं गात्रवलनलालित्यम् ।
काकुविभक्तार्थगिरो रसपुष्टिं वासनास्थैर्यम् ॥
सात्त्विकभावोन्मीलनमभिनयमनुरूपवर्तनाभरणम् ।
मिश्रामिश्रे नाट्ये लयाच्युतिं वर्णयन्ति मञ्जर्याः ॥ *K* 804-805.

ānukaraṇa-bheda-parimoṣa, 807). To show the *karuṇa* sentiment as distinct from the *vipralambha śṛṅgāra* sentiment even though the *anubhāvas* of the two are common was regarded as a great feat of dramatic performance.[1]

Now as regards the actual performance of the play. The staging of the play proper was preceded by singing accompanied by appropriate instruments. Verse 880 refers to the entry on the stage of a *sūtra-dhāra* and in the following stanza another *sūtra-dhāra* is said to have appeared on the stage after the music which was obviously in the nature of a benediction (*nāndī*). It would thus follow that there were actually two *sūtra-dhāras*, one of them was connected with *pūrva-raṅga* or prelude and recited the *nāndī* alone or in chorus, while the other entered the stage after the *nāndī* and remained there till the end of the *prastāvanā*, also called *āmukha*, i.e., introductory dialogue at the beginning of the play between the *sūtra-dhāra* and actress, jester or some other character which first gives an account of the dramatist and then introduces the audience to the incidents of the drama.[2]

All the roles, both male and female, in the drama were played by a troupe of women. These ladies were either ordinary courtesans or temple-maids. The role of princess Sāgarikā, daughter of the king of Siṁhala, was done by Mañjarī who was attached to the temple of Kalaśeśvara and was by far the best actress, while others, who have not been named, played the parts of the Vatsa king Udayana, his friend Vasantaka and queen Vāsavadattā (802-803). It may be noted in this connection that Bharata allows a woman to play the role of a female character and *vice versa*,[3] and in the third act of the *Priyadarśikā* of Harṣavardhana we find a woman acting the Vatsa king.

As pointed out above,[4] the play was staged strictly in

1. सदृशेऽप्यनुभावगणे करुणरसं विप्रलम्भतो भिन्नम् ।
दर्शयति निरभिकांक्षितसौख्य ननु गोचरापन्ना ॥ *Ibid.*, 809.

2. Tripathi calls the two *sūtra-dhāras* *nāndī-sūtra-dhāra* and *kathā-sūtra-dhāra* respectively. For full discussion on this point, vide his commentary on verse 881.

3. *Nāṭya-śāstra*, xii. 197-199.

4. *Supra*, p. 6.

conformity with the directions incorporated in the text of the drama as it has come down to us with only such minor modifications as were felt necessary.

It would appear from a perusal of the relevant stanzas that the performance was very much like an operette with plenty music and dancing. In the appreciative remarks of Samarabhaṭa also there is much greater stress on the musical part of of the performance than on other aspects. He enters into the technicalities of music and praises both singing and accompaniment. But for the appropriate changes of the dress by the actresses and faultless delivery he says nothing about acting as such. It has consequently been suggested that the performance of the *Ratnāvalī* was not much removed from that of the modern *swāngs* such as the *Rāma-līlā* acted annually all over Northern India or that of a *bhawāi* occasionally witnessed in Gujarati villages, and may be regarded as the earliest prototype of *bhawāi* or *swāṅg*.[1] But this observation cannot be accepted in its entirety; there is not only an explicit reference to acting (*abhinaya*) in connection with Mañjarī's performance (805), but there is much of it in the actual description of the enactment of the drama.

The dramatic art had fallen on evil days; it was cultivated mainly by courtesans who attached greater importance to their filthy profession than to dramatic performances. Their hearts being set on drinking, meat and men, they could not concentrate on this art which is so very essential for full success (794-799).

IV. OTHER ARTS

Patra-ccheda-vidhāna or making of various designs by cutting leaves was also a popular art. Fashionable men made a show of their proficiency in this art even though they did not actually know it and always carried a scissor (*patra-kartarī*).[2] It was

1. Vide Tripathi's commentary on verse 802; N.C. Mehta, "A Dramatic Production of the Eighth Century : the Development of the Modern," *JBORS*, xiv (1928), pp. 362-365.

2. पत्रच्छेदमजानन्जानन् वा कौशलं कलाविषये ।
प्रकटयति जनसमाजे बिभ्राणः पत्रकर्तरीं सततम् ॥ *K* 74.

regarded as an essential accomplishment of courtesans (124). This was one of the arts which Sundarasena is said to have learnt during his peregrinations (236).

There are only casual allusions to the art of painting (*ālekhya*, 236; *citra-kalā*, 535). It is said to have been practised by hetarai (124) and young men of fashion (235, 535).

Mention is also made of fashioning dolls or sculptures with a variety of materials (*pusta-karma*, 124, 235) including bees'wax (*siktha-karma*, 235).

V. ARCHITECTURE

Residential Architecture

Dāmodaragupta furnishes very meagre information of architectural interest. However, we come across a few interesting terms relating to ancient Indian palace architecture. *Prāsāda* (886, 887) was the most common word used to denote a palace. *Āsthāna* (921) or assembly hall was an important part of the palace complex where the king gave audience to the feudatory chiefs and other people.[1] *Dhaval-ālaya* (22) and *dhavala-gṛha* (539) denoted the principal residence of the royal couple inside the palace.[2] It was a *catuḥ-śāla* structure wherein rooms were built on the four sides of an open courtyard. Hindi *dhaurāhara* or *dharaharā* is a descendant of Sanskrit *dhavalagṛha*. *Pragrīvaka* (587) was one of the front rooms on the upper floor of the *dhavala-gṛha* used as drawing room. In the rainy season it could also be used as a bed-room.[3] In later times it came to be employed in the sense of a palace as a whole.[4] *Veśma* (26). *bhavana* (26), *mandira* (331) and *niśānta* (1046) are used in the sense of a residential structure in general. It is likely that *niśānta*, which is used with reference to the residence of prince Samarabhaṭa, had also something to do with palace architec-

1. There were two kinds of *āsthānas*, viz., *bāhy-āsthāna* and *bhukt-āsthāna*, corresponding to *darbār ām* and *darbār khās* of Mughal palaces. For details, vide V.S. Agrawala, *Harṣa-carita : Eka Sāṁskṛtika Adhyayana*; p. 205.

2. *Harṣa-carita : Eka Sāṁskṛtika Adhyayana*, pp. 91-92, 207-208.

3. Bhānuji Dīkṣita, on *Amara-kośa*, iii. 5. 35, explains *pragrīva* as *mukha-śālā* or *vātāyana* (window).

4. Cf. ग्रीवमस्त्री कलशे ग्रीवाप्रासादयोरपि । Keśava, quoted by T.M. Tripathi.

ture and probably corresponded to the *niśā-gṛha* mentioned in the *Rāmāyaṇa* (Sundarakāṇḍa, xii.1) in connection with Rāvaṇa's palace.[1] A well-decorated bed chamber, variously called *vāsak-āgāra* (141), *vāsaka-sthāna* (151), *vāsa-veśma* (391), *vāsa-bhavana* (357) and *vāsa-gṛha* (625), formed a constituent part of every well-to-do house.[2] Houses were provided with *jāla-mārgas* (520) or latticed windows to allow fresh air and light.

One of the most interesting architectural terms found in our work is *mattavāraṇa* (9). It has a long history and is frequently mentioned in the *Nāṭya-śāstra* in connection with the stage.[3] The term has been variously interpreted by scholars,[4] the most likely one being that suggested by H.R. Divekar, *viz.*, galleries on the two sides of the stage.[5] In the present context it appears to mean a *varāṇḍā* or gallery of a mansion or a large building.[6]

It is worthwhile to note in this context that most of the references appertaining architecture are made by our author in connection with courtesans, showing thereby that they led a luxurious life and lived in palatial buildings.

Town Planning

An ancient Indian city was usually surrounded by a rampart wall (*sāla*, 10). It was decorated with lofty temples, shining houses, parks and gardens, and tanks and step-wells.[7]

Villages were provided with wells for drinking water. They were furnished with wooden footholds on which one kept one of the feet while welling out water (868).

1. But cf. *Amara-kośa*, ii.2. 4-5, where it is taken to mean a house.
2. The *Bṛhat-saṁhitā*, lii. 9, 14, calls it *rati-bhavana*. Vide my *India as seen in the Bṛhatsaṁhitā of Varāhamihira*, p. 374.
3. *Nāṭya-śāstra*, ii. 63-65, 98-99; i. 90-91; iii. 41.
4. P. Subbarao, *Nāṭya-śāstra*, vol. i, second edition, introduction, p. 29; P.S. Sastri in *Mirashi Felicitation Volume*, p. 134; V.V. Mirashi in *Kolte Gaurava Grantha* (Marathi), pp. 1-8.
5. *JOI*, x, pp. 435-438.
6. Cf. *Viśva-prakāśa* cited by Tripathi.
7. See the descriptions of Vārāṇasī, Ābu and Pāṭaliputra. Also f.c vv. 665, 666, 857, 870.

APPENDIX

GEOGRAPHICAL REFERENCES

Although, as shown above, Dāmodaragupta, while composing the *Kuṭṭanī-mata*, had contemporary Kashmiri life before him, he deliberately eschewed mentioning Kashmir or any place therein. On the other hand, the poem contains some interesting topographical references indicating the author's (and probably Kashmiris') intimate knowledge of other parts of India.

The geographical horizon of the *Kuṭṭanī-mata* is wide enough to embrace not only a larger part of India but even some foreign lands. It mentions the snow-bound Himālayas in the north and the Malaya mountain in the south, Abu in the west and Pāṭaliputra in the east. Reference is also made to Ceylon and Eastern Turkistan.

These and other allusions have been incidentally noticed earlier in the book as demanded by the context, but fuller details about them are outlined in the lines that follow.

I. PHYSICAL FEATURES

1. *Mountains*

Arbuda

We get a beautiful description of the Arbuda mountain (modern Abu) in connection with the travels of Sundarasena and Guṇapālita (238-257). Possessed of streams of cool, clear water, Arbuda was traditionally regarded as the son of the Himālaya mountain which was pleased, as it were, to locate it (Arbuda) in the Maru region by taking mercy upon the people.[1] The antiquity of this belief is indicated by the fact that the Tīrthayātrāparvan of the *Mahābhārata* also describes it as the son of the Himavat and adds that earlier there was a deep crater or chasm in the earth at this point.[2] The belief is also

1. एष सुतः सानुमतः स्यन्दच्छीताच्छसलिलसंपन्नः ।
लोकानुकम्पयेव प्रालेयमहीभृता मरौ न्यस्तः ॥ *K* 240.

2. ततो गच्छेत धर्मज्ञ हिमवत्सुतमर्बुदम् ।
पृथिव्यां यत्र वै छिद्रं पूर्वमासीद् युधिष्ठिर ॥
Mahābhārata, iii. 82. 55.

Dr. V.S. Agrawala observes that the description of Abu as Himālaya's son is borne out by the fact that it represents the highest point between the Himālayas and the Nilgiris, its *guru-śikhara* being 5650 feet above the sea-level

mentioned in the Udepur Praśasti of the Rulers of Malwa[1] and an Abu inscription recording the construction of a temple of the Jain *tīrthaṅkara* Neminātha. The latter speaks of the Arbuda as the son of the mountain that is the father-in-law of the husband of Gaurī and as the brother-in-law of the moon-bearer (Śiva).[2]

There were caves in the mountain (241) as also cascades (246), ponds and rivers (257). It was haunted by the mythical beings called Vidyādhara (241) and was resorted to by ascetics performing austerities and living on wild fruits and wind striving to secure heaven after death (241, 248-249). The flora (*oṣadhi*, 245) growing on it included *saptapatra*, *palāśa*, *madana*, *tilaka*, *pīlu*, *arjuna*, *bāṇa*, *mrṣṭaka* (*v.l miṣṭaka*, *mastaka*) and *rohiṇī* (250-253). It was also rich in fauna which included the deer (250), bears (252), apes or lions (*hari*, 251), and the birds parrot, *hārīta* and *bharadvāja* (246). In beauty, says Dāmodaragupta, it surpassed even the heaven (255). It is so lofty, imagines the poet, that innocent poor ladies took the stars for flowers on tree-tops (242) and the Ursa Major appeared to be situated close to it (243). On its top were laid out stepped wells, ponds, parks and temples (257).

Today Abu is regarded as particularly sacred to the Jains and abounds in numerous Jain monuments. But as we have seen above,[3] Abu was a stronghold of Brāhmaṇical Hinduism, particularly Śaivism, from the late Gupta period to about the close of the first millennium B.C. The construction of the

As to the second point, he suggests that possibly like the Himālaya, Abu was also thrown up in one of the tectonic movements of the earth. Vide his Foreword to the *Holy Abu* by Muni Sri Jayanta Vijayaji, Engl. tr. by U.P Shah.

1. अस्त्युर्वीध्रः प्रतीच्यां हिमगिरितनयः सिद्धदंपत्यसिद्धेः ।
स्थानं च ज्ञानभाजामभिमतफलदोऽखर्व्वितः सोऽर्बुदाख्यः

EI, i. p. 234. verse 5.

2. गौरीवरश्वसुरभूधरसम्भवोऽय-
मस्त्यर्बुदः ककुदमद्रिकदम्बकस्य ।
मन्दाकिनीं घनजटे दधदुत्तमाङ्गे
यः श्यालकः शशिभृतोऽभिनयं करोति ॥

Ibid., viii, p. 210, verse 30.

3. *Supra*, p. 91

Vimala-vasahī in A.D. 1030 ushered in a new era in the history of the city which now became a prominent centre of the Jains.

Himācala

Referred to as Himācala (180), Prāleyanagādhirāja (18) and Prāleyamahībhṛt (240), it is the celebrated Himālaya mountain which constitutes the northern frontier of India. Pārvatī, Śiva's spouse, was traditionally regarded as his daughter (18), and Mt. Abu his son (240). It is said to have been a resort of the Gandharvas (180), and ascetics aiming at attainment of divine status also flocked there (966).

Malaya

Allusion to the cool breeze blowing from the Malaya mountain is commonplace in classical Sanskrit literature (299). It denoted the southern portion of the Western Ghats from the Nilgiris to Cape Comorin.[1]

Mandara

It is the mythical mountain said to have been used as the churning stick in the legend of the churning of the ocean (19).

Meru

It is said to have been haunted by the Kiṁpuruṣas (316). It denotes both a fabulous mountain which is the residence of gods and is supposed to be situated in the centre of Jambūdvīpa, and a portion of the Himālayas. Ancient texts place it in the northern division of India.[2] According to Monier-Williams, it is the highland of Tartary, north of the Himālayas.[3] B.C. Law takes it to be identical with the Rudra Himālaya in Garhwal where the Ganges rises.[4] Others take it to denote the Pamir range in Central Asia.

Udayataṭa (v.l.-naga)

It is the mythical mountain of the rising of the moon (926) and the sun.

1. Pargiter, *Markaṇḍeya Purāṇa*. Engl. tr., p. 285 & note.
2. *Bṛhat-saṁhitā*, xiv. 24. Also vide my *India as seen in the Bṛhatsaṁhitā of Varāhamihira*, p. 54.
3. *Sanskrit-English Dictionary, s. v. Meru.*
4. B.C. Law, *Historical Geography of Ancient India*, p. 111.

Vindhya

It is said to have abounded in mad elephants (9). Although the name is generally applied to the whole chain of mountains along the Narmadā, in a restricted sense it referred to its eastern part together with the hills standing south of the Narmadā and extending as far as the ocean.[1]

2. *Rivers*

Gaṅgā

The current of the water of the Gaṅgā is described as taking varied routes, expanding on the earth, breaking through mountains and sacred.[2] It is also called Nāka-vāhinī on the banks of which Vārāṇasī is situated (17). We also get an allusion to its confluence with the Yamunā at Prayāga (298).

Narmadā

Reference is made to the swiftness of its flow (192).

II. COUNTRIES

Devarāṣṭra

Samarabhaṭa, son of king Siṁhabhaṭa, is said to have governed a town (*niveśana*) connected with (i.e. situated in) Devarāṣṭra[3] (737). Nothing is known about Siṁhabhaṭa or his son Samarabhaṭa from any other source. They may as well be fictitious names. The earliest reference to Devarāṣṭra occurs in the Allahabad pillar inscription of Samudragupta who is said to have defeated and later reinstated its ruler Kubera.[4] It was formerly identified with Mahārāṣṭra,[5] but with the help of the Kasimkota plates of the Eastern Cālukya king Bhīma I which mentions Elamāñci-Kaliṅga-*deśa* as forming part of Devarāṣṭra-*viṣaya*[6] Jouveau-Dubreuil identified it with the

1. H.C. Raychaudhuri, *Studies in Indian Antiquities*, p. 106.
2. बहुमार्गो भङ्गयुतः कुसृतिपरो गोत्रभेदकरणपटुः ।
   गङ्गाजलप्रवाहः पुण्यवशात् केवलं तव समानः ॥
   K 776. भद्रयुतः and पुण्यदिशा are variants.
3. Tripathi follows the reading *Devarāja* which is a variant.
4. Fleet, *CII*. iii, p. 7, text line 20.
5. Fleet in *JRAS*, 1898, p. 369; V.A. Smith, *Early History of India*, 1957 reprint, p. 301. For an attempt to revive this theory, see *ABORI*, xxvi. p. 138.
6. *ASI, AR*, 1908-09, p. 123; *JAHRS*, viii, p. 153.

Yellamanchili region of the Visakhapatnam District of Andhra Pradesh.[1] In the time of Samudragupta Devarāṣṭra and Piṣṭapura were two separate kingdoms,[2] but later the latter was included in the former as would follow from the Srungavarapukota grant of *Mahārāja* Anantavrman which refers to Pīṣṭapura as the *adhiṣṭhanā* (capital) of Devarāṣṭra.[3]

Māru

The Arbuda mountain is situated in Maru (240), which corressponds to Marwar in Rajasthan.

Siṁhala

Sāgarikā, the heroine of Hhrṣavardhan's *Ratnāvalī*, was the daughter of the king of Siṁhala (803), modern Ceylon.

Turuṣka

The Turuṣka country, which was famous for its horses (10) and steel-made soles of shoes (64), is Eastern Turkistan. But as shown above,[4] the name was probably used for the Arabs also.

Vatsa

It corresponds to the country round Allahabad with Kauśāmbī, modern Kosam, on the Yamunā, as its headquarters. Its king Udayana, hero of Harṣa's *Ratnāvalī* (802, 807, 882, 886. 916), was a contemporary of Gautama Buddha.

III. LOCALITIES

Harinagara

While describing Pāṭaliputra, Dāmodaragupta says that it resembled Harinagara on account of sacrifiicial posts (*Hari-uagaraṁ kratu-yūpaiḥ*, 180). Tripathi suggests its identification with either Haridvāra or Ayodhyā, the city of Rāma (Hari),

1. J. Dubreuil, *Ancient History of the Deccan*, p. 60.

2. *CII*, iii, p. 7, text lines 19-20, where Piṣṭapura and Devarāṣṭra are spoken of as independent principalities.

3. *ASI, AR*, 1934-35, p. 65; *EI*, xxiii, p. 57 & text line 2 on p. 60. R.C. Majumdar suggests that Devapura from where Anantavarman's Siripurm grant was issued may have been the capital of Devarāṣṭra. See *ibid.*, p. 58.

4. *Supra*, p. 10.

where innumerable sacrifices were performed by the kings of the Solar lineage. For want of decisive evidence on the point none of these identifications can be regarded as certain. There is nothing to show that Ayodhyā was ever known as Harinagara. The identification with Hardwar is more likely.

Pāṭaliputra

Pāṭaliputra, also known as Kusumapura (234, 411, 495), of which we have a graphic account (176-192), was one of the most important cities of ancient India. Since the time the Haryaṅka king Udāyin (fifth century B.C.) made it his capital, it became a great politico-cultural centre. It saw the rise and fall of some of the greatest empires India can boast of. And even though after the Imperial Guptas it ceased to be the imperial metropolis of North India, for a long time afterwards it retained its reputation as an important cultural centre. Dāmodaragupta describes it as the crest-jewel of the surface of the earth (*mahī-tala-tilaka*), permanent habitation of the goddess of learning, and as a great city (*mahānagara*) that had put Indra's city (Amarāvatī) to shame.[1] It was so very perfect and beautiful as to make one imagine that Viśvakarman, the divine architect, had fashioned it as a model (*varṇaka*) in order to exhibit his skill to god Brahmā when the latter asked him to prove his ability of producing a city of the three worlds (177). It enjoyed a high reputation as a religious centre and as such had a chequered career. It was a stronghold of Buddhism during the Śaiśunāga and Maurya periods; but the Śuṅgas and Guptas converted it into a prominent centre of Brāhmaṇical Hinduism, and one could see there sacrificial posts (180) and the smoke rising from sacrificial fire floating in the sky (182). Although Pāṭaliputra was now under the Pālas who were staunch Buddhists themselves and gave lavish patronage to their religion, yet the Brāhmaṇical traditions nurtured by the Śuṅgas and Guptas were so deep-rooted as to continue unabated even under adverse conditions. Having enjoyed the status of the imperial capital of North India for well over a millennium, Pāṭaliputra had attained great prosperity, and our author states that it

1. अस्ति महीतलतिलकं सरस्वतीकुलगृहं महानगरम् ।
नाम्ना पाटलिपुत्रं परिभूतपुरन्दरस्थामम् ॥ *K* 176.

resembled ocean on account of its having heaps of a variety of gems and with its hoarded wealth rivalled the city of Kubera (179).[1]

Prayāga

The confluence of the twin rivers Gaṅgā and Yamunā at Prayāga has been regarded as highly sacred from a hoary antiquity, and the meeting of the white current of the former and the blue one of the latter is a sight pleasant enough to strike the imagination of a poet. Dāmodaragupta discerns a resemblance between the mixing of the clear, white sweat-water and the collyrium-stinted tears falling on the breasts of a fair lady on the one hand and the confluence on the other.[2]

Vārāṇasī

The *Kuṭṭanī-mata* is composed in the form of a dialogue between the courtesan Mālatī and the old cunning procuress Vikarālā, both of whom are represented as residents of the city of Vārāṇasī. The scene of the episode of the courtesan Mañjarī and prince Samarabhaṭa is also laid in the same city. We, therefore, naturally get a vivid description of Vārāṇasī, which is one of the most important and holiest places in whole India.

Dāmodaragupta speaks of Vārāṇasī as 'the ornament of the whole surface of the earth',[3] and compares it with the divine city of Amarāvatī.[4] The fame of Vārāṇasī as a centre of religion and learning had very early spread far and wide. From very ancient times the city has been regarded as a pilgrimage centre (*tīrtha-sthāna*, 800), and as such it was frequented by crowds of people hailing from far and near. It was in the course of one such pilgrimage that prince Samarabhaṭa of distant Devarāṣṭra fell into the clutches of Mañjarī.

1. For Pāṭaliputra as a centre of learning, see *supra*, p. 172.
2. वासिसितं स्वेदजलं कज्जलमलिनाश्रुवारिणा मिश्रम् ।
कुचतटपतितं तस्याः प्रयागसम्भेदसलिलमनुकुरुते ॥ *K* 298.
3. निखिलभूतलभूषणभूता, *ibid.*, 3.
4. नन्दनवनाभिरामा विबुधवती नाकवाहिनीजुष्टा ।
अमरावतीव याऽन्या विश्वसृजा निर्मिता जगति ॥ *Ibid.*, 17.

Vārāṇasī is the city of Śiva, and there are numerous places in it connected with Śaivite legends in some way or other. Of the Śaiva temples which must have existed in legion mention is made of only three, viz., Vṛṣabhadhvaja, Kalaśeśvara and Gambhīreśvara. Vaiṣṇavism also prevailed side by side, and the religious atmosphere appears to have been characterised by a catholic spirit.[1]

Vārāṇasī has been well-known as a centre of learning from time immemorial. In pre-Buddhist and Buddhist times its educational importance was next only to that of Takṣaśilā.[2] A number of seals and sealings found in archaeological excavations at Rajghat also reveal that Vedic studies were specially cultivated here in the Gupta period.[3] Grammar (12) and poetry (15) also found favour with the people. Fine arts like dance, music (10, 14) and dramaturgy (757, 793, 794), too, received special attention. Vārāṇasī maintined its high academic traditions in the medieval period also. Alberuni speaks of Vārāṇasī and Kashmir as 'high schools of sciences'.[4] The *Ukti-vyakti-prakaraṇa* of Dāmodara sheds welcome light on the system of education at Vārāṇasī in the 12th century A.D. and mentions grammar, particularly the *Kālāpa* of Śarvavarman as a favourite subject of study.[5] Abul Fazl also observed that 'from time immemorial it has been the chief seat of learning in Hindustan'.[6] The *Skānda Purāṇa* also refers to Kāśī as an abode of sciences.[7]

As at present, so in the past, Vārāṇasī presented a curious blending of both the aspects of life, a quest after the spiritual truth and a gay abandon to mundane, sensual pleasures. It

1. For religious importance of Vārāṇasī, see *supra*, pp. 90-91.

2. Cf. *Khuddaka-aṭṭhakathā*, p. 198; *Jātaka*, i, 109, 238, 463; ii, 100; iii. 18 ,233; iv. 237.

3. Motichandra, *Kāśī kā Itihāsa*, pp. 97-98; V.S. Pathak in *JNSI*, xx, pp. 195-201; xxvi, pp. 214-221.

4. E. Sachau, *Alberuni's India*, i, p. 173.

5. *Ukti-vyakti-prakaraṇa*, 2/7-8; 12/6-7. Vide also Motichandra's essay on material of Social and Historical Interest published as an introduction to it.

6. *Aine-Akbari*, ii,p 158.

7. विद्यानां सदनं काशी, *Kāśi-khaṇḍa*, xcvi. 121.

was famous for its hetairai (5) and fashionable ladies (7, 8). It has been known for its courtesans from quite early times. In the Buddhist literature we read of the courtesan Sāmā,[1] while Śyāmilaka's *Pāda-tāḍitaka* mentions the courtesan Parākramikā of Vārāṇasī.[2] In the 8th-9th centuries A.D. there was a regular colony of prostitutes, and our poet affords a vivid account of the conversation of courtesans, pimps and maids which Samarabhaṭa is represented to have heard while going to the temple (743-754). The assembly which gathered round Samarabhaṭa after the latter had offered worship to Śiva included prostitutes also (757). It is interesting to note in this connection that the Banaras inscription of Pantha belonging to the eighth century A.D. also notices this peculiar mixture of the spiritual and the worldly and refers to streets of prostitutes at Vārāṇasī.[3]

The prosperity of Vārāṇasī was announced by its lofty, shining buildings (9) and temples on the top of which fluttered flags (6). It was decorated with parks in which there were groves of *tamāla* plants (16). It was surrounded by a rampart wall (10).[4] Remains of this ancient surrounding wall have actually been traced from the confluence of the river Varana to the Adampur locality.[5]

1. *Jātaka*, iii.40-41. Pāli literature also mentions courtesan Aḍḍhakāsī of Vārāṇasī who went to Rājagṛha and charged a fee of 1000 for the night and 500 for the day. See G.P. Malalasekera, *Dictionary of Pali Proper Names*, p. 50.

2. *Caturbhāṇī*, pp. 187-188.

3. *EI*, ix, pp. 59 ff., verse 2. D.R. Sahni, who edited this inscription, is wrong in rendering *vividha-janapada-strī* as 'the wives of various inhabitants'. *Janapada-strī* is well known as a word meaning 'public woman'.

4. The Jātakas mention a moat (no. 164) and a rampart wall with four gates round Vārāṇasī which were closed at night (no. 155). Also vide A.S. Altekar, *History of Benares*. p. 14.

5. Shering, *The Sacred City of Benares*, London 1868, p. 299; Motichandra, *Kāśī kā Itihāsa*p. pp 6-7

SELECT BIBLIOGRAPHY

A. Original Sources

I. *Sanskrit and Prakrit Texts*

: *Āpastambīya Dharmasūtra*, ed. by G. Bühler, BSS, Bombay, 1892-94.

: *Āpastambīya Gṛhyasūtra*, ed. by Chinnaswami Shastri with the commentaries of Haradatta and Sudarśanācārya, Benares, 1928.

: *Āśvalāyana-gṛhyasūtra*, ed. by T. Ganapati Sastri with Haradatta's commentary, Trivandrum, 1923.

: *Baudhāyana-gṛhyasūtra*, ed. by R. Shamasastri, Mysore, 1920.

: *Bhāgavata-purāṇa*, 5th impression, Gita Press, Gorakhpur, V.S. 2021,

: *Chāndogya Upaniṣad*, with Śaṅkara's commentary and Hindi translation, 2nd edition, Gita Press, Gorakhpur, V. S. 2011.

: *Dipavaṁsa*, ed. and translated into English by H. Oldenberg, London, 1879.

: *Harivaṁśa*, ed. with Hindi translation by Ramanarayanadatta Shastri, Gita Press, Gorakhpur.

: *Jātaka*, ed. by V. Fausboll, 6 vols., London, 1877-97.

: *Kūrma-purāṇa*, ed. by Nilamani Mukhopadhyaya, BI, Calcutta, 1890.

: *Liṅga-purāṇa*, Venkateshwar Press, Bombay.

: *Mahābhārata*, with Nīlakaṇṭha's commentary, Chitrashala Press, Poona, 1929-33; Critical Edition, Bhandarkar Oriental Research Institute, Poona, 1927-66; Gita Press Edition, Gorakhpur, V.S. 2013-2015.

: *Mānava-gṛhyasūtra*, ed. with Aṣṭāvakra's commentary, by Ramakrishna Harshaji Shastri, G.O.S., Baroda, 1926.

: *Manu-smṛti*, ed. by J. Jolly, London, 1887; with Kullūka's commentary, NSP, Bombay, 1929; Engl. tr. by G. Bühler, SBE, Vol. 25, Oxford, 1886.

: *Mārkaṇḍeya-purāṇa*, translated into English by F. E. Pargiter, Calcutta, 1904.

: *Matsya-purāṇa*, ASS, Poona, 1907.

: *Nīlamata-purāṇa*, ed. by Ramlal Kanjilal and Jagaddhar Zadav, Lahore, 1924; critically edited by K.D. Vreese, Leiden, 1936 (unless otherwise stated, this edition has been used).

: *Padma-purāṇa*, 4 vols., ASS, Poona, 1893-94.

: *Parāśara-smṛti*, Bombay, 1893.

: *Rāmāyaṇa*, with Tilaka, Śiromaṇi and Bhūṣaṇa commentaries, 7 vols. Gujarāti Press, Bombay, 1912-1918; Gita Press Ed., Gorakhpur, V.S. 2020.

: *Śiva-purāṇa*, Venkateshwar Press, Bombay.

: *Viṣṇu-dharmaśāstra*, BI, Calcutta, 1881.

: *Viṣṇu-dharmottara*, Venkateshwar Press, Bombay, 1912.

: *Viṣṇu-purāṇa*, text with Hindi translation, Gita Press, Gorakhpur, V.S. 2009; Engl. tr. by H.H. Wilson, 5 vols., London, 1864-70.

: *Yājñavalkya-smṛti*, with Mitākṣarā commentary, 5th ed., NSP, Bombay, 1949.

Amarasiṁha : *Amara-kośa*, with Rāmāśramī commentary, NSP, Bombay, 1944.

Amaruka : *Amaru-śataka*, ed. with Kokasambhava's commentary by C. R. Devadhar, *ABORI*, XXXIX, pp. 226-265; XL. pp. 16-55

Ānandavardhana : *Dhvanyāloka*, with the Locana commentary, KSS, Vol. 135, Varanasi, 1940.

Aśvaghoṣa : *Saundarananda*, ed. and translated into English by E.H. Johnston, 2 vols., London, 1932.

Bāṇa : *Harṣa-carita*, edited with the Saṅketa commentary by Führer, BSS, Bombay, 1909.

" : *Kādambarī*, with the commentary of Bhānucandra and Siddhacandra, 9th edition, NSP, Bombay, 1948.

Bharata : *Nāṭya-śāstra*, ed. byM. Ramakrishna Kavi with Abhinavabhāratī, GOS, Vols. XXXVI, LXVIII, CXXIV CXLV, Baroda, 1954-64.

Bhāravi : *Kirātārjunīya*, with Mallinātha's Ghaṇṭāpatha gloss, Haridas Sanskrit Series, No. 105, Varanasi, 1939.

Bhavabhūti : *Mahāvīra-carita*, edited by Todarmal, and revised by A. A. Macdonell, Oxford, 1928.

" : *Uttararāma-carita*, ed. by S. K. Belvalkar, Poona, 1921.

Bilhaṇa : *Vikramāṅkadeva-carita*, ed. by G. Bühler, BSS, Bombay, 1875.

Dāmodaragupta : *Kuṭṭanī-mata*, edited by Tansukharam Manahsukharam Tripathi with his own Sanskrit commentary, Bombay, 1924 (unless otherwise stated, this edition has been used); critically edited by Madhusudan Kaul, BI, Calcutta, 1944.

Dāmodaraśarman : *Uktivyakti-prakaraṇa*, edited by Muni Jinavijaya, Singhi Jain Granthamala, Bombay, 1953.

Daṇḍin : *Daśa-kumāra-carita*, NSP, Bombay, 1928.

Hāla : *Gāthā-satta-sai*, edited with a Marathi introduction and translation by S. A. Joglekar, Poona.

Halāyudha : *Abhidhāna-ratnākara*, Varanasi, Śaka 1879.

Harṣa : *Nāgānanda*, ed. by P. V. Ramanujaswami, Madras, 1932.

" : *Priyadarśikā*, ed. by Nariman, Jackson and Ogden, Columbia University Indological Series, No. 10, New York, 1923.

" : *Ratnāvalī*, 4th ed., NSP, Bombay, 1938.

Hemacandra : *Abhidhāna-cintāmaṇi*, Bhavanagar, Vira Era 2441.

" : *Kāvy-ānuśāsana*, ed. by R. C. Parikh with Alaṅkāra-cūḍāmaṇi and Viveka, Bombay, 1938.

Īśvaradatta : *Dhūrta-viṭa-saṁvāda*, included in the *Śṛṅgāra-hāṭa* or *Caturbhāṇī* edited with a Hindi translation by Motichandra and V. S. Agrawala (Bombay, 1959), pp. 63-120.

Jalhaṇa : *Sūkti-muktāvali*, GOS, Baroda, 1938.

Kalhaṇa : *Rāja-taraṅgiṇī*, ed. by M. A. Stein, Delhi, 1960; Engl. translation by M. A. Stein, Delhi, 1961.

Kālidāsa : *Abhijñāna-Śākuntala*, with Rāghavabhaṭṭa's commentary, 12th edition, NSP, Bombay, 1958.

" : *Mālavikāgnimitra*, BSS, 2nd edition, Bombay, 1889.

Kālidāsa : *Raghu-vaṁśa*, with Mallinātha's Sañjīvanī commentary, 7th ed., NSP, Bombay, 1916.

" : *Ṛtu-saṁhāra*, 6th ed., NSP, Bombay, 1922.

" : *Vikramorvaśīya*, ed. by H. D. Velankar, Sahitya Akadami, Delhi, 1961.

Kauṭilya : *Arthaśāstra*, text edited by R. P. Kangle, Bombay, 1960; Engl. translation by R. P. Kangle, Bombay, 1963.

Kṛṣṇamiśra : *Prabodha-candrodaya*, NSP, Bombay, 1924.

Kṣemendra : *Bṛhatkathā-mañjarī*, ed. by Śivadatta and K. P. Parab, 2nd ed., Bombay, 1931.

" : *Kalā-vilāsa*, included in the *Kṣemendra-laghu-kāvya-saṅgraha* compiled by Aryendra Sharma, Hyderabad, 1961.

" : *Deśopadeśa*, included in the *Kṣemendralaghu-kāvya-saṅgraha*.

" : *Kavi-kaṇṭhābharaṇa*, included in the *Kṣemendra-laghu-kāvya-saṅgraha*.

" : *Samaya-mātṛkā*, included in the *Kṣemendra-laghu-kāvya-saṅgraha*.

Kṣīrasvāmin : *Kṣīra-taraṅgiṇī*, ed. by Yudhishthira Mimamsaka and R. S. Bhaṭṭacharya, Amritsar, V. S. 2014. Introduction only.

Lakṣmīdhara : *Kṛtya-kalpataru*, Vol. VIII : Tīrthavivecana-kāṇḍa, GOS, No. XCVIII Baroda, 1942.

Mammaṭa : *Kāvya-prakāśa*, ed. by R. D. Karmarkar, Poona, 1960.

Maṅkha : *Alaṅkāra-sarvasva*, 2nd ed., TSS, No. XLI, Trivandrum, 1926.

" : *Maṅkha-kośa-ṭīkā*, ed. by T. Zachariae, Bombay, 1897.

Māyurāja Anaṅgaharṣa : *Tāpasa-Vatsarāja*, ed. by Yadugiri Yatiraja, Bangalore, 1929.

Padmaśrī : *Nāgara-sarvasva*, ed. with Jagajjyotirmalla's commentary by Tansukharam Manahsukharam Tripathi, Bombay, 1921.

Pāṇini : *Aṣṭādhyāyī*, ed. by Sankaradeva Pathak, Vrindavan, V. S., 1996.

Patañjali : *Mahābhāṣya*, Vol. IV, NSP, Bombay, 1942.

Rājaśekhara : *Karpūramañjarī*, critically edited by Sten Konow and translated into English with notes by C.R. Lanman, 2nd Issue, Delhi, 1963.

" : *Kāvya-mīmāṁsā*, ed. by C. D. Dalal and R. A. Sastry and revised and enlarged by K. S. Ramaswami Sastri Siromani, 3rd ed., GOS., No. 1, Baroda, 1934.

" : *Viddhaśālabhañjikā*, ed. by J. B. Chaudhuri with the Camatkāra-taraṅgiṇī and Prāṇa-pratiṣṭhā commentaries, Calcutta Oriental Series, No. 10, Calcutta, 1943.

Śaraṇadeva : *Durghaṭa-vṛtti*, ed. by Louis Renou with French notes, Paris, 1945.

Śārṅgadhara : *Śārṅgadhara-paddhati*, ed. by P. Peterson, BSS, No. 37, Bombay, 1881.

Soḍḍhala : *Udayasundarī-kathā*, GOS, Baroda, 1920.

Somadeva : *Kathā-sarit-sāgara*, ed. by Durga Prasad and K. P. Parab, 4th ed., Bombay, 1930; Engl. Tr. by H. C. Tawney and Introduction, notes, etc. by N. M. Penzer, 10 Vols., London, 1924-28.

Somadevasūri : *Yaśastilakacampū*, 2 vols., NSP, Bombay, Vol. II, 1903; Vol. I, 2nd ed., 1916.

Subandhu : *Vāsavadattā*, edited with English Translation by H. Gray, Indian Issue, Delhi, 1962.

Śūdraka : *Mṛcchakaṭika*, with Pṛthvīdhara's commentary, 7th ed., NSP, Bombay, 1936.

Śūdraka : *Padma-prābhṛtaka*, included in the *Śṛṅgāra-hāṭa* or *Caturbhāṇī* edited with Introduction and Hindi rendering by Motichandra and V. S. Agrawala, pp. 1-61, Bombay, 1959.

Śyāmilaka : *Pāda-tāḍitaka*, included in *Śṛṅgāra-hāṭa* or *Caturbhāṇī*, pp. 149-259.

Vākpati : *Gauḍa-vaho*, ed. by S. P. Pandit and re-edited by N. B. Utgikar, BSS, No. XXXIV, Poona, 1927.

Vallabhadeva : *Subhāṣitāvali*, ed. by P. Peterson, 2nd ed., Poona, 1961.

Varāhamihira : *Bṛhatsaṁhitā*, ed. with Bhaṭṭotpala's commentary by Sudhakara Dvivedi, Varanasi, 1895-97.

Vararuci : *Ubhayābhisārikā*, included in *Śṛṅgāra-hāṭa* or *Caturbhāṇī*, pp. 121-147.

Vardhamāna : *Gaṇaratna-mahodadhi*, ed. by J. Eggling, Delhi, 1963.

Vātsyāyana : *Kāma-sūtra*, with Yaśodhara's Jayamaṅgalā commentary, KSS, No. 29, Varanasi, 1920.

Veṇīdatta : *Padya-veṇī*, ed. by J. B. Chaudhuri, Calcutta, 1944.

Vidyākara : *Subhāṣita-ratna-kośa*, ed. by D. D. Kosambi and V. V. Gokhale, HOS, Vol. XLII, 1957.

Viśākhadatta : *Mudrārākṣasa*, ed. by K. T. Telang, 3rd ed., NSP., Bombay, 1900.

Viśvavānāthatripāṭhin : *Praśasti-Kāśikā*, ed. by K.V. Sarma, Vishweshwaranand Indological Series, No. 39, Hoshiarpur, 1967.

Yāska : *Nirukta*, critically edited by Mukund

Jha Bakshi with Durgācārya's commentary, NSP, Bombay, 1930.

II. *Inscriptions**

Altekar, A.S. : Barnala Yūpa Inscription, B, Kṛta Year 335, *EI*, XXVI, p. 123.

Banerji, R. D. : Kadambapradaka grant of Naravarman, *ibid.*, XX, pp. 105 ff.

Bühler, G. : Udepur Praśasti of the Kings of Malwa, *ibid.*, I, pp. 222-38.

Bhandarkar, D. R. : Nadol Inscription of Chāhamāna Jojalladeva, *ibid*, XI, p. 28.

„ „ : *List of Inscriptions of Northern India*, *ibid*, XIX-XXII, Appendix.

Fleet, J. F. : Allahabad Pillar Inscription of Samudragupta, *Inscriptions of the Early Gupta Kings and their Successors*, *CII*, III, pp. 1-17.

„ „ : Gangdhar Stone Inscription of Viśvavarman, Mālava year 481, *ibid.*, pp. 72-79.

„ „ : Alina Plates of Śīlāditya VII, Year 447, *ibid.*, pp. 171-191.

Ghoshal, R. K. : Santa Bomilla Plates of Indravarman, Gaṅga Year 87, *EI*, XXV, pp. 194 ff.

Katare, S. L. : Kalanjar Inscription of V.S. 1147, *ibid.*, XXXI, pp. 163-66.

Kielhorn, F. : Khalimpur Plate of Dharmapāla, *ibid.*, IV, pp. 247-251.

„ „ : Pandukeshwar Plate of Lalitaśūra, *IA*, XXV, pp. 178-181.

„ „ : Twenty-one Copper-Plates of the Kings of Kanauj, *EI*, IV, pp. 97 ff.

Lüders, H. : Jaina Inscriptions at the Temple of Neminātha on Mt. Abu, *ibid.*, III, pp. 200 ff.

*Only such of the inscriptions as have been specifically mentioned in the text have been listed here.

Majumdar, N. G. : Ramganj Plate of Mahāmāṇḍalika Īśvaraghoṣa, *Inscriptions of Bengal*, III, pp. 149 ff.

Majumdar, R. C. : Gwalior Praśasti of Bhoja I, *EI*, XVIII, pp. 99 ff.

" " : Sringavarapukota Grants of Mahārāja Anantavarman, *ibid.*, XXIII, pp. 56 ff.

Mirashi, V. V. : Pattan Plates of Pravarasena II, *Inscriptions of the Vākāṭakas*, *CII*, V, pp. 57-52.

Sahni, D. R. : Banaras Inscription of Pantha, *EI*, IX, pp. 59-62

Sastri, Hiranand : Brāhmī Inscription from a Wooden Pillar from Kirari, *ibid*, XVIII, pp. 152-157.

Sircar, D. C. : *Select Inscriptions*, Vol. I, 2nd ed., Calcutta, 1965.

" " : Ghumli Plates of Bāṣkaladeva, V.S. 1045, *EI*, XXXI, pp. 11-16.

" " : Modasa Plates of Paramāra Bhoja, V.S. 1067, *ibid.*, XXXIII, 192-198.

" " : Mandar Hill Inscription, *ibid.*, XXXVI, p. 305.

" " : Pāṇḍukeśvara Grant of Padmaṭadeva, *ibid.*, XXXI, pp. 284-290.

III. *Coins*

Altekar, A. S. : *The Coinage of the Gupta Empire*, Varanasi, 1957.

Cunningham, A. : *Coins of Mediaeval India*, Varanasi, 1967.

Singh, J. P. : Observations on the So-called Khaḍga-trātā Coin-type of Kumāragupta I, *JNSI*, XXV, 29-35.

Smith, V. A. : *Catalogue of Coins in the Indian Museum*, Calcutta, I, Oxford, 1906.

Sohoni, S. V. : "Khaḍga-trātā" Coins of Kumāragupta I, *JNSI*, XVIII, pp. 178-186.

IV. *Foreign Sources.*

Beal, S. : *Si-yu-ki or Buddhist Records of the Western World*, 2 vols., London, 1906.

Giles, H. A. : *The Travels of Fa-hsien* (399-414 *A.D.*) or *Record of Buddhist Kingdoms*, Cambridge, 1923.

Takakusu, J. : *A Record of the Buddhist Religion as Practised in India and the Malay Archipelago*, Oxford, 1896.

Watters, T. : *On Yuan Chwang's Travels in India*, 2 vols., London, 1904-05.

Yule, H. : *Travels of Marco Polo*.

B. *Modern Works*

Agrawal, Urmila : *Khajuraho Sculptures and their Significance*, Delhi, 1964.

Agrawala, V. S. : *Harṣa-carita: Eka Sāṁskṛtika Adhyayana*, Patna, 1953.

" " : *Kādambarī : Eka Sāṁskṛtika Adhyayana*, Varanasi, 1958.

Altekar, A. S. : *History of Benares*, Varanasi, 1937.

Boner, A., Sarma, S. R. and Das, S, P. ; *New Light on the Sun Temple of Koṇārka*, Varanasi, 1972.

Chakladar, H. C. *Social Life in Ancient India, A Study in Vātsyāyana's Kāmasūtra*, 2nd ed., Calcutta, 1924.

Chattopadhyaya, S. : *Early History of Northern India*, 2nd ed., Calcutta, 1968.

Choudhury, P. C. : *The History of Civilization of the People of Assam to the Twelfth Century* A. D., Gauhati, 1959.

Cunningham, A. : *The Ancient Geography of India, the Buddhist Period*, Varanasi, 1963.

Dasgupta, S.N and De, S.K. : *A History of Sanskrit Literature*, Classical Period, Vol. I, 2nd ed., Calcutta, 1962.

De, S.K. : *History of Sanskrit Poetics*, 2nd ed., Calcutta, 1960.

" " : *Ancient Indian Erotics and Erotic Literature*, Calcutta, 1959.

Deo, S. B. : *Mārkaṇḍi Temples*, Nagpur, 1973.

Dubreuil, J. : *Ancient History of the Deccan*, translated from French into English by V.S.S. Dikshitar, Pondicherry, 1920

Gangoli, O. C. : *Koṇārk*, Calcutta, 1972.

Handiqui, K. K. : *Yaśastilaka and Indian Culture*, Sholapur, 1949.

Jain, Gokulchandra : *Yaśastilaka kā Sāṁskṛtika Adhyayana* Amritsar, 1967.

Jain, J. C. : *Life in Ancient India as Depicted in the Jain Canon*, Bombay, 1947.

Jamkhedkar, A. P. : *Cultural History from the Vasudevahiṇḍī*, Ph.D. thesis, University of Poona. (unpublished).

Jayanta Vijay, Muni : *Holy Abu*, translated from Gujarati into English with an Introduction by U.P. Shah and a Foreword by V.S. Agrawala. Bhavnagar V.S.210.

Jayaswal, K. P. : *The Hindu Polity*, 2nd ed. Bangalore, 1943.

Joshi, N.P. : *Life in Ancient Uttarāpatha, Varanasi* 1967.

Kak, R. C. : *A Handbook of the Archaeological and Numismatic Sections of the Sri Pratap Singh Museum, Srinagar*, Calcutta, 1923.

" " : *Ancient Monuments of Kashmir*, London 1933.

Kane, P. V. : *History of Dharmaśāstra*, Vols. II-IV, Poona, 1941-53.

" " : *History of Sanskrit Poetics*, Delhi, 1961.

Kangle, R. P. : *The Kauṭilīya Arthaśāstra* : A Study, Bombay, 1965.

Keith, A. B. : *Sanskrit Drama*, Oxford, 1924.

" " : *A History of Sanskrit Literature*, Oxford, 1956.

Krishnamachariar, M. : *History of Classical Sanskrit Literature*, Madras, 1937.

Lal, Kanvar : *Immortal Khajuraho*, Delhi. 1965.

Law, B.C. : *Historical Geography of Ancient India*, Paris, 1954.

Majumdar, G. P. : *Upavana-vinoda*, Calcutta, 1935.

Majumdar, R. C. (Ed.) : *The Age of Imperial Unity*, 2nd ed., : Bombay, 1953.

,, ,, : *The Classical Age*, Bombay, 1954.

Majumdar, R.C. (Ed.) : *The Age of Imperial Kanauj*, Bombay, 2nd ed., 1964.

Mirashi, V. V. : *Inscriptions of the Kalachuri-Chedi Era*, *CII*, IV, Ootacamund, 1953 (Introduction only).

Motichandra : *Kāśī kā Itihāsa*, Bombay, 1962.

,, : *Prācīna Bhāratīya Veśa-bhūṣā*, Prayag, 1950.

,, : *The World of Courtesans*, Delhi, 1973.

,, : *Costumes, Textiles, Cosmetics and Coiffure in Ancient and Mediaeval India*, Delhi, 1973.

Pandey, K. C. : *Abhinavagupta : An Historical and Philosophical Study*, Varanasi, 1963.

Panigrahi, K. C. : *Archaeological Remains at Bhubaneswar, Calcutta*, 1961.

Pant, Pratinidhi : *Ajiṇṭhā* (Marathi).

Pathak, V. S. : *Ancient Historians of India*, Bombay, 1966.

Pramod Chandra : *Stone Sculptures in the Allahabad Museum*, Poona, 1970.

Prater, S. H. : *The Book of Indian Animals.*

Ray, S. C. : *Early History and Culture of Kashmir*, Calcutta, 1957.

Raychaudhuri, H. C. : *Studies in Indian Antiquities*, 2nd ed., Calcutta, 1958.

Shastri, Ajay Mitra : *India as seen in the Bṛhatsaṁhitā of Varāhamihira*, Delhi, 1969.

Shering : *The Sacred City of Varanasi*, London, 1868.

Sinha, S.N. & Basu, N.K. : *History of Prostitution in India*, Vol. I, Calcutta.

Sircar, D. C. : *Indian Epigraphy*, Delhi, 1965.

Sivaramamurti, C. : *Amaravati Sculptures in the Madras Government Museum, Bulletin of the Madras Government Museum*, New Series, General Section, Vol. IV, Reprinted, Madras, 1956.

Sanskrit Literature and Art Mirrors of Indian Culture, *MASI*, No. 73.

Smith, V. A. : *Early History of India*, Oxford, 1957.

Tripathi, R. S. : *History of Kanauj*, Varanasi, 1937.

Ved Kumari : *The Nīlamata Purāṇa : A Cultural and Literary Study of a Kāśmīrī Purāṇa*, Srinagar-Jammu, 1968.

Vidya Prakash : *Khajuraho*, Bombay, 1967.

Vogel, J. Ph. : *Catalogue of Archaeological Museum at Mathura*, Allahabad, 1910.

Zannas, E. and Auboyer, J. : *Khajurāho*, The Hague, 1960.

C. Articles

Bhise, Usha R. : The Importance of Nāman in the Ṛgveda, *Summaries of Papers*, All-India Oriental Conference, 25th Session (1969), pp. 2-3.

De, S. K. : A note on the Kunda-mālā, *JRAS*, 1924, pp. 663-664.

Dhavalikar, M.K. : A Note on the Tilaka Mark, *JOI*, XVIII, pp. 71-73.

Gai, G. S. : A Note on the Tilaka Mark and Kaṅkaṇa, *BDCRI*, XX, pp. 300-301.

Ghosh, M. M. : Origin and Antiquity of the Sanskrit Name Cīna as the Name of China, *ABORI*, XLII (1961), pp. 150-154.

Kane, P. V. : The Tilaka Mark, *JBBRAS*, New Series, XXI (1945), pp. 33-37.

Kavi, M. R. : Tāpasa-Vatsarāja, *JAHRS*, I, pp. 155 ff.

Kielhorn, F. : Pādamūla, Pādamūlika, *IA*, XXVII (1898), p. 252.

Mehta, N. C. : A Dramatic Production in the Eighth Century, The Development of the Modern, *JBORS*, XIV (1928), pp. 358 ff.

Mirashi, V. V. : Mattavāraṇī, *Dr. KolteGaurava Grantha*, Amraoti, 1969, pp. 1-8.

Pandey, Chandrabali : Mṛcchakaṭika kā Parivrājaka, *Nai Dhārā*, October, 1952, pp. 3-4.

Pathak, V. S. : Religious Sealings from Rajghat, *JNSI*, XIX, pp. 168-179.

Ray, S. C. : The identity of Toramāṇa Coins of Kāśmīra, *ibid.*, XIV, pp. 152-157.

Shastri, Ajay Mitra : Historical Data in the Kuṭṭanī-mata of Dāmodaragupta, *JIH*, XLVI, pp. 357-367.

" " : Coins and Media of Exchange in the Kuṭṭanī-mata of Dāmodaragupta, *JNSI*, XXX ; pp. 118-121.

" " : Reading and Interpretation of a Verse in Dāmodaragupta's Kuṭṭanī-mata in the Light of Puranic and Archaeological Evidence, *Purāṇa*, XII, pp. 160-66.

Shastri, B. N. : Is Bhāskaravarman, the King of Kāmarūpa, referred to in the Kuṭṭanī-mata of Dāmodaragupta? *Summaries of Papers, All-India Oriental Conference*, 23rd Session, p. 17.

Sternbach, Ludvik : Veśyā : Synonyms and Aphorisms, *BV*, IV, pp. 104-114; V, pp. 115-143.

Svamin, Bhaṭṭanātha : Māyurāja, *IA*, XLI (1912), pp. 139-143.

Yun-Hua, Jan : Some Fresh Reflections on Yaśovarma of Kanauj and Muktāpīḍa of Kashmir, *JIH*, XLV (1967), pp. 161 ff.

D. *Dictionaries*

Bhattacharya, Tāranātha : *Vācaspatyam*, 6 vols., Varanasi, 1962.

Malalasekera, G. P. : *Dictionary of Pali Proper Names*, 2

vols., London, 1934, 1938.

Monier Williams : *Sanskrit-English Dictionary*, Oxford, 1899.

Radhakantadeva Bahadur: *Śabda-kalpa-druma*, 5 vols., Delhi, 1961.

Rhys-Davids, T. W. & Stede, William : *Pali-English Dictionary*, Pali Text Society.

Sircar, D. C. : *Indian Epigraphical Glossary*, Delhi, 1966.

E. Manuscript Catalogues

Eggling : *Catalogue of Sanskrit Manuscripts in the India Office Library*, III, London, 1891.

Peterson, P. : *Report on the Search of Sanskrit Manuscripts in the Bombay Circle for* 1883-84.

Rangacharya, M. : *Descriptive Catalogue of Sanskrit Manuscripts in the Government Oriental Manuscripts Library, Madras*, IV, Madras, 1907-08.

Rangacharya, M., and Sastri, S. Kuppuswami : *Descriptive Catalogue of the Sanskrit Manuscripts in the Government Oriental Manuscripts Library, Madras*, Vol. XVII, Madras, 1914.

Sastri, H. P. : *A Descriptive Catalogue of Sanskrit Manuscripts in the Collections of the Asiatic Society of Bengal*, VII, Calcutta, 1934.

———

INDEX*

*The following abbreviations have been used in the index : *l.*=locality; t.=text.

ADDITIONS

P. 134, note 1 : Add "It may be mentioned, however, that the word *paṭakā*, which has probably descended from *paṭikā*, is applied for a waist-band in Hindi and a light head-band in Marathi. According to Tripathi, *paṭikā* is the same as the modern *khesa*, while Motichandra takes it to mean loin-cloth (*Costumes, Textiles, Cosmetics and Coiffure in Ancient and Mediaeval India*, p. 105) But the context seems to favour the use of the word in the sense of a particular textile. However, the possibility of its use in the other senses cannot be altogether ruled out."

P. 135, note 1 : Add "Motichandra takes *tauruṣkika* to mean 'painted with storax' (*Costumes*, etc., p. 105). But his statement that the shoes were embroidered with gold (*ibid.*) is not borne out by the text."

P. 141 : Add at the end of line 2 "It seems to have been a kind of earring with sharp point-like projections along the edge of the ring and is sometimes found represented in sculpture (Pl. XIII.24). Since Dāmodaragupta clearly describes it as worn on the ears (*lamba-śravaṇa-niveśita*), Motichandra's suggestion to take it in the sense of 'comb' (*ibid.*, p. 105) appears untenable."

P. 141 : Add at the end of paragraph 2 "It seems to have comprised a large number of pendents with their shape resembling *ṭiṭṭibha*. The peculiarity of the *ṭiṭṭibha* bird is that it lies supine with legs raised up. The pendents appear to have reflected this peculiarity. Mention must in this connection be made of a *vaikakṣyaka* with pendents alternatively shaped like goad (*aṅkuśa*) and what looks like a bird with its legs raised up found depicted in Bharhut sculpture (Pl. XIII. 26). Motichandra, however, takes it to refer to a necklace with two *ṭiṭṭibhaka* birds facing each other (*ibid.*, p. 105)."

P. 161 : Add at the end of paragraph 2 "It is perhaps represented by a modern toy modelled like a cart consisting of a covered terracotta casket (*samudgaka*) and a mechanical device attached to the axle which strikes the cover of the casket and makes sound at regular intervals as the wheels are in motion (Pl. XXI. 43). It is very popular among children in North India and is particularly favoured on the Makarasaṅkrānti festival."

1. 

2 

1. Clay sealing of Kalaśeśvara, Rajghat
2. Kāma with Rati and Prīti, Bhuvaneswar

Pl. II

3. Andhakāsuravadha, Ellora

4. Śiva and Pārvati Playing Chausar, Ellora

5

6

5. Pārvatī with Alakāvali and Dhammilla hair-styles, Ahichchhatra
6. Huntsman on horseback, Harvan

7 

8 

9 

7-8. Hunting Scenes, Harvan
9. Wild Boar Hunt, Koṇārka

Pl. VI

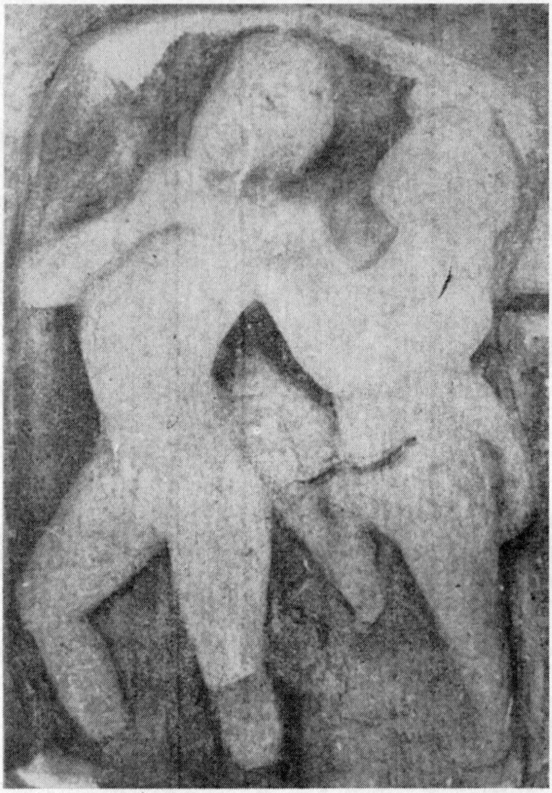

10

11

10. Wrestling Scene. Paunar
11. Hunting Scene, Harvan

12. School Scene, Khajuraho

13. Dancing School, Khajuraho

14

15 ↑

14. Nartakāchārya (Dance Master), Koṇārka
15. Music Scene, Harvan

16. Viṭa, Kumrahar

17. Female figure with mirror, Bhuvaneswar

Pl. XII

18

19

18. Female Chauri-bearer wearing half-sleeved jacket, Ajanta
19. Female Chauri-bearer wearing full-sleeved jacket, Ajanta

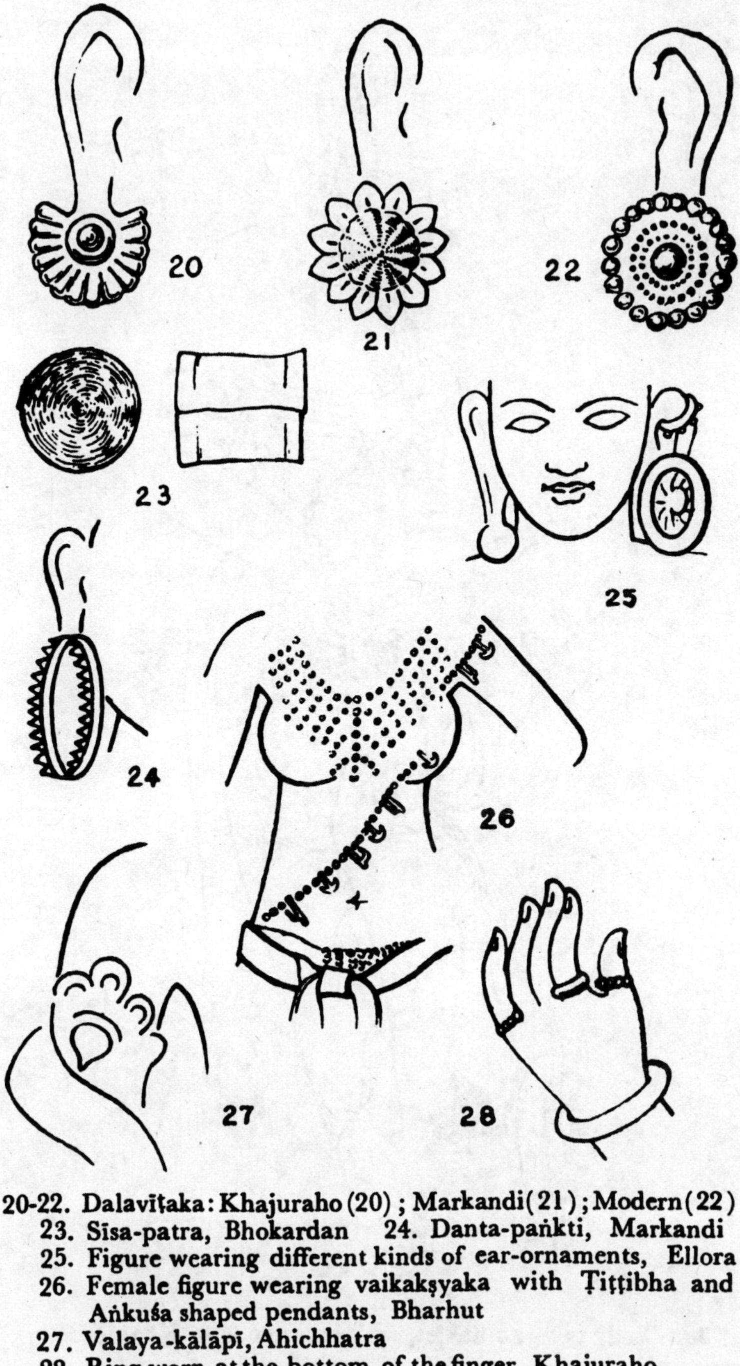

20-22. Dalavīṭaka: Khajuraho (20); Markandi (21); Modern (22)
23. Sīsa-patra, Bhokardan 24. Danta-paṅkti, Markandi
25. Figure wearing different kinds of ear-ornaments, Ellora
26. Female figure wearing vaikakṣyaka with Ṭiṭṭibha and Aṅkuśa shaped pendants, Bharhut
27. Valaya-kālāpī, Ahichhatra
28. Ring worn at the bottom of the finger, Khajuraho

30. Lady tying an anklet, with an attendant, Khajuraho

Pl. XIV

29. Lady tying an anklet, Jamsot

Pl. XVI

31. Lady with a veil, Ajanta 32. Lady with two Veṇīs, Mathura
33. Lady with Dhammilla hair-style, Ajanta
34. Lady with Alakāvali hair-style, Ajanta
35. Gaṅgā with Alakāvali and Dhammilla hair-styles, Paunar

36

37

36. Lady applying lac-dye to the sole of her foot. Khajuraho
37. Lady applying collyrium, Khajuraho

Pl. XVIII

39

38

38-39. Lady playing with ball, Sirsa (39) ; Khajuraho (38)

40. Ram-fight, Ajanta

Pl. XX

41. Female figure playing with a parrot, Markandi

42. Female figure playing with a śārikā, Markandi

Pl. XXI

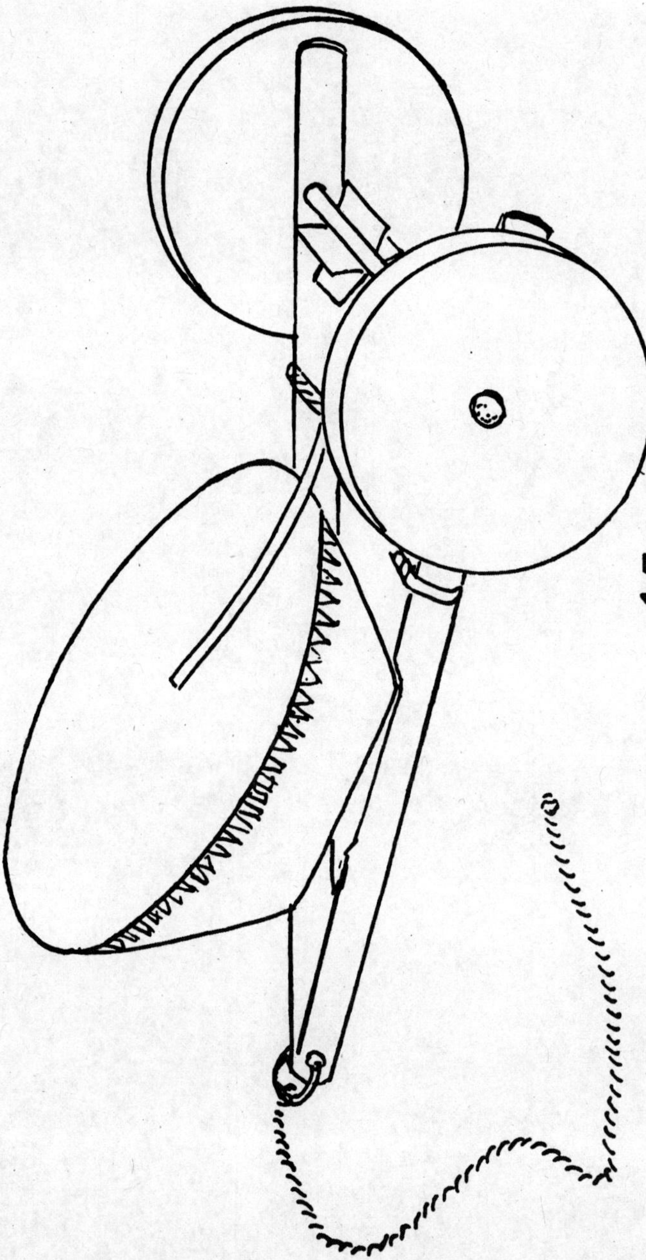

43

43. Samudgikā